AA ROA ATL

C000259878

IRELAND

Scale 1:200,000
3.16 miles to 1 inch
2km to 1cm

4th edition January 2010

© AA Media Limited 2010
Original edition printed 2004

Cartography:
All cartography in this atlas edited, designed and produced by
the Mapping Services Department of AA Publishing (A04258).

 **Land & Property Services.** This is based upon Crown Copyright
and is reproduced with the permission
of Land & Property Services under
delegated authority from the
Controller of Her Majesty's Stationery
Office, © Crown copyright and database rights 2010. Licence
No. 100,363. Permit number 90143.
This product includes RCDI by permission of Land & Property
Services on behalf of the Controller of Her Majesty's
Stationery Office © Crown Copyright 2010.

© Ordnance Survey Ireland/Government of Ireland Copyright
Permit No. 8544.

Published by AA Publishing (a trading name of AA Media
Limited, whose registered office is Fanum House, Basing
View, Basingstoke, Hampshire RG21 4EA, UK. Registered
number 06112600)

ISBN: 978 0 7495 6539 8

A CIP catalogue record for this book is available from
The British Library.

Disclaimer:
The contents of this atlas are believed to be correct at the
time of the latest revision. However, the publishers cannot be
held responsible for loss occasioned to any person acting or
refraining from action as a result of any material in this atlas,
nor for any errors, omissions or changes in such material.
This does not affect your statutory rights. The publishers
would welcome information to correct any errors or omissions
and to keep this atlas up to date. Please write to the
Cartographic Editor, Publishing Division, The Automobile
Association, Fanum House, Basing View, Basingstoke,
Hampshire RG21 4EA, UK.
E-mail: *roadatlasfeedback@theaa.com*

Many place names in the main-map section of this atlas are
given in English and Irish. The names shown are those
approved by the Land & Property Services and Ordnance
Survey Ireland.

Acknowledgements:
The AA would like to acknowledge the following bodies and
agencies for information used in the creation of this atlas:
The Environment & Heritage Service, Heritage of Ireland,
RSPB, Department of Agriculture & Rural Development,
An Roinn Gnóthaí Pobail, Tuaithe agus Gaeltachta,
GaelSaoire, Coillte Teoranta, The National Trust, An Taisce,
Roads Service and The National Roads Authority. Relief map
image supplied by Mountain High Maps ® Copyright © 1993
Digital Wisdom, Inc.

Printer:
Printed in China by Leo Paper Products.

Atlas contents

Map pages	inside front cover
Route planning	II–VI
Route planner	II
Ferry ports	III
Distance chart	IV
The shape of the land	V
Language and dialects	VI
Key to map symbols	1
Road maps 1:200,000 scale	2–68
Town plans	69–76
Key to town plans	69
Motorways	77–86
Key to motorway maps	77
Index to place names	87–98
County and administrative areas	87
Freshwater fishing	inside back cover

Route planner

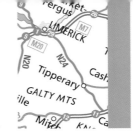

Legend:
- Toll-free motorway — See atlas pages for opening dates
- Toll motorway
- Primary route (NI) / National primary route (IRL)
- A road (NI) / National secondary route (IRL)
- Car ferry
- Catamaran car ferry

Ferry ports

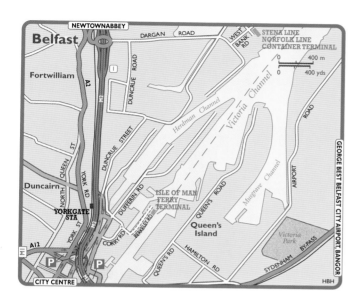

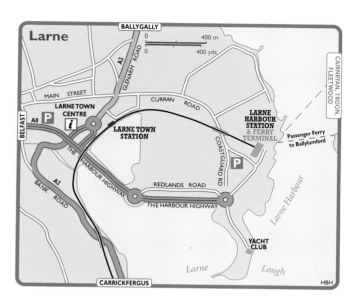

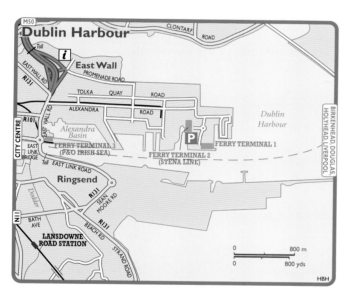

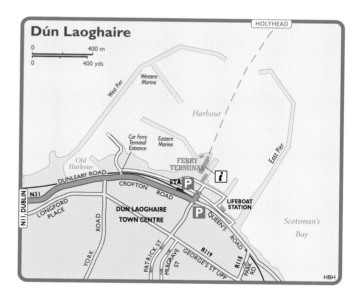

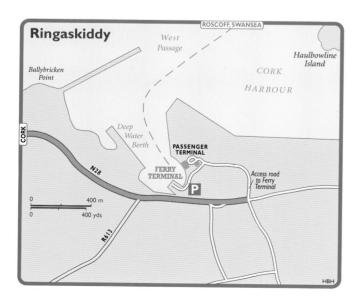

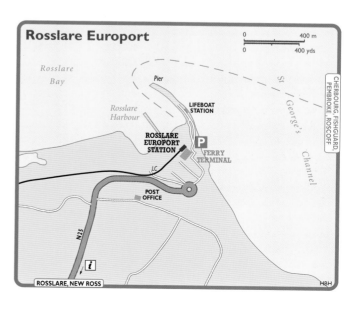

Distance chart

This chart shows distances, in both miles and kilometres, between two towns along AA-recommended routes. Using motorways and other main roads this is normally the fastest route, though not necessarily the shortest.

For example, the distance between Cork and Omagh is 395 kilometres or 245 miles (8 kilometres is approximately 5 miles).

To reflect the distances shown on road signs, distances shown on the road maps in this atlas are in miles in Northern Ireland and kilometres in the Republic of Ireland.

distances in miles

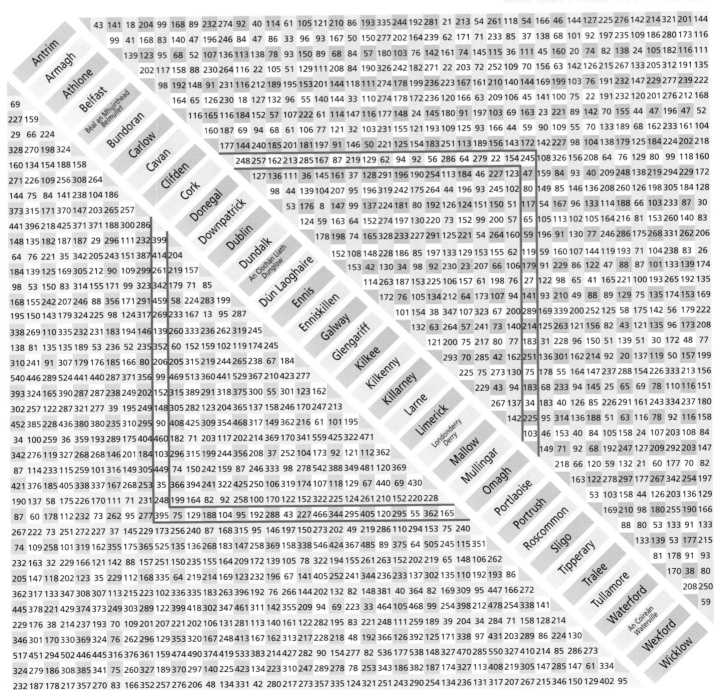

distances in kilometres

The shape of the land

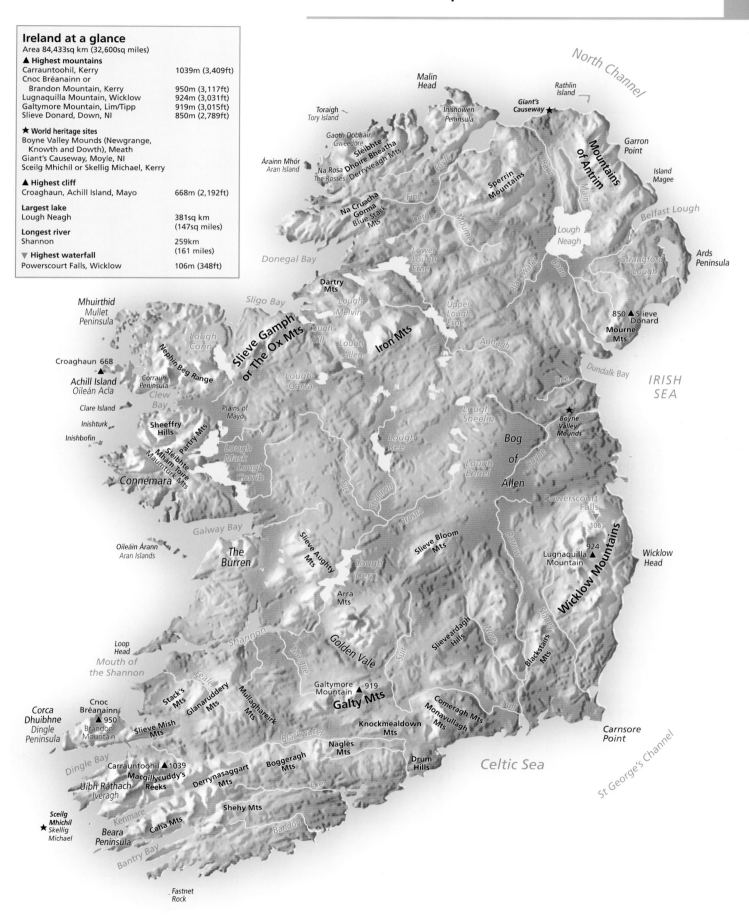

Ireland at a glance

Area 84,433sq km (32,600sq miles)

▲ **Highest mountains**

Carrauntoohil, Kerry	1039m (3,409ft)
Cnoc Bréanainn or Brandon Mountain, Kerry	950m (3,117ft)
Lugnaquilla Mountain, Wicklow	924m (3,031ft)
Galtymore Mountain, Lim/Tipp	919m (3,015ft)
Slieve Donard, Down, NI	850m (2,789ft)

★ **World heritage sites**

Boyne Valley Mounds (Newgrange, Knowth and Dowth), Meath
Giant's Causeway, Moyle, NI
Sceilg Mhichíl or Skellig Michael, Kerry

▲ **Highest cliff**

Croaghaun, Achill Island, Mayo   668m (2,192ft)

Largest lake

Lough Neagh   381sq km (147sq miles)

Longest river

Shannon   259km (161 miles)

▼ **Highest waterfall**

Powerscourt Falls, Wicklow   106m (348ft)

North Channel

Malin Head

Toraigh Tory Island

Inishowen Peninsula

Rathlin Island

Giant's Causeway ★

Mountains of Antrim

Garron Point

Island Magee

Gaoth Dobhair Gweedore

Sléibhte Dhoire Bheatha

Árainn Mhór Aran Island

Na Rosa The Rosses

Derryveagh Mts

Sperrin Mountains

Bann

Belfast Lough

Foyle

Finn

Derg

Mourne

Ards Peninsula

Na Cruacha Gorma Blue Stack Mts

Lower Lough Erne

Lough Neagh

Strangford Lough

Donegal Bay

Dartry Mts

Lough Melvin

Upper Lough Erne

Blackwater

Bann

850 ▲ Slieve Donard

Mourne Mts

Mhuirthid Mullet Peninsula

Sligo Bay

Slieve Gamph or The Ox Mts

Lough Gill

Iron Mts

Annagh

Dee

Dundalk Bay

IRISH SEA

Lough Conn

Lough Allen

Croaghaun 668

Achill Island Oileán Acla

Nephin Beg Range

Lough Garra

Lough Ree

Boyne Valley Mounds ★

Clare Island

Corraun Peninsula

Clew Bay

Plains of Mayo

Lough Sheelin

Bog of Allen

Boyne

Inishturk

Sheeffry Hills

Partry Mts

Lough Mask

Lough Corrib

Lough Ennel

Inishbofin

Sléibhte Mhám Toirc Maumturk Mts

Powerscourt Falls ▼

106

Connemara

Suck

Shannon

Brosna

Barrow

Lugnaquilla Mountain 924 ▲

Wicklow Mountains

Galway Bay

The Burren

Slieve Aughty Mts

Lough Derg

Slieve Bloom Mts

Wicklow Head

Oileán Árann Aran Islands

Arra Mts

Slieveardagh Hills

Nore

Slaney

Loop Head

Shannon

Maigue

Golden Vale

Suir

Slievardagh Hills

Blackstairs Mts

Mouth of the Shannon

Feale

Galtymore Mountain ▲ 919

Galty Mts

Comeragh Mts

Carnsore Point

Corca Dhuibhne Dingle Peninsula

Cnoc Bréanainn ▲ 950 Brandon Mountain

Stack's Mts

Glanaruddery Mts

Mullaghareirk Mts

Knockmealdown Mts

Monavullagh Mts

Celtic Sea

Slieve Mish Mts

Blackwater

Nagles Mts

Drum Hills

St George's Channel

Dingle Bay

Carrauntoohil ▲ 1039

Boggeragh Mts

Macgillycuddy's Reeks

Derrynasaggart Mts

Lee

Sceilg Mhichíl ★ Skellig Michael

Shehy Mts

Uibh Ráthach Iveragh

Kenmare

Caha Mts

Bandon

Beara Peninsula

Bantry Bay

Fastnet Rock

0	10	20	30	40	50 miles
0		20	40	60	80 km

Teanga agus canúintí
Langue et dialectes
Sprache und Dialekte

Language and dialects

An Ghaeltacht

Gaeltacht is an Irish language term for those areas of Ireland where the Irish language is still spoken as a community language. The Irish language word for the language itself is *Gaeilge*. When you see the road sign **An Ghaeltacht**, it means that you are about to enter a Gaeltacht area. Many traffic signs in the Gaeltacht are in the Irish language only.

In order to match the road signs on the ground, the place name spellings for places in Gaeltacht areas used in this atlas are in official Irish. For example, 'An Daingean' is used rather than 'Dingle' for the town in west county Kerry. However, in order to assist those unfamiliar with Irish, the English language version of the name is also shown on the maps and for ease of reference both versions are listed alphabetically in the index.

According to the 2006 census, over 50,000 Irish people speak Irish on a daily basis while 1.65 million people have the ability to speak at least some Irish. It is one of two official languages in the Republic of Ireland (the other being English). Irish is taught at all stages in Irish primary and secondary schools. However, it survives as the first community language only in the Gaeltacht areas, most of which are in the west of Ireland.

The English spoken in Ireland is similar to the English spoken in Britain. There are a number of dialect variations to be found in different parts of the country. The main dialect boundary separates the west and south from the north which has a strong lowland Scots element in vocabulary and markedly different vowel sounds. Some consider Ulster-Scots or Ullans to be a separate language.

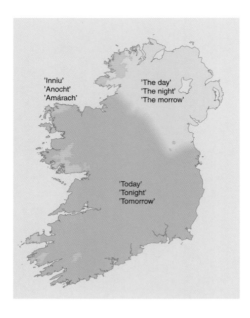

'Inniu' 'Anocht' 'Amárach'

'The day' 'The night' 'The morrow'

'Today' 'Tonight' 'Tomorrow'

GAELTACHT
Ceantair Ghaeltachta
La région Gaeltacht
Gaeltacht-Regionen

Scottish influence
Tionchar Albanach
Influence Ecossaises
Schottisches Beeinflusst

Gaeilge influence
Tionchar Ghaeilge
Influence Gaeilge
Gaeilge Beeinflusst

ANGLO-IRISH
Angla Éireannach
Anglo-Irlandaise
Anglo-Irisch

GÉILL SLÍ

Major road ahead – give way to traffic on it

Comhartha tráchta ag ordú duit GÉILL nó GÉILL SLÍ roimh an trácht ar an bpríomhbhóthar romhat.

Panneau routier indiquant YIELD ou CEDER LE PASSAGE aux usagers de la route principale.

Bei diesem Verkehrsschild müssen Sie dem Verkehr auf der Hauptverkehrsstraße die VORFAHRT GEWÄHREN.

*Is téarma Gaeilge í Gaeltacht do na ceantair sin in Éirinn ina bhfuil an Ghaeilge fós á labhairt mar theanga pobail. Is í Gaeilge an focal ar an dteanga féin. Nuair a fheiceann tú comhartha bóthair **An Ghaeltacht**, ciallaíonn sé go bhfuil tú ag dul isteach i gceantar Gaeltachta. Go leor comharthaí tráchta i gceantair Gaeltachta, is i nGaeilge amháin atá siad.*

Ar an atlais seo, litrítear na logainmneacha do áiteanna sa nGaeltacht de réir an chaighdeán oifigiúil Ghaeilge chun teacht leis na comharthaí bóthair atá sna ceantair sin. Mar shampla, úsáidtear 'An Daingean' seachas 'Dingle' i gcás an bhaile in iarthar chontae Chiarraí. Tá an leagan Béarla den logainm luaite ar an léarscáil chomh maith mar chúnamh dóibh siúd nach bhfuil taithí acu ar an nGaeilge agus ar mhaithe le soiléireacht tá an dá leagan liostáilte in ord abítearach san innéacs.

De réir daonáireamh na bliana 2006, labhraíonn os cionn 50,000 Gaeilge go laethúil agus tá de chumas ag 1.65 milliún duine ar a laghad roinnt Gaeilge a labhairt. Tá sí ar cheann de dhá theangacha oifigiúla Phoblacht na hÉireann (is é an Béarla an ceann eile). Múintear Gaeilge ag gach leibhéal sna bunscoileanna agus meánscoileanna in Éirinn. Tá sí fós ina príomh teanga pobail in sna ceantair Gaeltachta amháin, áfach, a bhfuil a bhformhór acu in iarthar na hÉireann.

Tá an Béarla a labhraítear in Éirinn cosúil leis an mBéarla a labhraítear sa Bhreatain. Ta roinnt éagsúlachtaí canúna le fáil i gcodanna éagsúla den tír. Deighleann an príomh-teorainn canúna an iarthar agus an deisceart ón dtuaisceart ina bhfuil tionchar láidir ag teanga na n-ísealchríoch Albanach ar an mBéarla ann ó thaobh na bhfoclóra agus fhuaimniú na ngotaí de. Dar le roinnt daoine, is teanga ar leith í Albainis Uladh nó Ultais.

Gaeltacht est un terme irlandais pour les région de l'Irlande où l'irlandais est encore parlé dans les communautés. En irlandais le mot désignant la langue irlandaise est *Gaeilge*. Si vous rencontrez le panneau indicateur **An Ghaeltacht**, cela signifie que vous êtes sur le point de pénétrer dans une région Gaeltacht. Beaucoup de panneaux de signalisation du Gaeltacht ne sont qu'en irlandais.

Afin que les panneaux de signalisation de l'atlas correspondent à ceux sur le terrain, les noms des lieux utilisés dans l'atlas pour les régions du Gaeltacht sont donnés dans la langue irlandaise officielle. Par exemple 'An Daingean' est utilisé au lieu de 'Dingle' pour désigner la ville du Kerry situé dans l'ouest du pays. Cependant la version anglaise des noms figure également sur les cartes pour aider ceux qui ne connaissent pas l'irlandais. Pour un système de référence plus facile les deux versions sont données en ordre alphabétique dans l'index.

Selon le recensement de 2006 plus de 50 000 Irlandais parlent quotidiennement l'irlandais et 1,65 million de personnes sont capables de parler un peu l'irlandais. C'est l'une des deux langues officielles de la République d'Irlande (l'autre étant l'anglais). L'irlandais est enseigné à tous les niveaux du primaire et du secondaire dans les écoles irlandaises. Mais l'irlandais ne survit en tant que langue communautaire que dans les régions du Gaeltacht qui se situent principalement à l'ouest de l'Irlande.

L'anglais parlé en Irlande est similaire à celui parlé en Grande-Bretagne. Il existe un certain nombre de dialectes dans différentes parties du pays. La principale frontière dialectique sépare l'ouest et le sud du nord qui comporte dans son vocabulaire un fort élément des Basses-Terres écossaises et des voyelles dont le son est nettement différent. Certains considèrent que l'écossais d'Ulster, aussi appelé Ullans, est une autre langue.

Gaeltacht ist ein Begriff in der irischen Sprache für die Regionen in Irland, in denen die irische Sprache noch gesprochen wird. In der irischen Sprache wird die Sprache als *Gaeilge* bezeichnet. Wenn Sie das Verkehrsschild **An Ghaeltacht** sehen, fahren Sie in eine Gaeltacht-Region. Viele Verkehrsschilder in der Gaeltacht-Region sind nur in der irischen Sprache.

Damit die Ortsnamen den Verkehrsschildern vor Ort entsprechen, erscheinen in diesem Atlas die Ortsnamen in den Gaeltacht-Regionen in der offiziellen irischen Sprache. So wird beispielsweise 'An Daingean' anstatt von 'Dingle', der Stadt in der Grafschaft Kerry im Westen Irlands, verwendet. Um das Verständnis für diejenigen zu erleichtern, die der irischen Sprache nicht mächtig sind, erscheint der englische Name ebenfalls auf den Karten und im Ortsverzeichnis sind beide Versionen in alphabetischer Reihenfolge aufgeführt.

Laut der Volkszählung in 2006 sprechen über 50.000 Personen täglich die irische Sprache und 1,65 Millionen Personen können zumindest etwas Irisch sprechen. Sie ist eine der beiden offiziellen Landessprachen in der Republik Irland (die andere Sprache ist Englisch). Irisch wird in allen Stufen von Grundschulen und weiterführenden Schulen in Irland gesprochen. Sie ist nur in den Gaeltacht-Regionen, die sich zum Großteil im Westen Irlands befinden, noch die Muttersprache.

Das Englisch, das heute in Irland gesprochen wird, ist dem Englisch, das in Großbritannien gesprochen wird, sehr ähnlich. In verschiedenen Teilen des Landes gibt es unterschiedliche Dialekte. Die Hauptdialektgrenze trennt den Westen und Süden vom Norden, in dem beim Vokabular und mit deutlichen Unterschieden bei den Vokalauten ein starkes schottisches Element vorherrscht. Von manchen wird Ulster-Schottisch oder Ullans sogar als eine eigene Sprache betrachtet.

Key to map symbols
Eochair *Légende* *Legende*

Motoring information

Mótarbhealach saor in aisce / Autoroute gratuite	M1	**Toll-free motorway** / Mautfreie Autobahn
Mótarbhealach le híoc / Autoroute à péage	M1	**Toll motorway** / Mautpflichtige Autobahn
Acomhal lán (1), srianta (2) / Échangeur (1), Échangeur partiel (2)	(1) (2) (1) (2)	**Full (1), restricted junction (2)** / Vollwertige (1), eingeschränkte Anschlussstelle (2)
Mótarbhealach á dhéanamh / Autoroute en construction		**Motorway under construction** / Autobahn in Bau
Carrbhealach dúbailte / Double voie		**Dual carriageway** / Straße mit getrennten Fahrbahnen
Carrbhealach singil / Une voie		**Single carriageway** / Straße mit einem Fahrstreifen
Bóthar á dhéanamh / Route en construction		**Road under construction** / Straße in Bau
Mionbhóthar / Route secondaire		**Minor road** / Nebenstraße
Droichead nó bóthar le híoc / Péage pont ou routier	Toll	**Bridge or road toll** / Brücken- oder Straßenmaut
Carrchaladh / Car-ferry	or	**Car ferry** / Autofähre
Carrchaladh catamaran / Catamaran-ferry		**Catamaran car ferry** / Katamaran-Autofähre
ealach iarainn, stáisiún, crosaire comhréidh / Voie de chemin de fer, gare, passage à niveau		**Railway, station, level crossing** / Eisenbahn, Bahnhof, Bahnüber
Aerfort, aerpháirc / Aéroport, aérodrome	✈	**Airport, airfield** / Flughafen, Flugplatz
Cathair, baile mór, baile beag nó ceantar / Grande ville, ville, village ou localité	○	**City, town, village or locality** / Großstadt, Stadt, Dorf oder Ort
Créamatóiriam / Crématorium	C	**Crematorium** / Krematorium
Airde i méadair, timpeall / Altitude en mètres, col	628 ▲ •	**Height in metres, pass** / Höhenangabe in Metern, Pass

Príomh cheann cúrsa (roghnaithe) / Destination primaire (sélectionnée)	CORK	**Primary destination (selected)** / Hauptziel (ausgewählt)
Bóthar priomha náisiúnta (IRL) / Route nationale (IRL)	N17	**National primary route (IRL)** / Nationalstraße erster Ordnung (IRL)
Bóthar tánaisteach náisiúnta (IRL) / Route départementale (IRL)	N56	**National secondary route (IRL)** / Nationalstraße zweiter Ordnung (IRL)
Bóthar réigiúnach (IRL) / Route communale (IRL)	R182	**Regional road (IRL)** / Regionalstraße (IRL)
Faid i gciliméadar (IRL) / Distance en kilomètres (IRL)	▼ 8 ▼	**Distance in kilometres (IRL)** / Entfernung in Kilometern (IRL)
Bóthar príomha (NI) / Route nationale (NI)	A4	**Primary route (NI)** / Straße erster Ordnung (NI)
Bóthar A (NI) / Catégorie A (NI)	A21	**A road (NI)** / Nationalstraße (NI)
Bóthar B (NI) / Catégorie B (NI)	B75	**B road (NI)** / Nebenstraße (NI)
Faid i mílte (NI) / Distance en miles (NI)	▼ 5 ▼	**Distance in miles (NI)** / Entfernung in Meilen (NI)
Tollán bóthair / Tunnel routier	=======	**Road tunnel** / Straßentunnel
Teorainn idirnáisiúnta / Frontière internationale		**International boundary** / Staatsgrenze
Teorainn eile / Autre frontière		**Other boundary** / Andere Grenze
Trá, cladach eile / Plage, autre rivage		**Beach, other foreshore** / Strand, sonstige Uferbereiche
Abhainn, canáil, loch / Rivière, canal, lac		**River, canal, lough** / Fluss, Kanal, See
Uimhir leanúnach an leathanaigh / Numéro de continuation de page	23	**Page continuation number** / Nummer der Anschlussseite

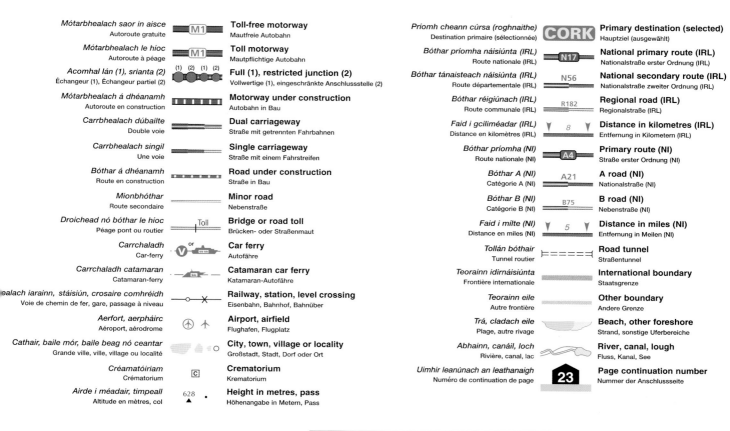

Touring information

Ionad eolais turasóireachta, séasúrach / Office de tourisme, saisonnier	𝑖	**Tourist information, seasonal** / Fremdenverkehrsamt, während der Saison
Ionad cuartaíochta / Centre pour visiteurs	V	**Visitor centre** / Besucherzentrum
Láithreán campála AA / Terrain pour camping homologué AA		**AA approved campsite** / Mit AA ausgezeichneter Campingplatz
Láithreán carbhán eile / Autre terrain pour caravanes		**Other caravan site** / Sonstiger Wohnwagenplatz
Mainistir, ardeaglais nó prióireacht / Abbaye, cathédrale ou monastère		**Abbey, cathedral or priory** / Abtei, Kathedrale, Priorei
ullóg mainistreach, ardeaglais nó prióireacht / Ruines d'abbaye, de cathédrale ou de monastère		**Ruined abbey, cathedral or priory** / Abtei-, Kathedralen-, Priorei-Ruine
Caisleán, dún / Château, fortifications	♜	**Castle, hill-fort** / Schloss, Festung
Iarsmalann nó dánlann / Musée ou galerie	M	**Museum or gallery** / Museum oder Kunstgalerie
Gairdín, páirc tuaithe / Jardin, parc	❋ ⚘	**Garden, country park** / Garten, Landschaftspark
Zú, fiabheatha nó páirc éanlaithe / Zoo, réserve naturelle ou parc ornithologique		**Zoo, wildlife or bird park** / Zoo, Tier- oder Vogelpark
Dúlra, tearmann éin / Réserve naturelle, ornithologique	RSPB	**Nature, bird reserve** / Natur-, Vogelschutzgebiet
Slíbhealach le comharthaí / Promenade banalisée		**Waymarked walk** / Ausgeschilderter Weg
Ionad dearctha, láithreán picnicí / Panorama, aire de pique-nique		**Viewpoint, picnic site** / Aussichtspunkt, Picknick-Platz
Ar liosta AA, galfchúrsa eile / Terrain de golf homologué AA, non homologué AA	▷	**AA listed, other golf course** / Mit AA ausgezeichneter, sonstiger Golfplatz
Bealach radharcach / Itinéraire pittoresque		**Scenic route** / Landschaftlich schöne Strecke

Rásaí capall, ciorcad rásaí cairr / Hippodrome, circuit automobile		**Horse racing, motor-racing circuit** / Pferde-, Motorrennbahn
Lúthchleasaíocht idirnáisiúnta, aontas rugbaí / Événements athlétiques internationaux, rugby		**International athletics, rugby union** / Internationale Leichtathletik-, Rugby-Union
Gníomhaíocht sciála, bádóireacht / Activités nautiques, ski		**Boating, skiing activities** / Wassersport, Ski
Áitreabh Taisce Náisiúnta / Propriété du National Trust	AT	**National Trust property** / Eigentum des National Trust
Teach nó foirgneamh stairiúil / Bâtiment ou maison historique		**Historic house or building** / Historisches Haus oder Gebäude
Leacht réamhstairiúil / Monument préhistorique		**Prehistoric monument** / Prähistorisches Denkmal
Suim tionsclaíoch / Point d'intérêt industriel		**Industrial interest** / Industriedenkmal
Láithreán catha le dáta / Champ de bataille avec date	✕ 1690	**Battle site with date** / Schlachtfeld mit Datum
Leacht, áit eile suimiúil / Monument, autre lieu d'intérêt	⚱ ★	**Monument, other place of interest** / Denkmal, anderer interessanter Ort
Léiríonn comharthaí le boscaí tarraingtí laistigh de cheantair uirbeacha / Les symboles encadrés signalent un lieu d'attraction en zone urbaine	☐	**Boxed symbols indicate attractions within urban areas** / Eingerahmte Symbole bezeichnen Attraktionen innerhalb der Stadtgebiete
Ceantair Ghaeltachta / La Gaeltacht région		**Gaeltacht (Irish language area)** / Gaeltacht-Regionen
Páirc Náisiúnta / Parc national		**National Park** / Nationalpark
Páirc Foraoise / Parc forestier		**Forest Park** / Parkwald
Foraois / Forêt		**Woodland** / Wald

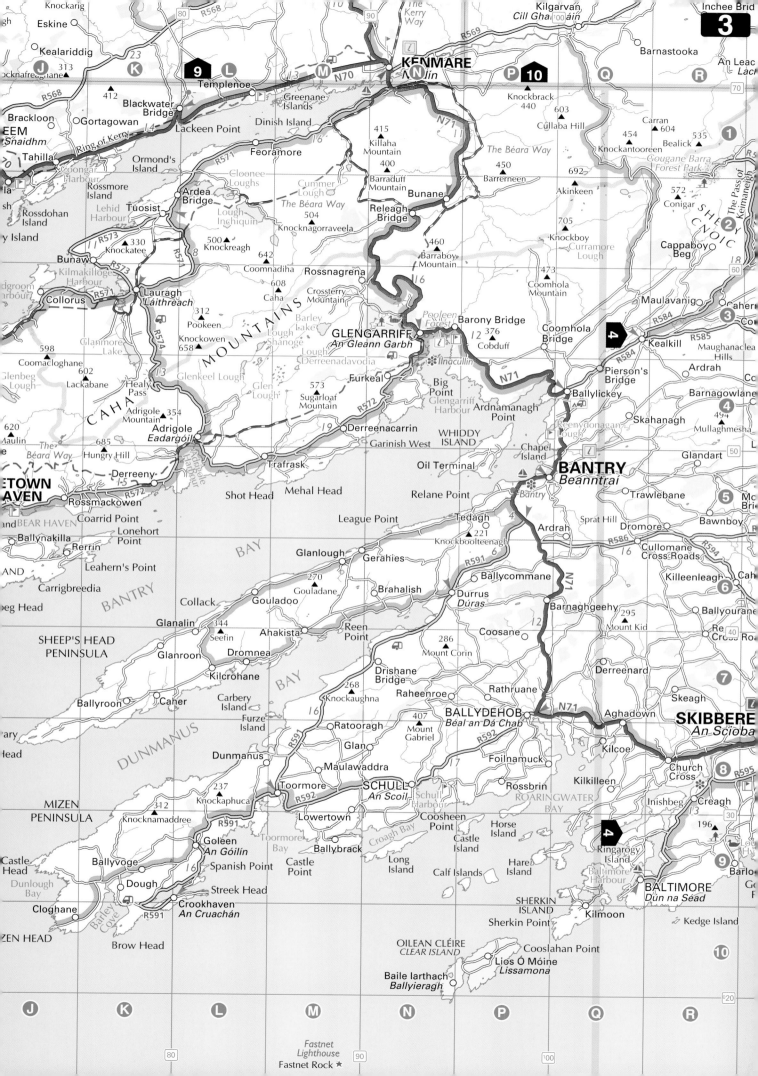

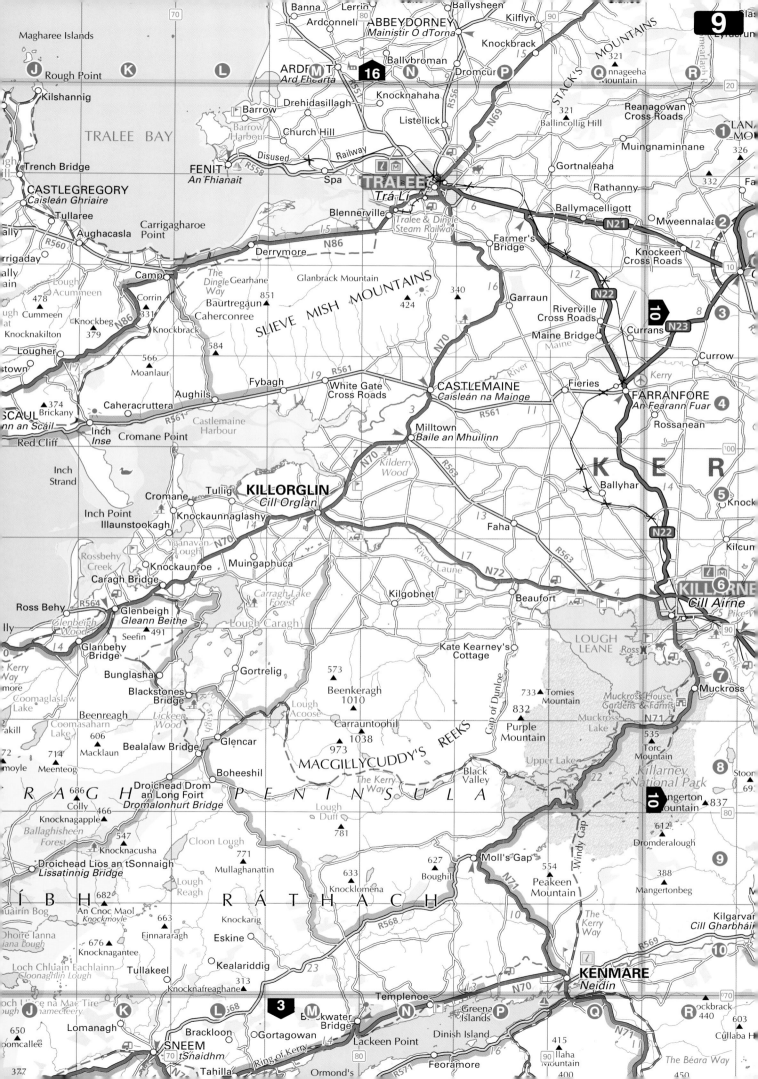

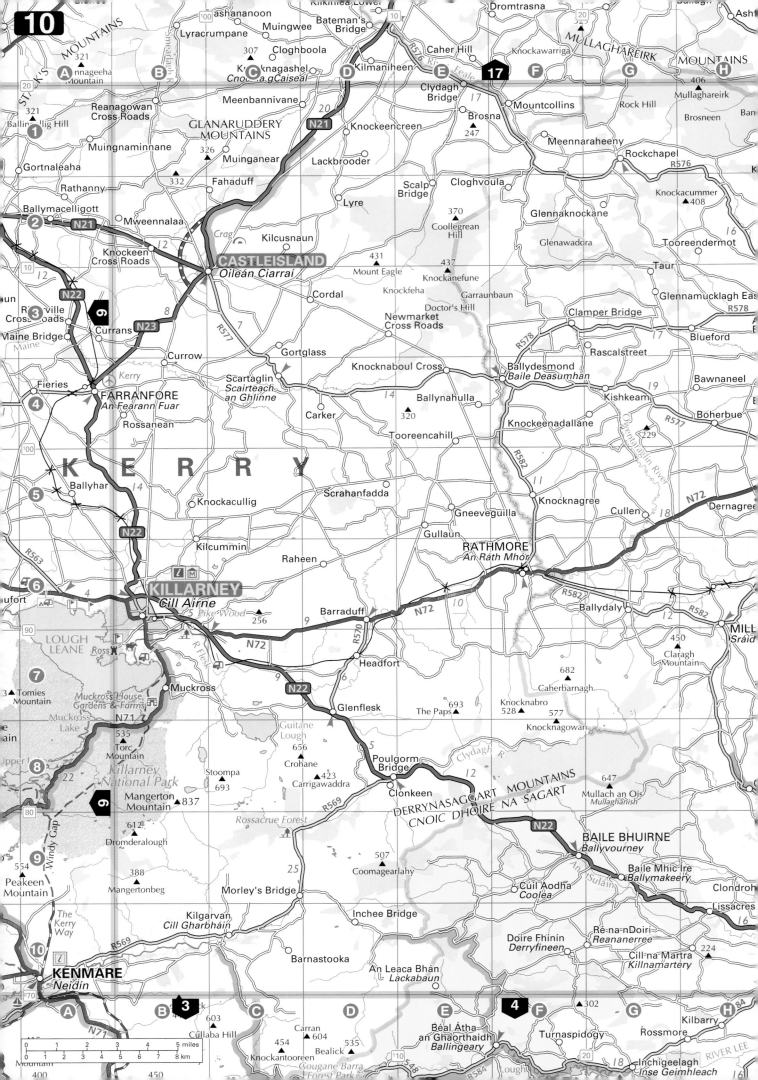

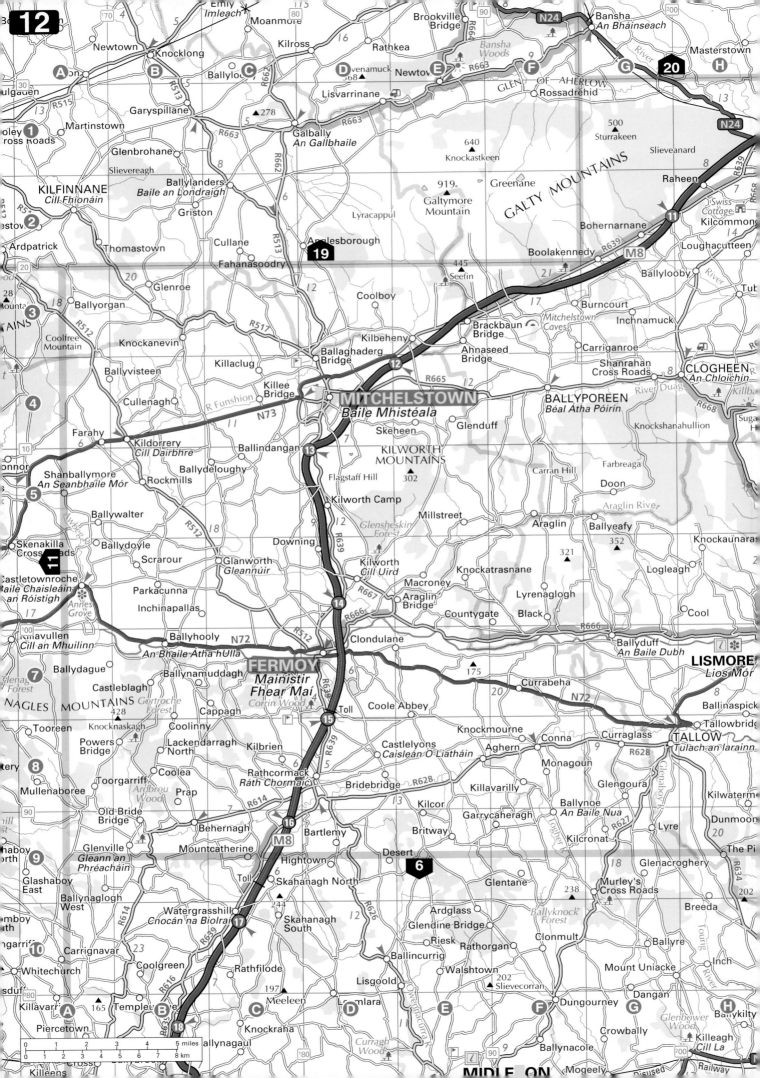

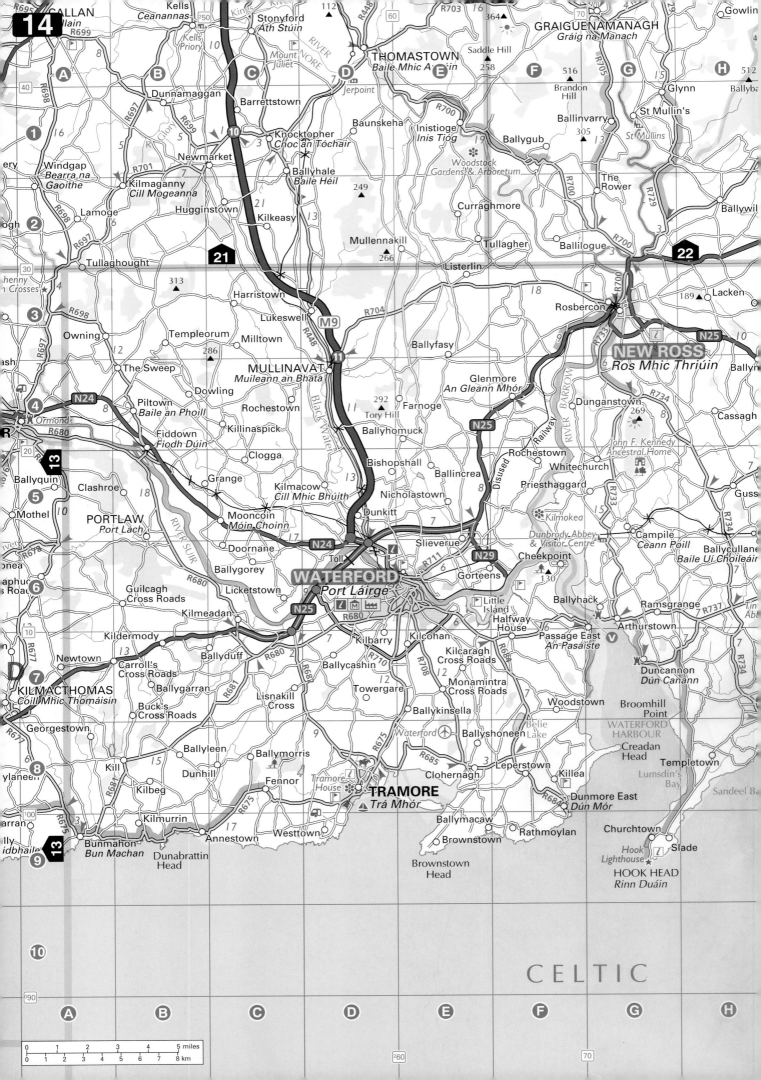

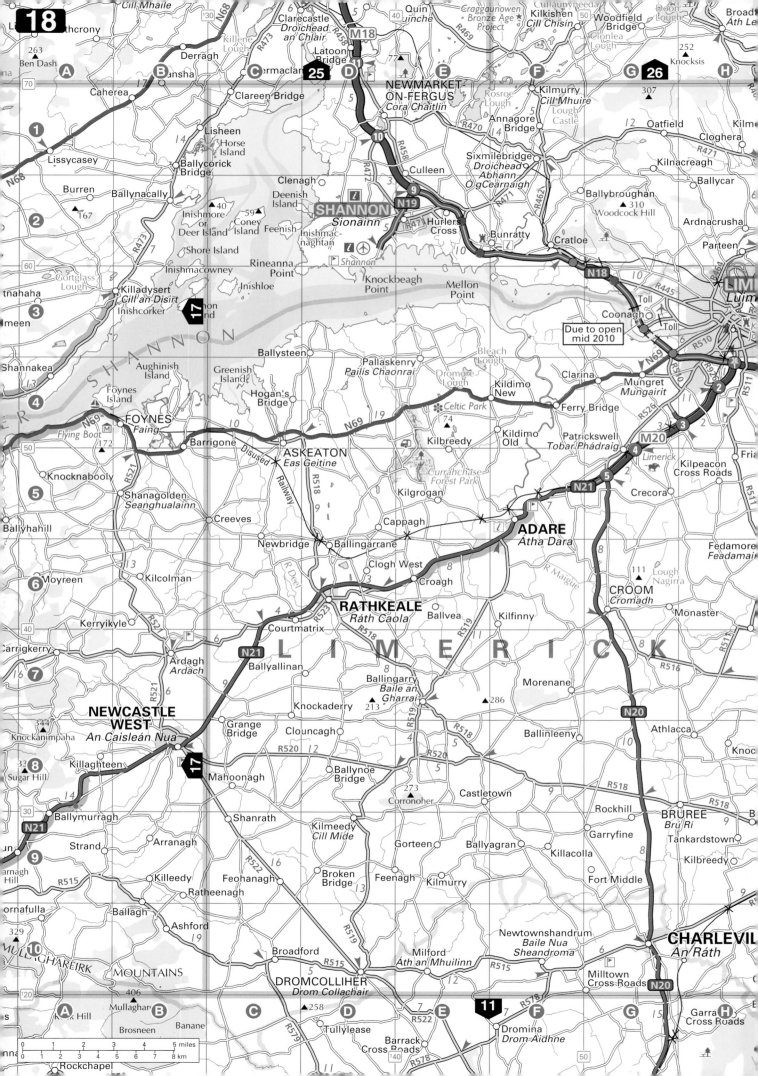

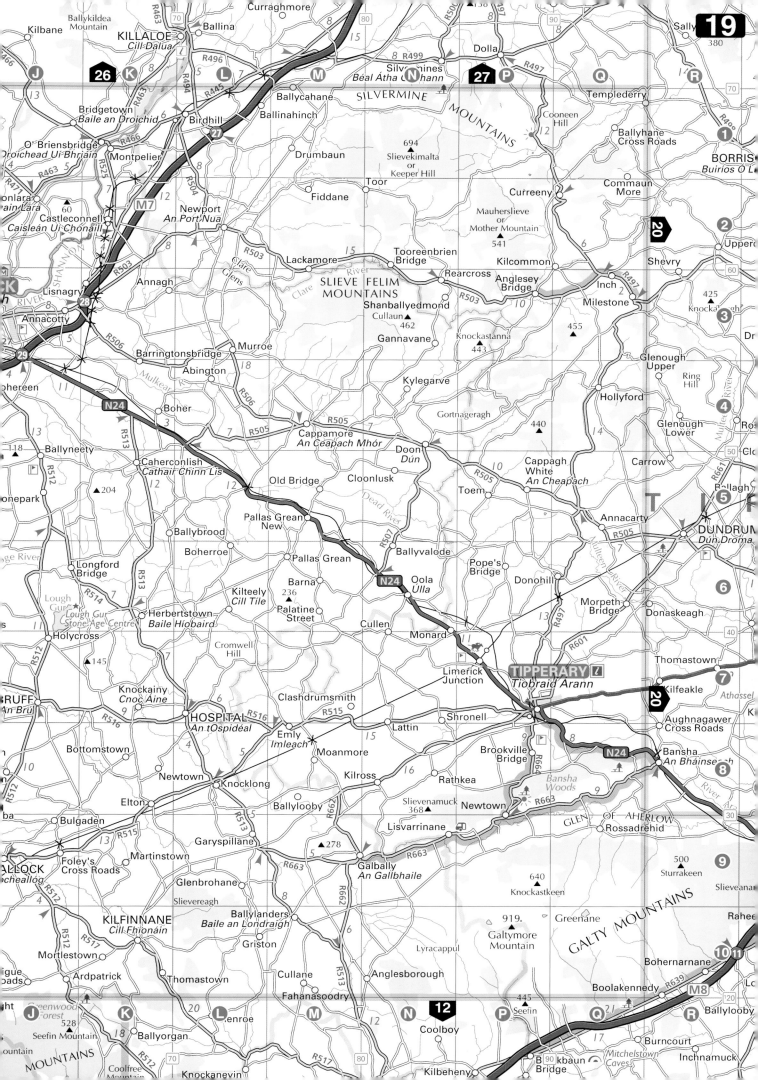

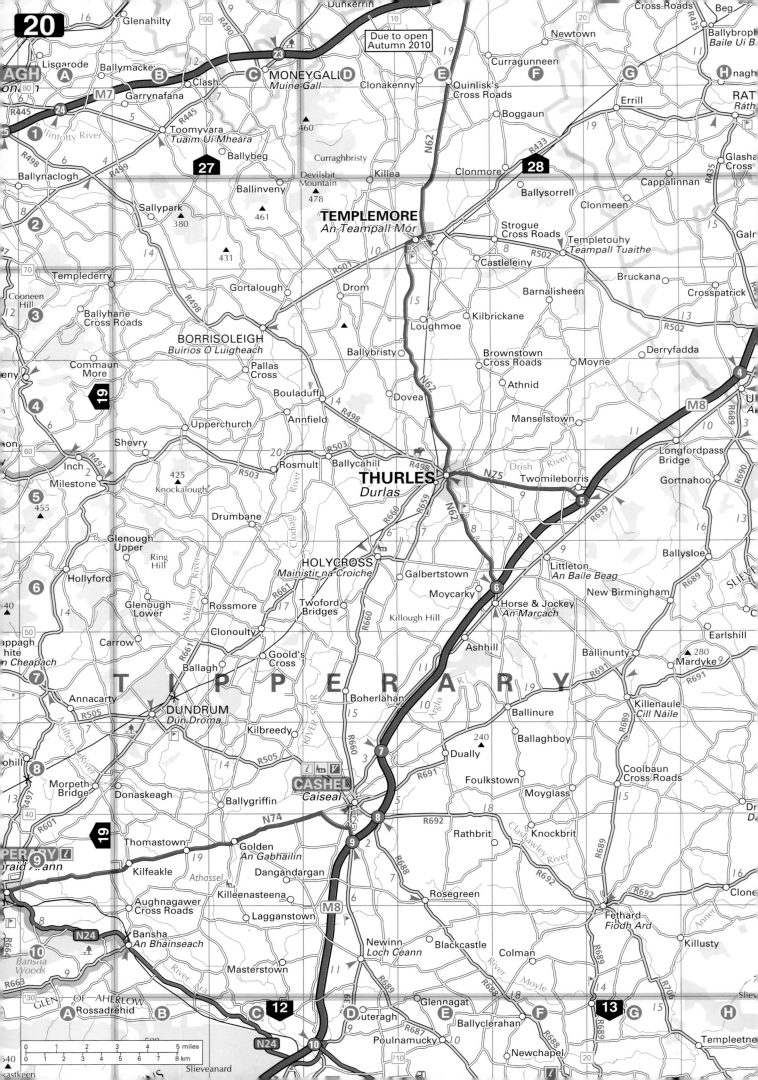

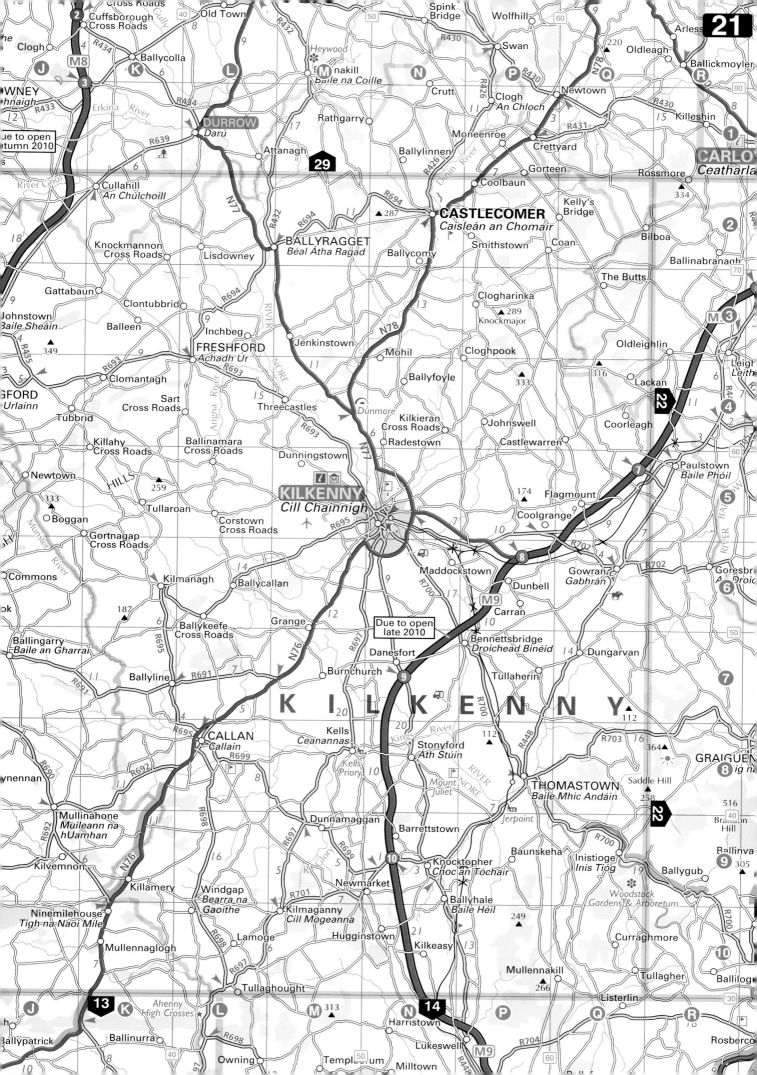

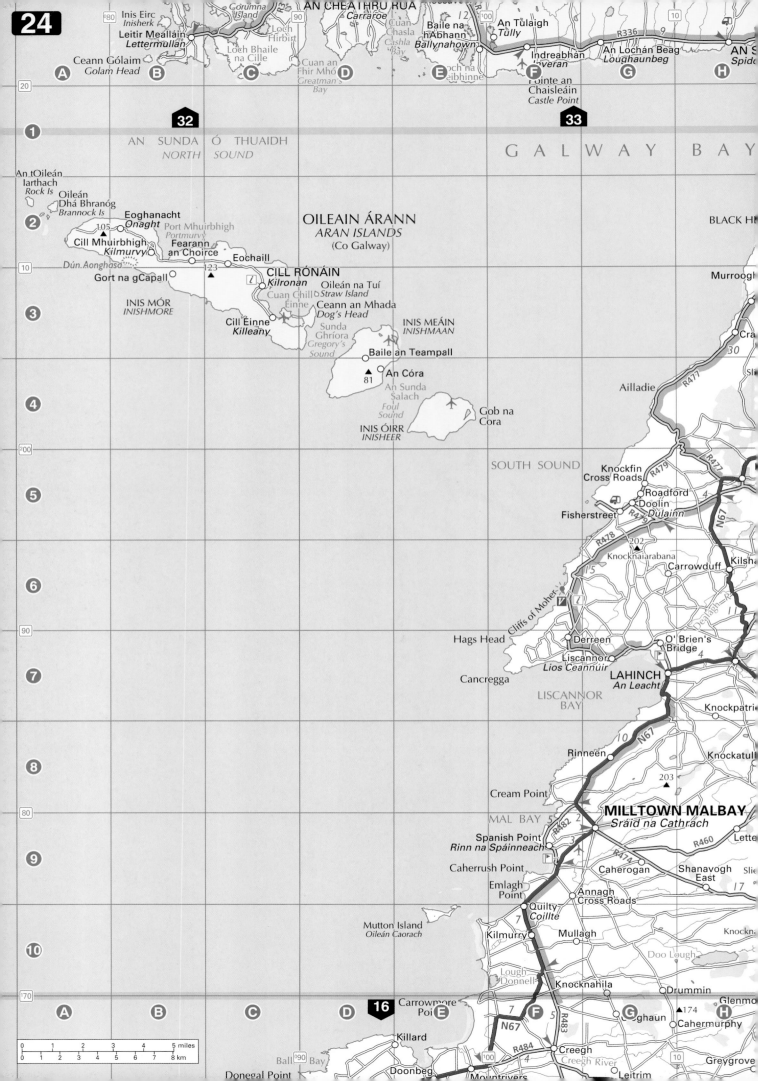

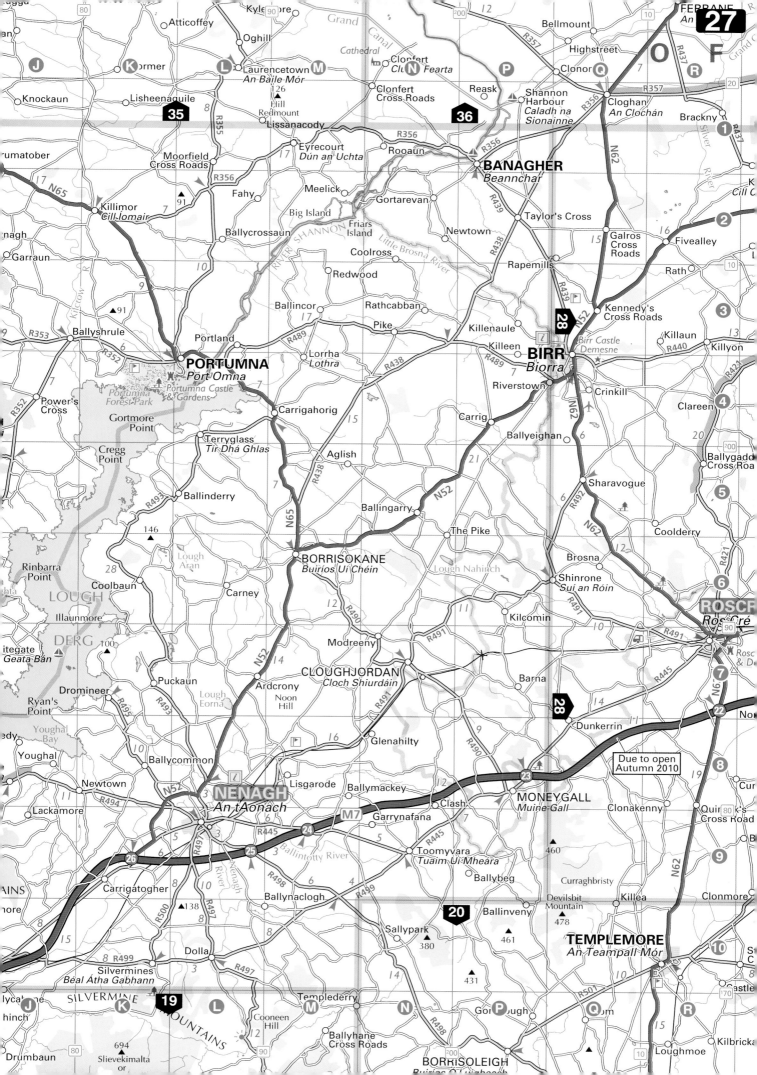

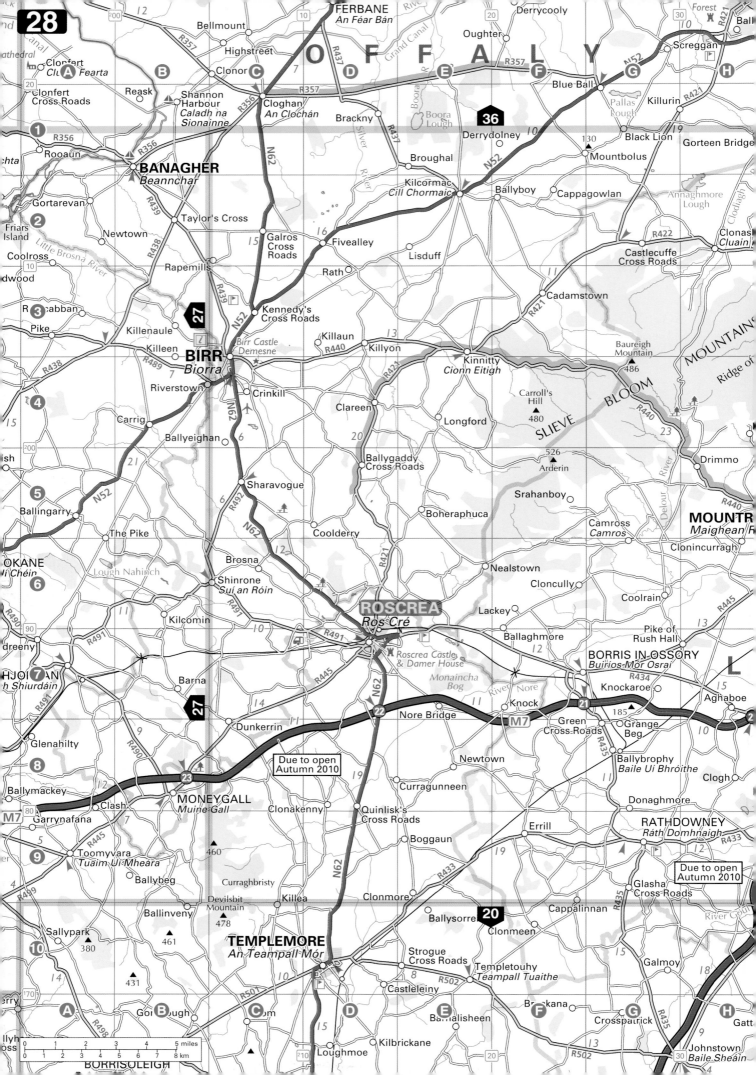

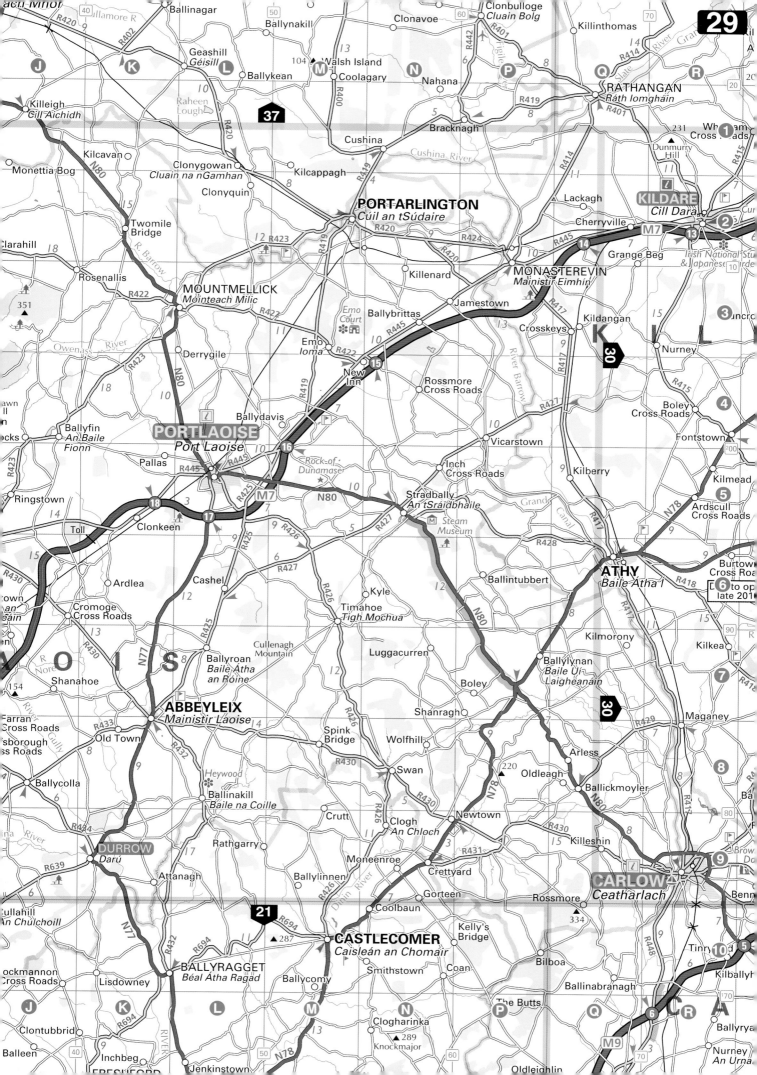

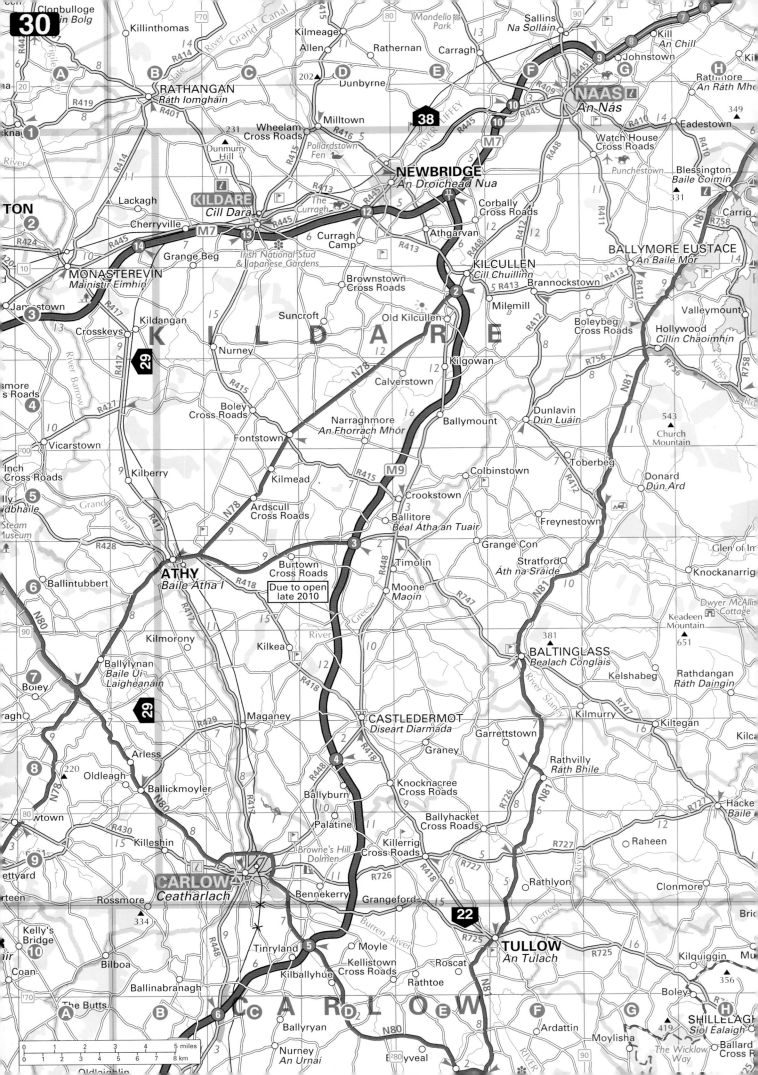

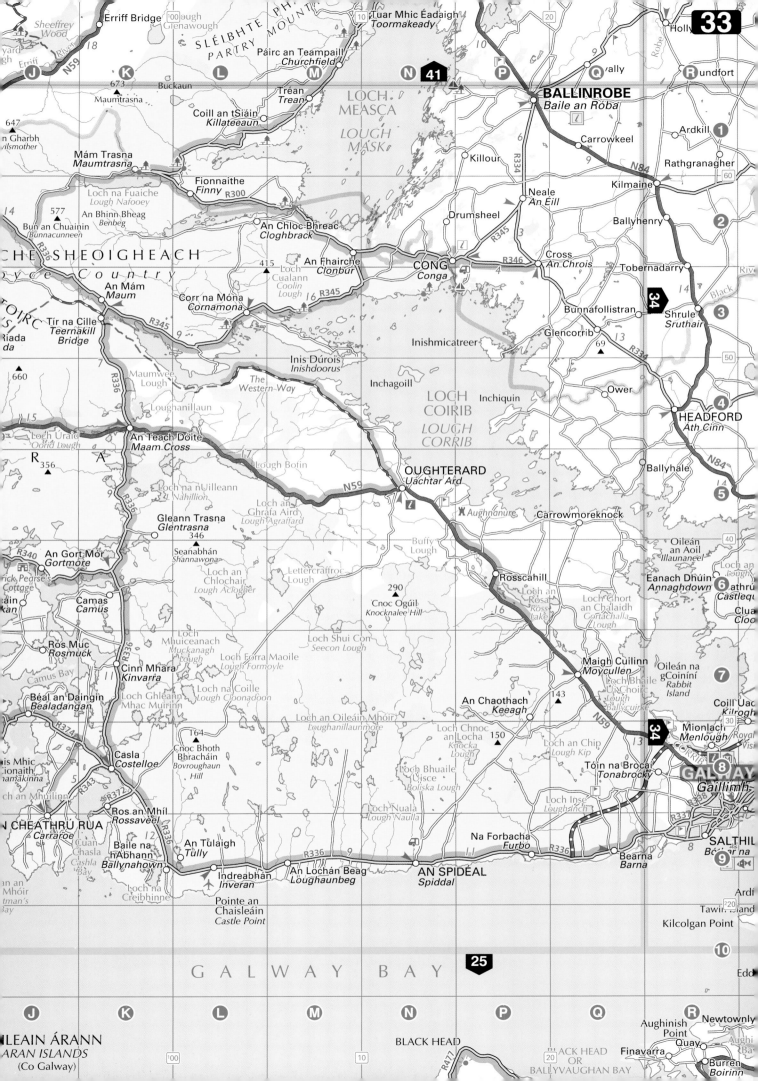

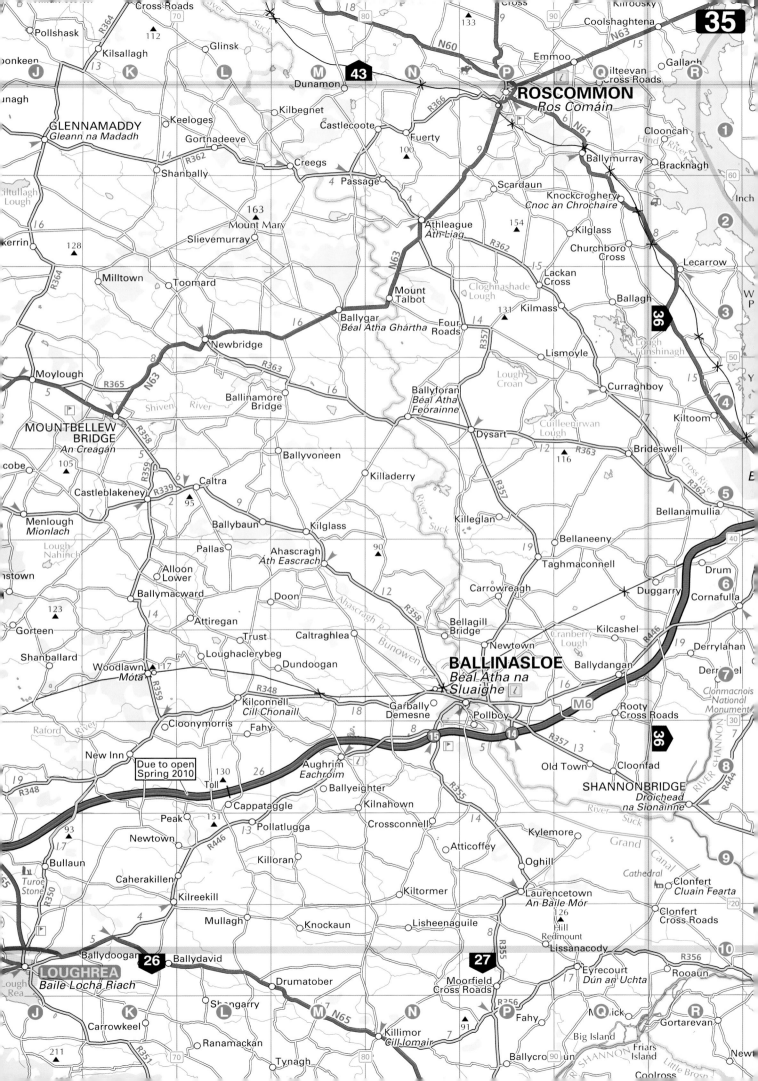

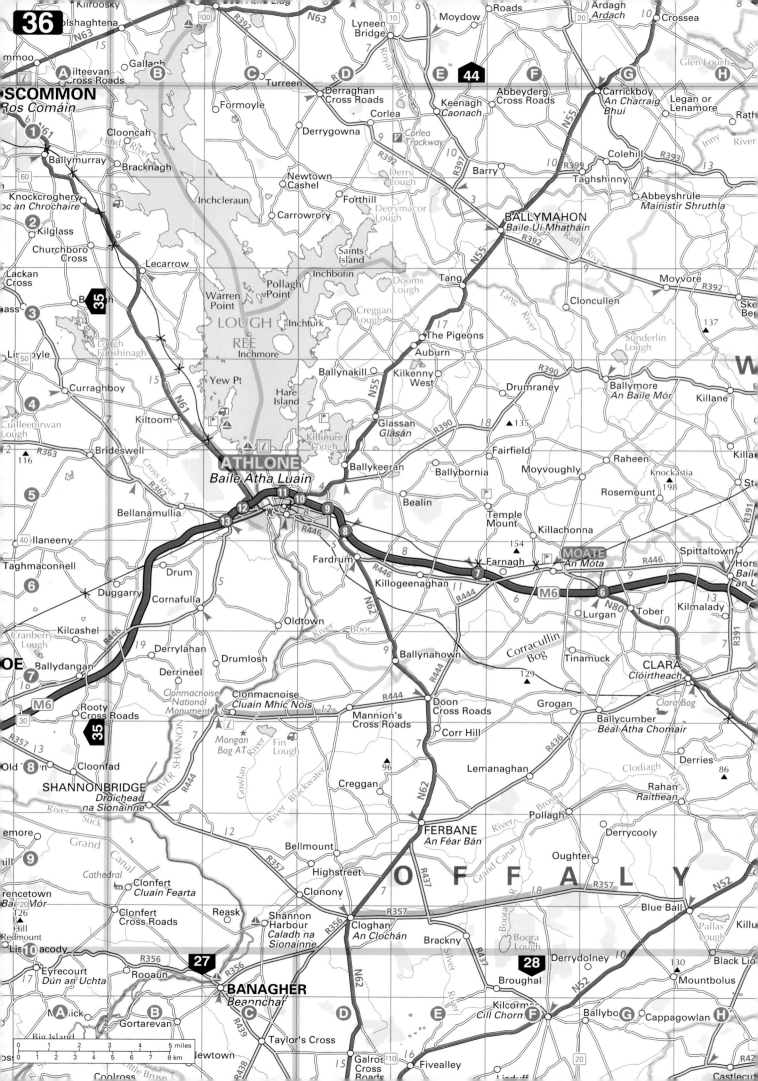

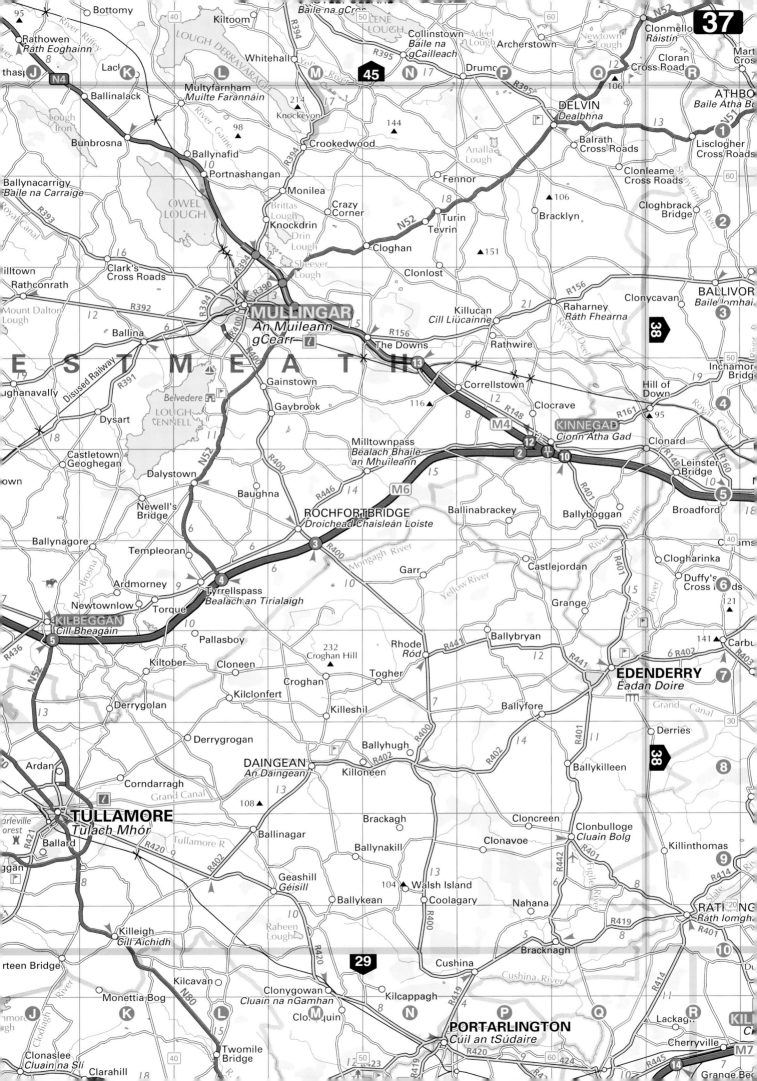

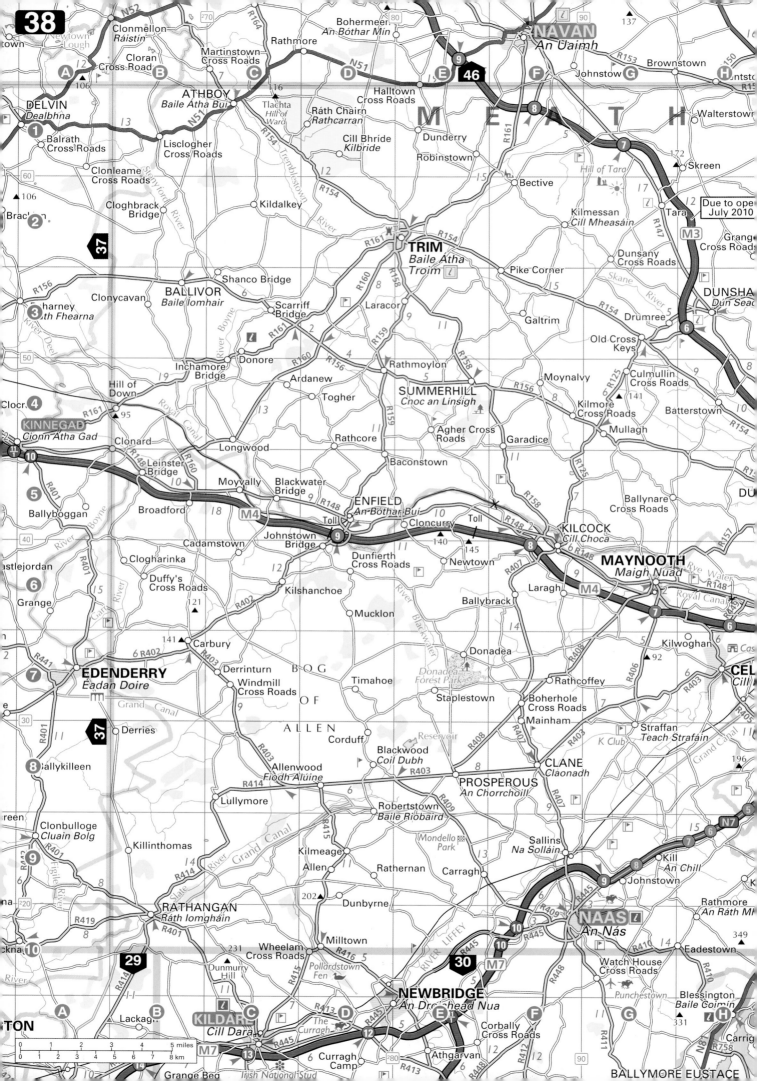

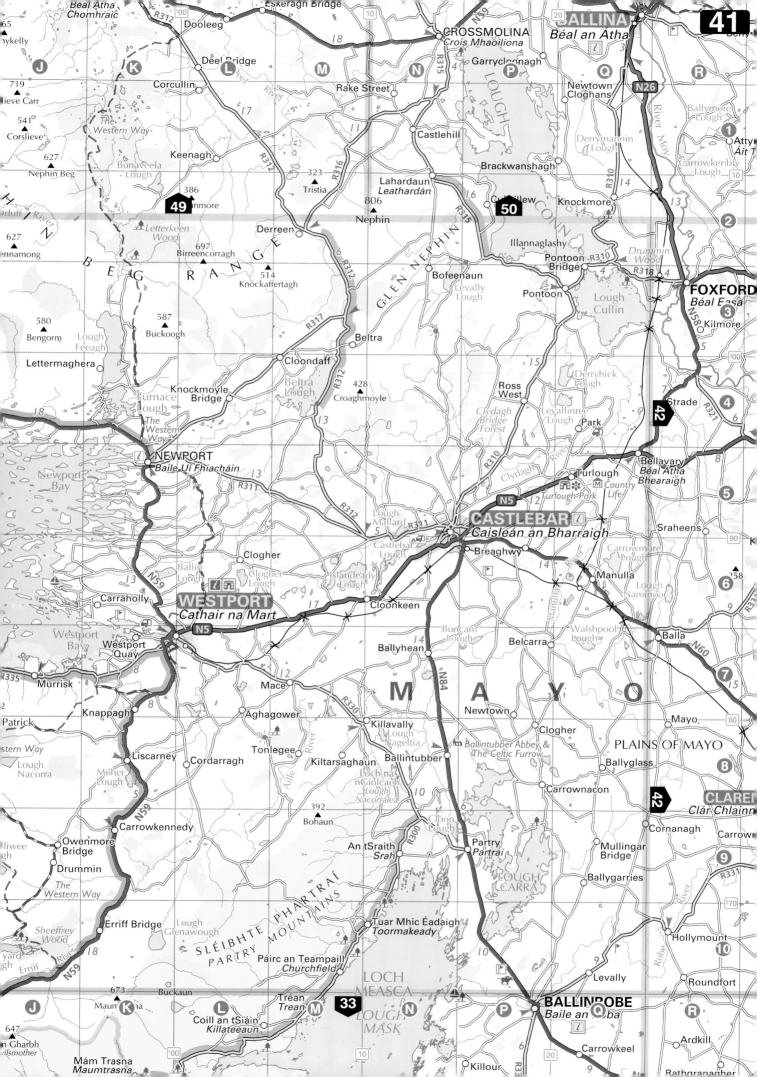

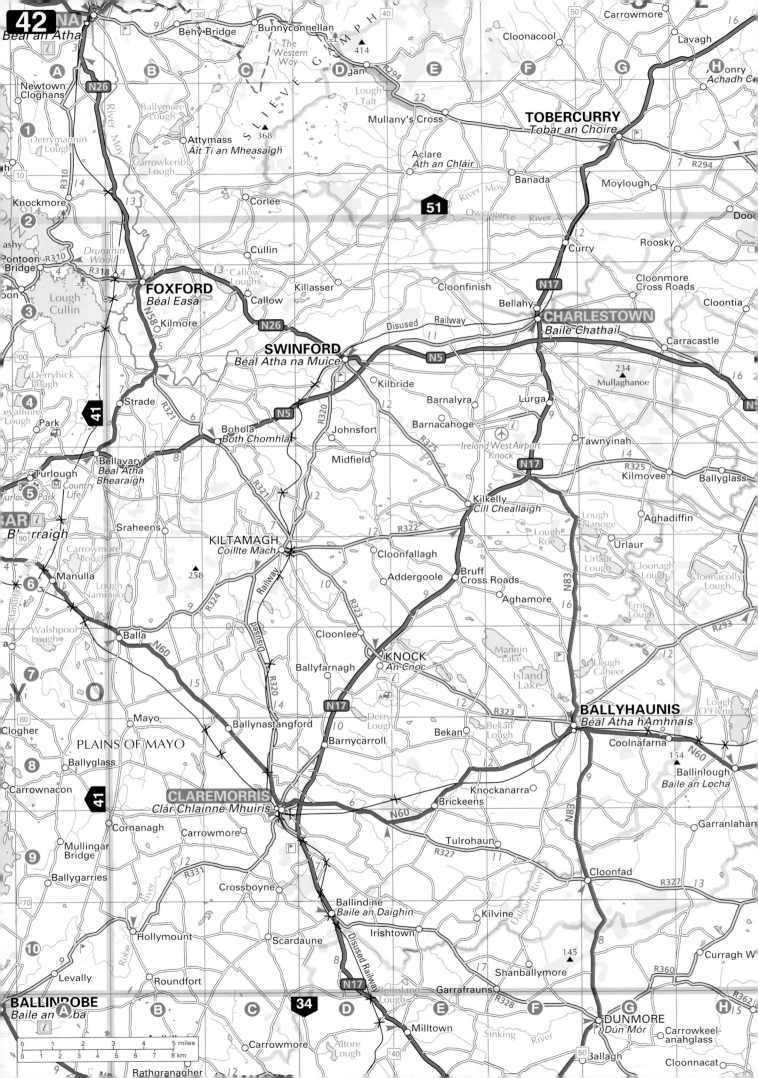

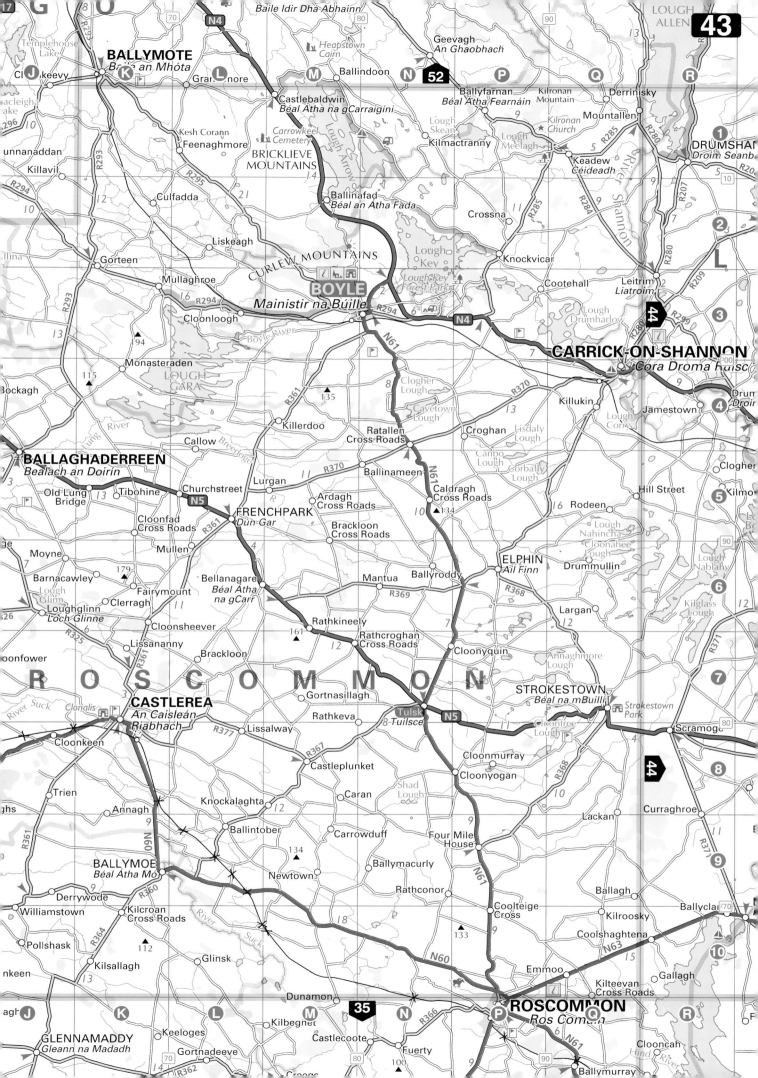

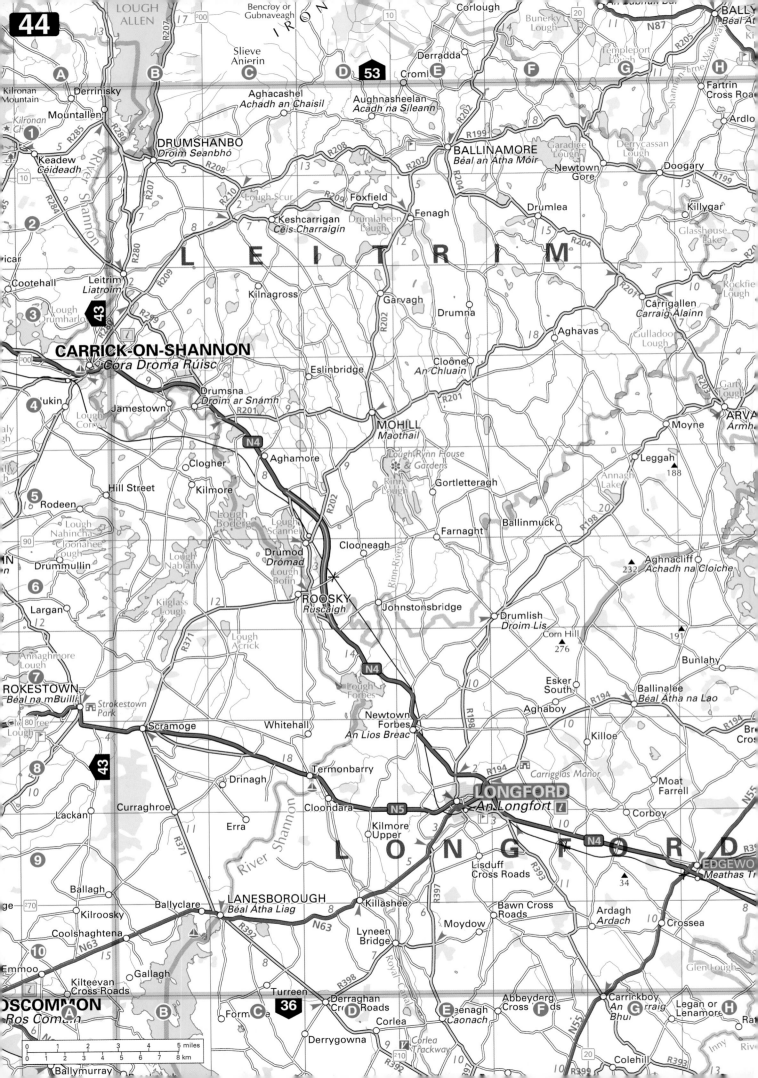

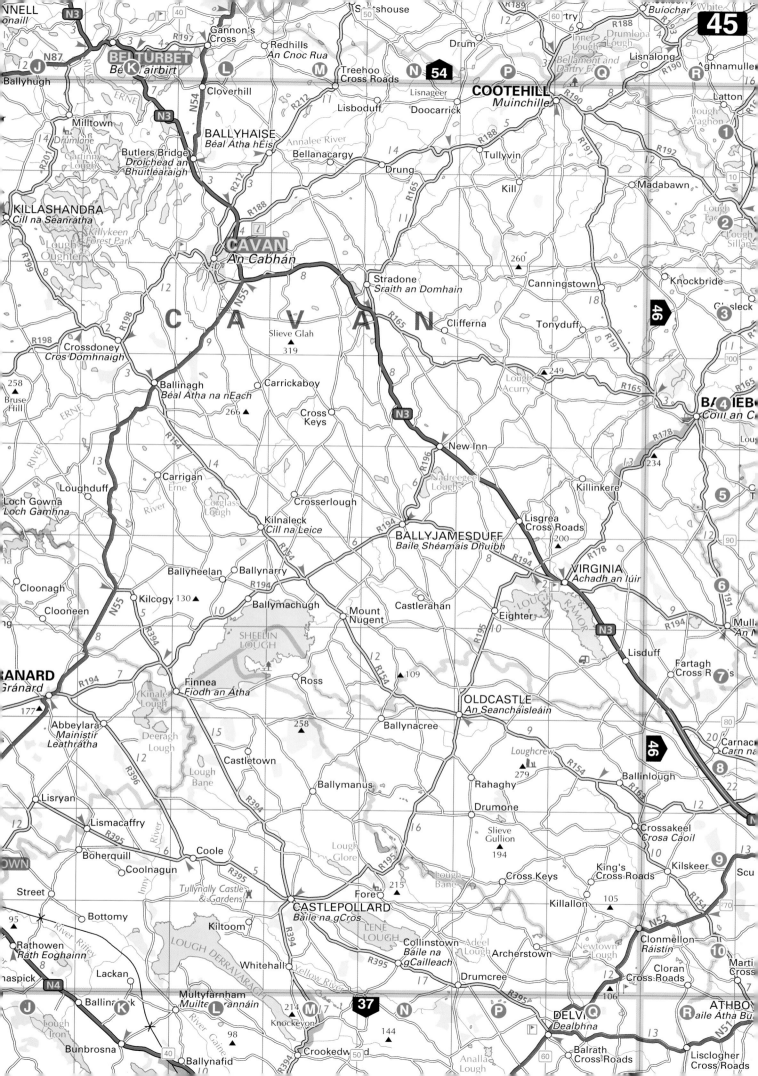

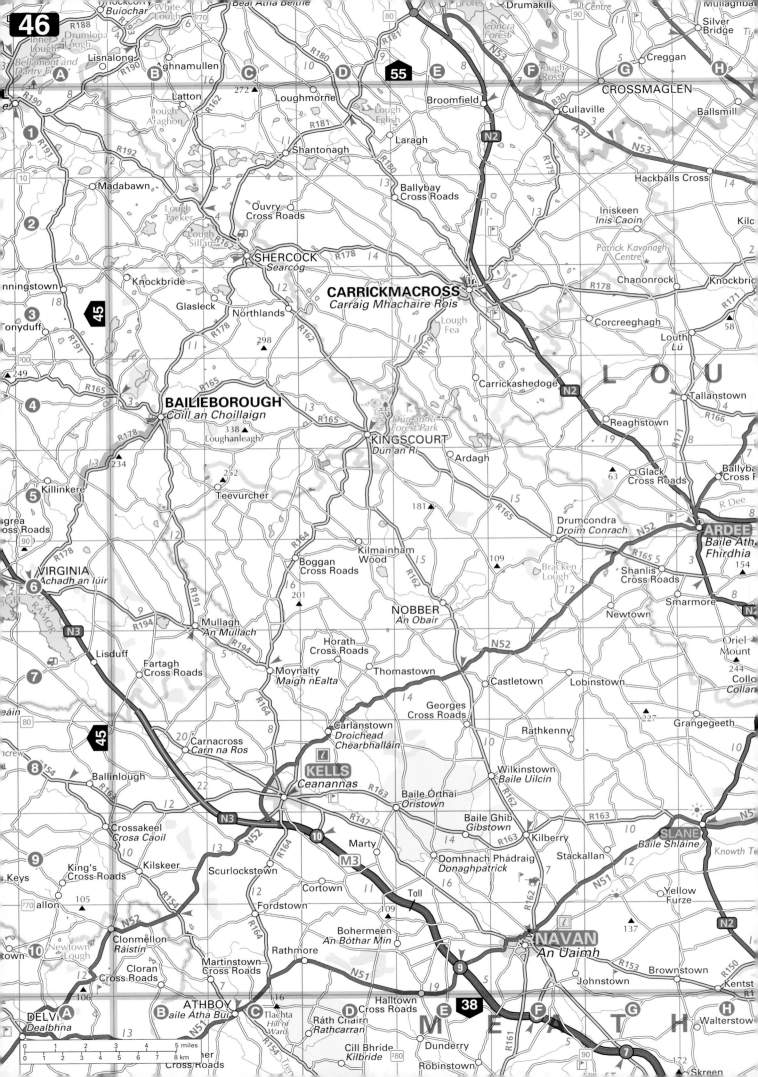

Ná Stac
Stags o
Broad Ha

BARRE NA
BINNE BUÍ
BENWEE
HEAD

Oileán Mionnán
Kid Island

Ceathrú Thaidhg
Carrowteige

CEANN IORRAIS
ERRIS HEAD

Ceann Ghleann
Doire
Glendorragh
Point

Gob a' Stuacáin
Gubastuckaun

CUAN AN
INBHIR MHÓIR
Broadhaven

Achadh
Aghadoon

Oileán na nIolrach
Eagle Island

Ceann Dhún Bhíle
Duveel Point

Ros
Ros

Ceann Dhún Modha
Doonamo Point

Corrchloch
Corclogh

Cnoc a' Túir
Tower Hill
130

Cnocán na Líne
Knocknalína

264

Poll a' tSóma
Pollatomish

Ceann Eanach
Annagh Head

Loch Tearmáinn
Carrach

An Carn
Carn

Maigh Raithin
Moyrahan

Cnoc na Lobhar
Knocknalower

Annagh Marsh

BÉAL AN
MHUIRTHEAD
Belmullet

Barr na Trá
Barnatra

Inis Gluaire
Inishglora

Ceann na
Croise
Cross
Point

9

R314

6

Inis Caorach
Inishkeeragh

An Geata Mór
Binghamstown

Loch na
Croise
Cross Lough

R313

Bun na hAbhna
Bunnahowen

Cnoc Ghleann
Chaisil
Glencastle Hill

Lo
Ceath

Ceann na
Chorráin
Corraun
Point

Bá na Trá Móire
Trawmore Bay

229

237

Carr
Le

LEITHINIS AN
MHUIRTHID
Mullet Peninsula

Loch Léime
Leam Lough

15

Gob na
hAirde
Móire

An tSráith
Srah

Cnoc na Scolb
Knocknascollop

R313

15

Bearánach
Barranagh Is

Cuan Oiligh

Ceann Tir Áine
Tiraun Point

R313

Gob Ard Oiligh
Ardelly Point

Srahm

Inis Gé Thuaidh
Inishkea North

An Clochar
Clógher

Gob Mhaigh Ratha
Moyrahan Point

Gaoth Sáile
Gweesalia

67

An Eachléim
Aghleam

Inis Gé Theas
Inishkea South

Dumha Dhearc
Dooyork

102

An Fód Dubh
Blacksod

An Tearmann

Ceann
Bhinn
Altái
Kanfinalta

Tullachán Dubh
Tullaghanduff

Tullagham
Bay

Dubh Oileán Mór
Duvillaun More

Cnoc a' Rátha
Rath Hill
61

An Tor
Black Rock

Dubh Oileán Beag
Duvillaun Beg

Ceann
Reamhar
Kinrovar

Dumha Thuama
Doohooma

Srahnamanrag
Bridge

CUAN AN FHÓID DHUIBH
Blacksod Bay

Doona

Fahy Lough

Ballycroy
Baile Chruaich

ACHILL ISLAND
Oileán Acla

Ceann a' Droime
Ridge Point

N59

17

Saddle Head

671
Slievemore

Doogort
Dumha Goirt

Loch Sruthair
Sruhill Lough

Inis Bigil
Inishbiggle

10

Castlehill

N59

ACHILL
HEAD

665
Croaghaun

DOOAGH
Dumha Acha

KEEL
An Caol

40

Keel
Lough

R319

Bun an Churraigh
Bunacurry

Annagh
Island

Claggan

14

Moyteóge
Head

Inishgalloon

An Caiseal
Cashel

Tóin re Gaoth
Tonregée

19

464

An Mhaoilinn
Mweelin

An Cnoc Mór
Knockmore
337

Gob an Choire
Achill Sound

380
lagga
Mounta

Ceann D na Éige
Dooega Head

Dumha Éige
Dooega

Na Sraithiní
Sraheens Bridge

R319

M
A

Ba Phort na hAille
Portnahally Bay

n Doirín
Derreen

524

540
Sliabh an

0 1 2 3 4 5 miles
0 1 2 3 4 5 6 7 8 km

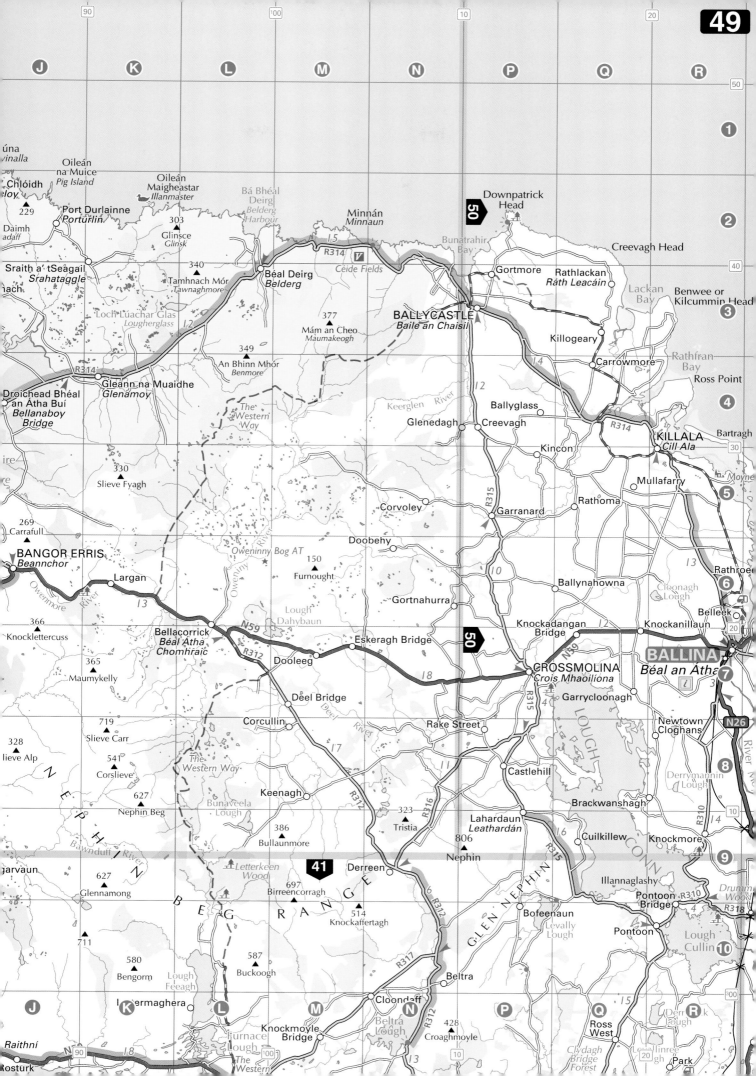

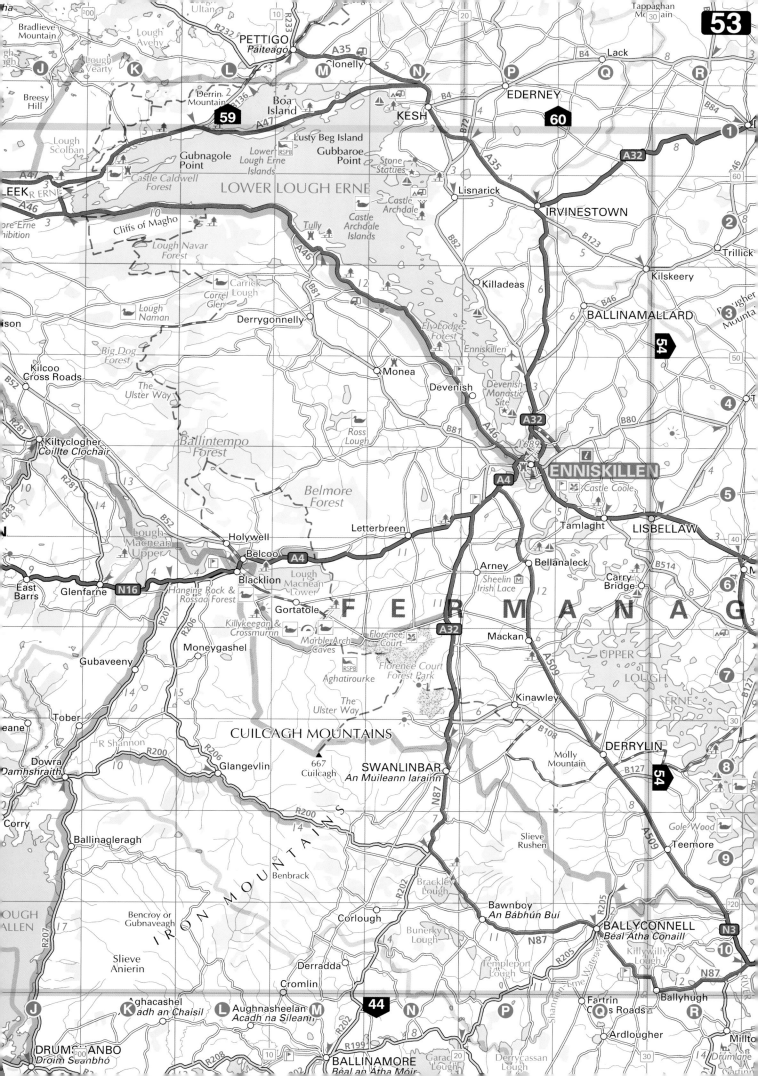

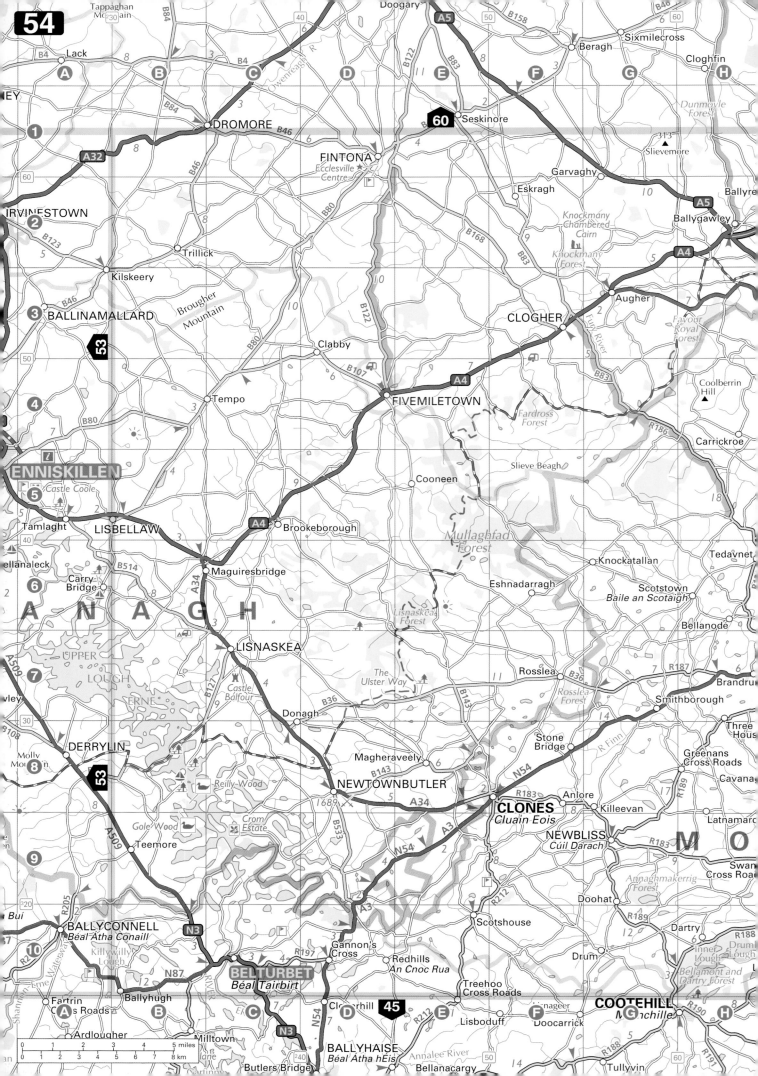

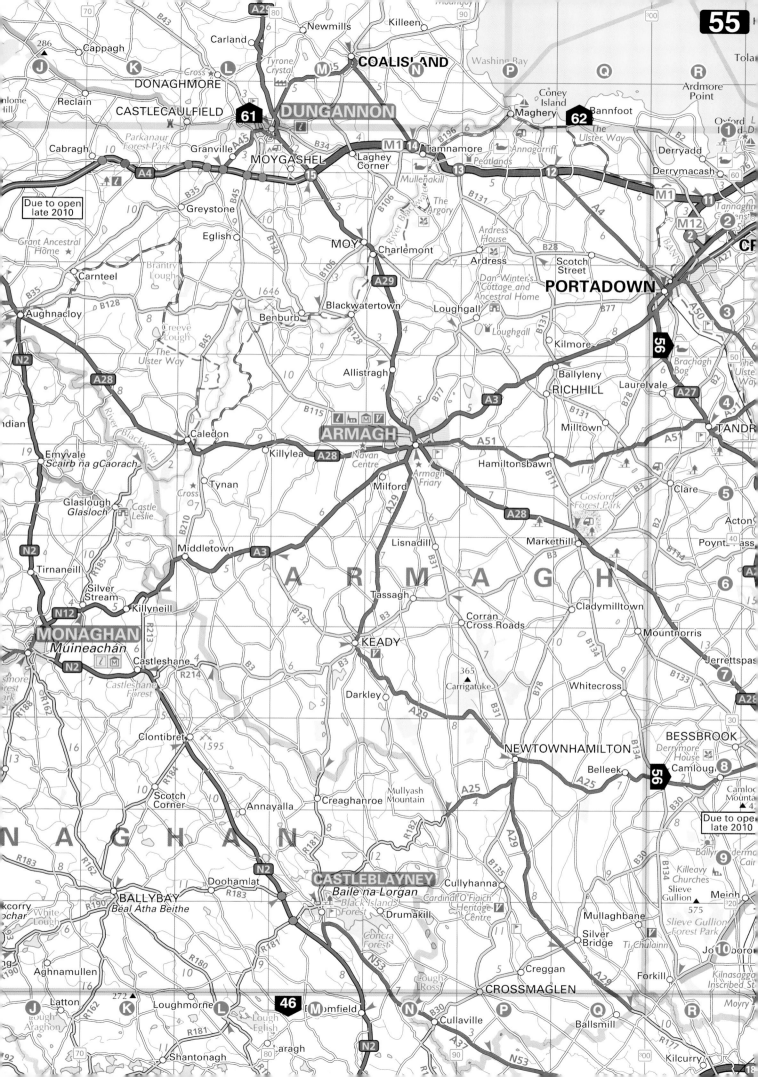

1

2

3

4

5

6

7

8

9

10

an Doirn
Rut **70** I-Island

Loch Mhic
Lough Meela

AN CLOCHÁN LIATH
Gunglow

Inis Caorach
Inishkeeragh

Inis Fraoigh
*Inishfree
Upper*

An T_____?

R259

Loch Crathaí
Lough Craghy

Cionn na Cruaiche
Crohy Head

An Machaire
Maghery

R252

N56

Mín na Croise
Meenacross

An Dú
De

Loch
Leaca Mór
*Lough
Valeck-More*

Roaninish

An Dumhaigh
Dooey Point

BÉAL AN BHEARA
Gweebarra Bay

Loch Mhic A
Lough Machug

Dunmore
Head

Inishkeel

Leitir Mhic an Bhaird
Lettermacaward

16

Derkbeg
Hill

Portnoo
Port Nua

Naran

Clooney

Dawros Head

Rossbeg

Kiltooris
Lough

Máas

Sheskinmore
Lough

R261

Lough Aderry

N56

6

GLENT
Na Glean

Inishbarnog

LOUGHROS MORE BAY

Loughros
Point

Lough
Machugh

Kilrean

R253

3

Loughros Beg
Bay

15

Heritage
Centre

7

Crockbrack

An Tor Mór
Tormore Island

472
▲
Sliabh Thuaidh
Slievetooey

Loch-na-
Luchramán
*Lough
Nalugraman*

ARDARA
Ard an Ratha

Ivy Bridge

90

Sturróg
Sturall

Cruach an Chuilinn
Croaghacullion

Crockuna

Glengesh Pass
Forest

R230

Common
Bridge

Maol Mosóg
*Mulmosog
Mountain*

Binbar

Cionn Ghlinne
Glen Head

Father McDyers
Folk Village &
Heritage Centre

Mín na Croise
Meenacross

Gleann Gheise

13

N56

R262

Ceann Ros Eoghain
Rossan Point

M

R230

Ghlinne

Mín an Aoire
Meenaneary

Crocknapeast

Killin Hill

Gleann Cholm Cille
Glencolumbkille

R263

Málainn Mhóir
Malin More

Abhainn

Glen River

Maol na nDamh
Mulnanaíf

473
▲

Croagh

Bá Mhálainne
Malin Bay

Loch
Onna
*Lough
Inna*

Bungosteen
Bridge

8

9

80

Málainn Bhig
Malin Beg

An Charraig
Carrick

Inver
Inbhear

Reachlainn Uí Bhirn
*Rathlin O'Birne
Island*

Sliabh
Slieve

Liag
League

595
▲

Teelin
Teileann

Crownasillagh
Forest

494
▲

Crownarad

3

Bruckles

15

Dunkineely
Dún Clonnaola

Cionn an Charraigín
Carrigan Head

Cill Charthaigh
Kilcar

R263

17

Largy

KILLYBEGS
Na Ceala Beaga

Cionn Mhucrois
Muckros Head

Fintragh
Bay

Drumanoo
Head

Carntullagh
Head

McSwyne's
Bay

Inver Bay

Inishduff

Doorin
Point

70

St John's
Point

DONEGAL BAY

Kildoney
Point

Co

51

52

Mullaghmore
Head

BUNDORAN
Bun Dobhrain

Tullaghan

N15

Mullaghmore

Roskeeragh
Point

70

Castlegal

0 1 2 3 4 5 miles
0 1 2 3 4 5 6 7 8 km

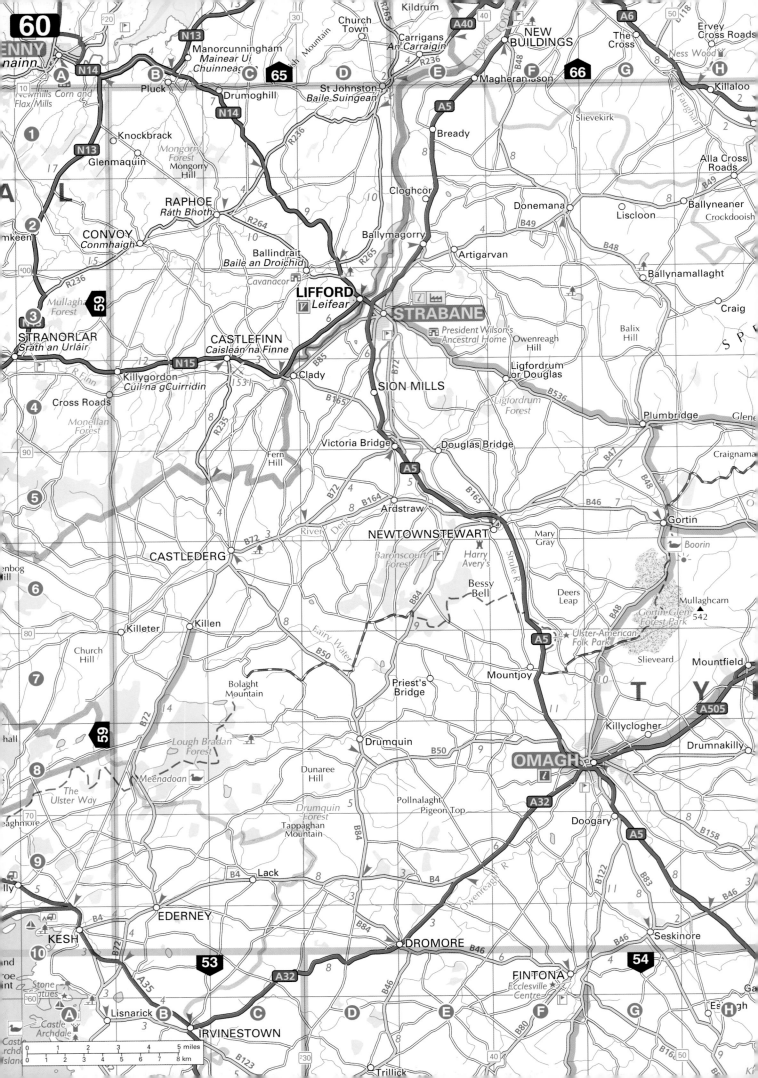

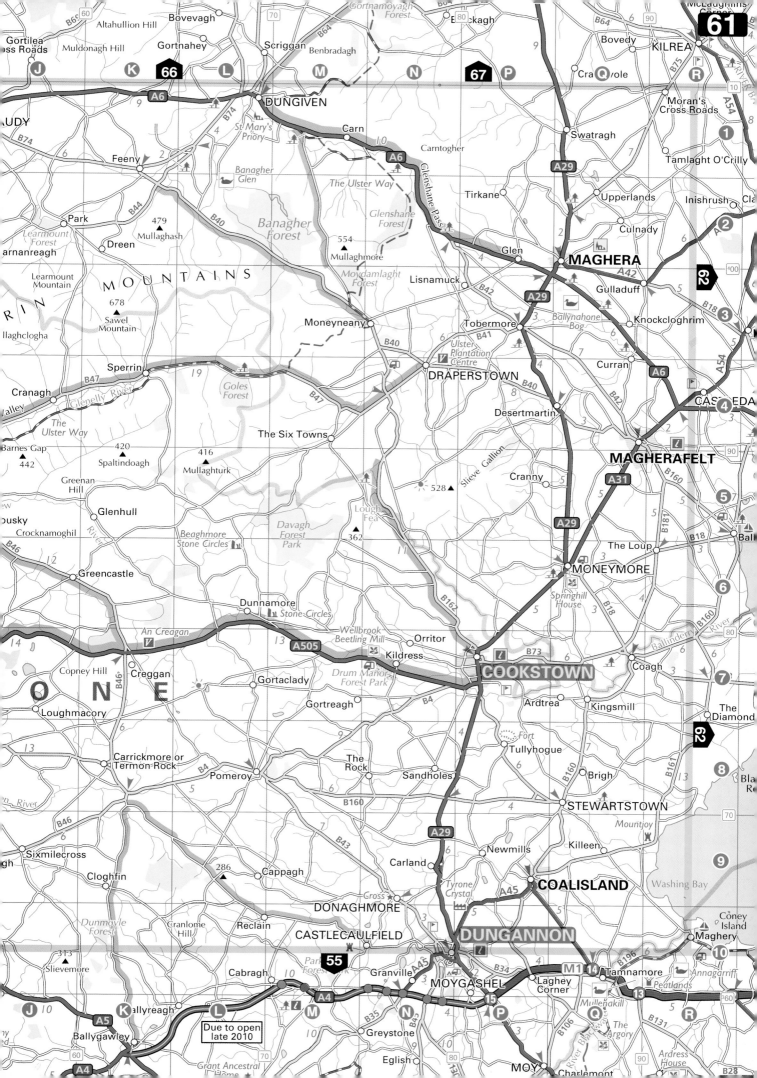

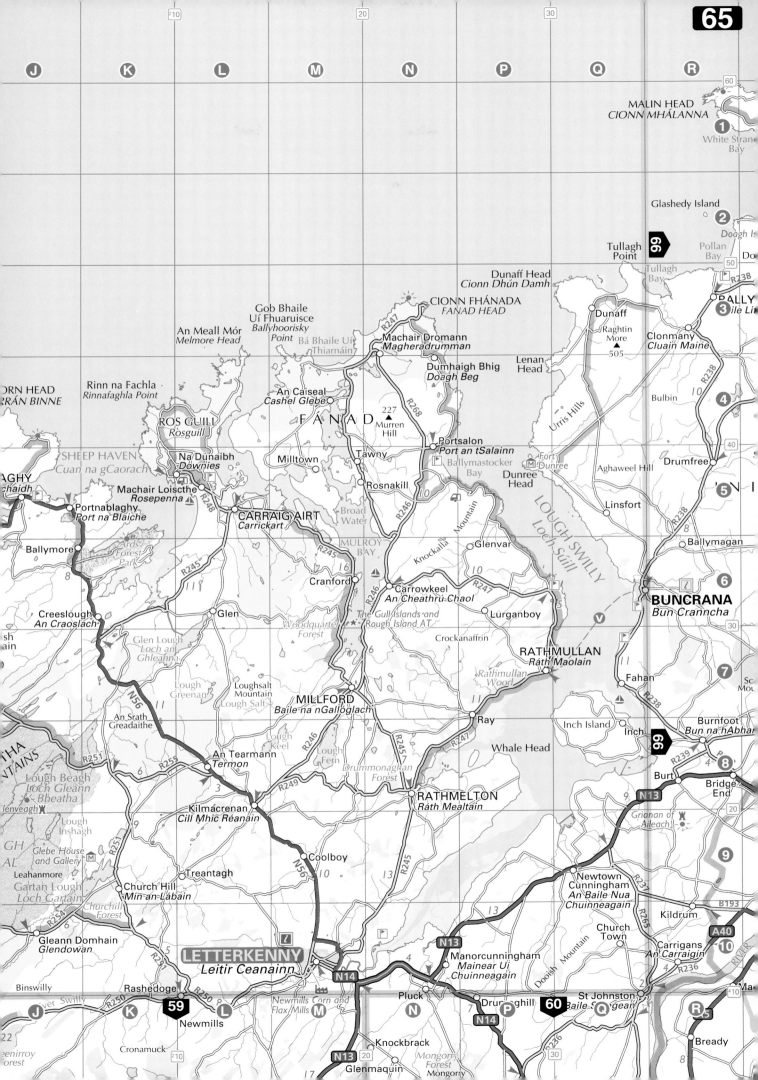

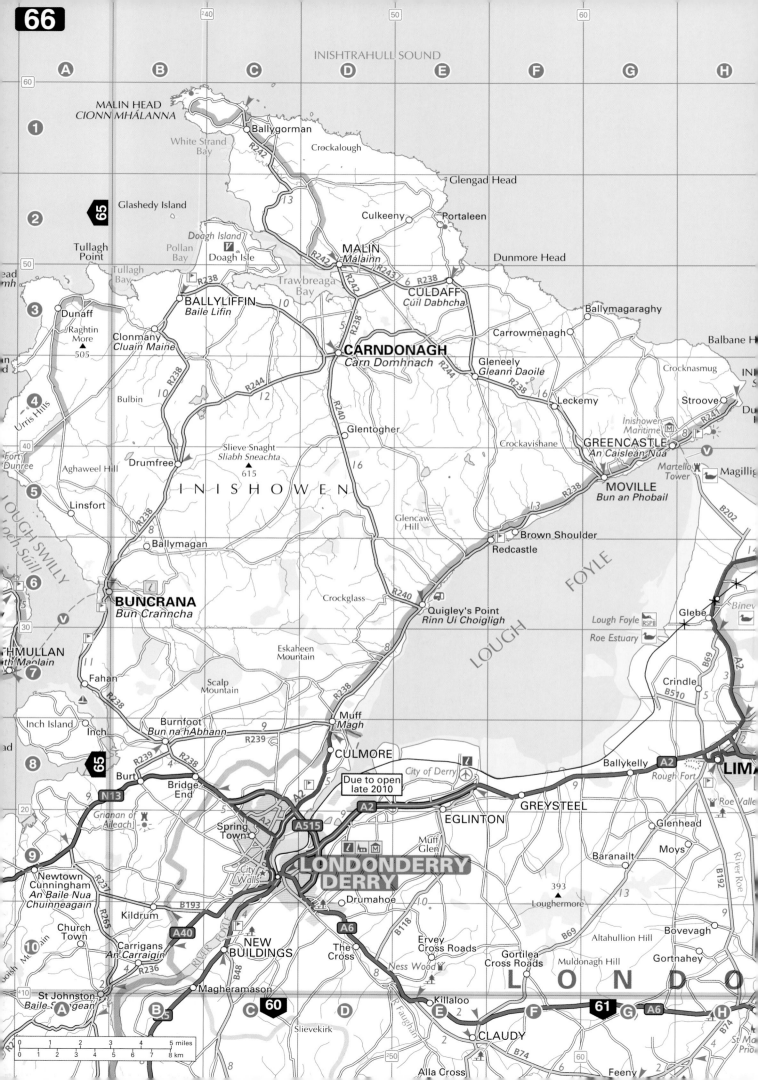

Town plans

Town plans

Page 70 .... Belfast
71 .... Cork
72–73 ..... Dublin
74 .... Galway
74 .... Kilkenny
74 .... Killarney
75 .... Limerick
75 .... Londonderry
76 .... Sligo
76 .... Waterford

⛴ Port plans

Page III .... Belfast
III .... Dublin Harbour
III .... Dún Laoghaire
III .... Larne
III .... Ringaskiddy
III .... Rosslare Europort

Key to town plans
Eochair   Légende   Legende

Bóthar príomha náisiúnta (IRL) Nationalstraße erster Ordnung (IRL)	**N4**	**National primary route (IRL)** Route nationale (IRL)
Bóthar príomha (NI) Straße erster Ordnung (NI)	**A12**	**Primary route (NI)** Route nationale (NI)
Bóthar tánaisteach náisiúnta (IRL) Nationalstraße zweiter Ordnung (IRL)	**N69**	**National secondary route (IRL)** Route départementale (IRL)
Bóthar A (NI) Nationalstraße (NI)	**A501**	**A road (NI)** Catégorie A (NI)
Bóthar réigiúnach (IRL) Regionalstraße (IRL)	**R118**	**Regional road (IRL)** Route communale (IRL)
Bóthar B (NI) Nebenstraße (NI)	**B123**	**B road (NI)** Catégorie B (NI)
Bóithre eile Andere Straßen		**Other roads** Autres routes
Crios coisí Fußgängerzone		**Pedestrian zone** Zone piétonne
Bealach fithiseach istigh Innere Ringstraße		**Inner orbital route** Périphérique interne
Foirgneamh Suimiúil Interessantes Gebäude	COLLEGE	**Building of interest** Bâtiment d'intérêt historique
Eaglais, séipéal Kirche, Kapelle	†	**Church, chapel** Église, chapelle
Páirc nó spás oscailte Park oder Freifläche		**Park or open space** Parc ou espace ouvert
Páirceáil Parkplatz	P	**Car parking** Parking
Leithris Toiletten		**Toilets** Toilettes
Sráid aon-bhealach Einbahnstraße	←	**One-way street** Sens unique
Ionad eolais turasóireachta Fremdenverkehrsamt	*i*	**Tourist information** Office de tourisme
Gluaiseacht siopaí Mobilität für Behinderte beim Einkaufen		**Shopmobility** Magasin ambulant
Siopa AA AA Geschäft	AA	**AA shop** Magasin de AA

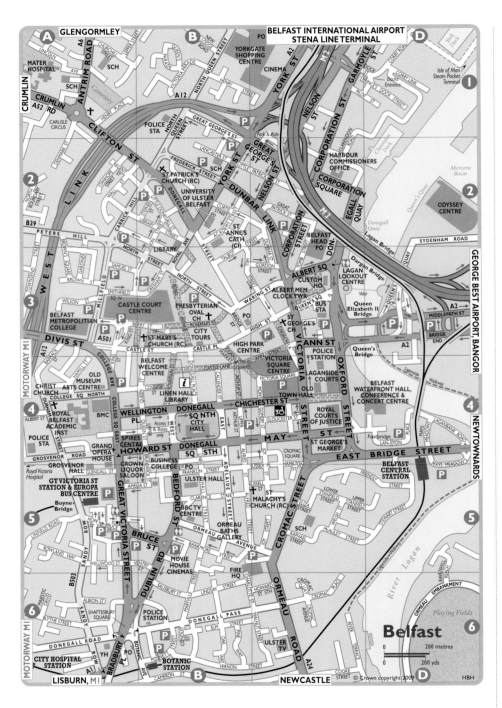

D1	Corry Road
C6	Cromac Avenue
C6	Cromac Place
C6	Cromac Quay
C4	Cromac Square
C5	Cromac Street
A1	Crumlin Road
B2	Curtis Street
A2	Denmark Street
A3	Divis Street
D1	Dock Street
B6	Donegall Pass
B4	Donegall Place
C3	Donegall Quay
A6	Donegall Road
B4	Donegall Square East
B4	Donegall Square North
B4	Donegall Square South
B4	Donegall Square West
B2	Donegall Street
B6	Dublin Road
B2	Dunbar Link
C2	Dunbar Street
A4	Durham Street
C4	East Bridge Street
C5	Eliza Street
B6	Elm Street
B4	Fountain Street
B5	Franklin Street
B2	Fredrick Street
D5	Friendly Street
A3	Gardiner Street
C1	Garmoyle Street
A5	Glengall Street
C4	Gloucester Street
C3	Gordon Street
B1	Great George's Street
C2	Great Patrick Street
A5	Great Victoria Street
B3	Gresham Street
A4	Grosvenor Road
A4	Hamill Street
C5	Hamilton Street
A1	Henry Place
B1	Henry Street
C3	High Street
B3	Hill Street
A5	Hope Street
A4	Howard Street
C6	Howard Street South
C4	Joy Street
A3	King Street
D4	Laganbank Road
B2	Lancaster Street
D4	Lanyon Place
A1	Lepper Street
B2	Library Street
A1	Lincoln Avenue
B6	Lindsay Street
B4	Linen Hall Street
A5	Linfield Road
B2	Little Donegall Street
C2	Little Patrick Street
C5	Lower Stanfield Street
A6	Majestic Drive
B6	Maryville Street
C4	May Street
D4	Mays Meadows
C5	McAuley Street
D3	Middlepath Street
A3	Millfield
C4	Montgomery Street
C2	Nelson Street
B1	New Lodge Road
A2	North Boundary Street
B1	North Queen Street
B3	North Street
B6	Oak Way
B5	Ormeau Avenue
D6	Ormeau Embankment
C6	Ormeau Road

C4	Oxford Street
A2	Peters Hill
C1	Pilot Street
B6	Pine Way
B6	Posnett Street
D1	Prince's Dock Street
B4	Queen Street
B1	Queen's Parade
D3	Queen's Quay
C3	Queen's Square
C5	Raphael Street
D6	Ravenhill Reach
A2	Regent Street
C6	River Terrace
B3	Rosemary Street
A5	Rowland Way
B3	Royal Avenue
C5	Russell Street
B6	Salisbury Street
A3	Samuel Street
A6	Sandy Row
A6	Shaftesbury Square
A3	Smithfield Square North
A2	Stanhope Street
B2	Stephen Street
D5	Stewart Street
C5	Sussex Place
D2	Sydenham Road
B3	Talbot Street
C3	Tomb Street
A3	Townsend Street
B2	Union Street
B4	Upper Arthur Street
B4	Upper Queen Street
C5	Upper Stanfield Street
B5	Ventry Street
B6	Vernon Street
B1	Victoria Parade
C4	Victoria Square
C3	Victoria Street
A2	Wall Street
C6	Walnut Street
C3	Waring Street
A4	Wellington Place
A5	Wellwood Street
C5	Welsh Street
A3	West Link
A3	Wilson Street
B2	York Street

Belfast

Belfast is found on atlas page **63 J8**

B2	Academy Street
B5	Adelaide Street
C3	Albert Square
A4	Albert Street
A6	Albion Street
B5	Alfred Street
A5	Amelia Street
C3	Ann Street
A1	Antrim Road
B4	Arthur Square
B4	Arthur Street
B5	Bankmore Street

A4	Barrack Street
B5	Bedford Street
A3	Berry Street
A6	Blythe Street
A6	Botanic Avenue
A6	Bradbury Place
D3	Bridge End
B3	Bridge Street
A3	Brown Street
A3	Brown's Square
B5	Bruce Street
B4	Brunswick Street

B4	Callender Street
B6	Cameron Street
A1	Carlisle Circus
A2	Carrick Hill
B4	Castle Lane
B3	Castle Place
B3	Castle Street
B6	Charlotte Street
B4	Chichester Street
C3	Church Lane
A1	Churchill Street
B5	Clarence Street

C2	Clarendon Road
A1	Clifton Street
A4	College Avenue
A4	College Square East
A4	College Square North
B4	College Street
B6	Conduit Street
C6	Cooke Street
B4	Cornmarket
C2	Corporation Square
C2	Corporation Street
D1	Corry Link

Cork

Cork is found on atlas page **6 A5**

B5	Abbey Street	A4	Greenville Place
B3	Academy Street	A4	Hanover Street
A4	Adelaide Street	A6	Hartlands Road
D4	Albert Quay	A4	Henry Street
D3	Albert Road	D5	High Street
D4	Albert Street	D3	Horgan's Quay
D1	Alexandra Road	B5	Industry Street
D3	Alfred Street	D5	Infirmary Road
C3	Anderson Quay	B3	John Redmond Street
D4	Anglesea Street	B2	John Street
B1	Assumption Road	B2	John Street Upper
B2	Audley Place	B5	Kevin Street South
A4	Bachelor's Quay	B3	Kyle Street
D1	Ballyhooly New Road	A3	Kyrl's Quay
A6	Bandon Road	A5	Lancaster Quay
B5	Barrack Street	D5	Langford Row
C4	Beasly Street	C3	Lapp's Quay
C2	Bellevue Park	B3	Lavitt's Quay
C2	Bellview Crescent	B2	Leitrim Street
A5	Bishop Street	B4	Liberty Street
B1	Blackpool Bypass	A6	Lough Road
A3	Blarney Street	A1	Lover's Walk
B5	Bonaventure Place	D2	Lower Glanmire Road
B3	Camden Place	D2	Mahony's Avenue
B3	Camden Quay	B4	Marlborough Street
D6	Capwell Road	A3	Mary Aikenhead Place
B3	Carrolls Quay	C4	Mary Street
A3	Castle Market Avenue	C3	Maylor Street
B4	Castle Street	C3	McCurtain Street
A2	Cathedral Road	C3	Merchants Quay
A2	Cathedral Street	D2	Military Hill
A2	Cathedral Walk	C1	Military Road
A3	Church Street	A2	Monastery Road
B3	Coal Quay	C4	Morrison's Quay
B3	Coburg Street	B5	Mount Carmel Road
A5	College Road	C6	Mount Pleasant
C6	Congress Road		Avenue
A5	Connaught Avenue	C6	Mount Pleasant Road
B4	Cook Street	B5	Mount Sion Road
C4	Copley Street	A3	Newsom's Quay
B3	Corn Market Street	C5	Nicholas Road
B5	Cove Street	A5	Noonan Road
D6	Curragh Road	A3	North Main Street
A5	Dean Street	A3	North Mall
B6	Deerpark Road	D6	O'Connell Avenue
C6	Derrynane Road	A2	O'Connell Street
B5	Desmond Square	D5	Old Blackrock Road
B3	Dominick Street	A3	Old Market Place
C5	Douglas Street	D4	Old Station Road
C6	Doyle Road	B4	Oliver Plunkett Street
C4	Dunbar Street	C3	Oliver Plunkett Street
A4	Dyke Parade		Lower
B3	Eason's Hill	C3	Parnell Place
B3	Emmet Place	B4	Paul Street
D6	Evergreen Road	C3	Penrose's Quay
B5	Evergreen Street	B3	Pope's Quay
A3	Fair Street	B1	Pope's Road
C6	Father Mathew Road	B6	Pouladuff Road
B5	Fort Street	B5	Presentation Place
C4	Friar Matthew Quay	B4	Princess Street
B5	Friar Street	B5	Proby's Quay
C6	Friars Road	C5	Quaker Road
C6	Friars Walk	D3	Railway Street
D1	Gardiners Hill	B2	Rathmore Park
D4	Gas Works Road	C1	Rathmore Road
C4	George's Quay	A2	Redemption Road
A2	Gerald Griffin Avenue	B5	Reed Street
A2	Gerald Griffin Street	B2	Richmond Hill
A5	Gill Abbey Street	D4	Rockborough Road
D2	Glanmire Road	B2	Roman Street
B1	Glen Avenue	C5	Rutland Street
A3	Glen Ryan Road	A5	St Finbars Road
A6	Gould's Road	D2	St Luke's Cross
B4	Grand Parade	A2	St Mary's Road
A4	Grattan Street	B2	St Patrick's Hill
A1	Great William O'Brien	C3	St Patrick's Quay
	Street	C6	St Patrick's Road
B6	Green Street	B4	St Patrick's Street
A6	Greenmount Avenue	B3	St Paul's Avenue

C4	Sawmill Street	D5	Southern Road	A4	Washington Street West
A1	Seminary Road	B4	Sullivan's Quay	B1	Watercourse Road
A3	Shandon Street	D2	Summer Hill	C2	Wellington Road
A5	Sharman Crawford	C5	Summer Hill South	C5	White Street
	Street	B5	Tower Street	D5	Windmill Road
A4	Sheares Street	B5	Townsend Place	A2	Wolfe Tone Street
C2	Sidney Park	B4	Tuckey Street	A4	Woods Street
C4	Smith Street	C4	Union Quay	C3	York Street
D4	South City Link Road	B5	Vicar Street	C2	Youghal Old Road
B4	South Main Street	D3	Victoria Road		
C4	South Mall	A4	Wandesford Quay		
C4	South Terrace	B4	Washington Street		

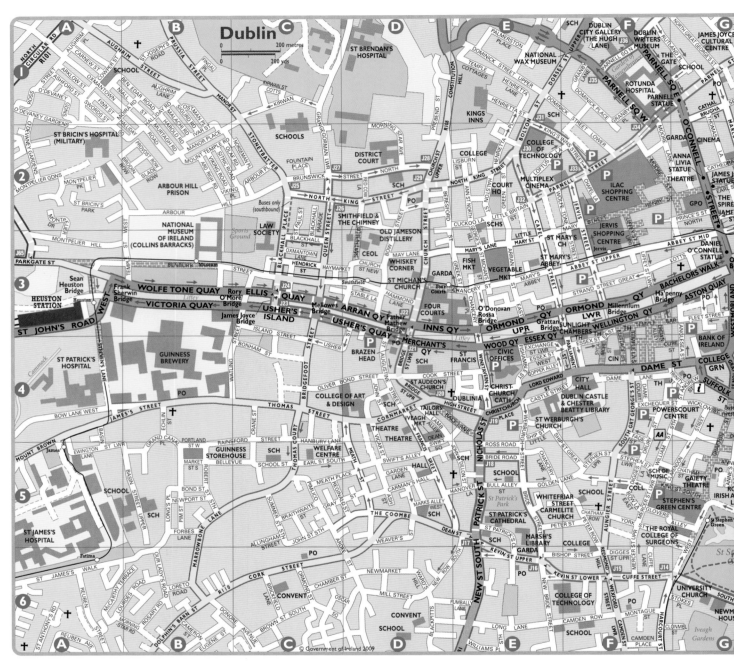

Dublin

Dublin is found on atlas page **39 M7**

G2	Abbey Street Lower	G3	Bachelors Walk	C6	Brickfield Lane	E5	Chancery Lane	H1	Corporation Street	F5	Drury Street
G3	Abbey Street Middle	D4	Back Lane	E5	Bride Road	E3	Chancery Place	A1	Cowper Street	G4	Duke Lane Lower
G3	Abbey Street Old	J6	Baggot Street Lower	E5	Bride Street	E3	Chancery Street	C4	Crane Street	G4	Duke Street
F3	Abbey Street Upper	L5	Barrow Street	C4	Bridgefoot Street	F2	Chapel Lane	L6	Cranmer Lane	G2	Earl Street North
L2	Abercorn Road	A4	Basin Street Lower	D4	Bridge Street Lower	F5	Chatham Row	J3	Creighton Street	C5	Earl Street South
K5	Albert Court	B5	Basin Street Upper	D4	Bridge Street Upper	G5	Chatham Street	K2	Crinan Strand	J5	East Merrion Square
C5	Allingham Street	J1	Beaver Street	B2	Brodin Row	E4	Christchurch Place	F3	Crown Alley	K5	Eblana Villas
J2	Amiens Street	H1	Bella Street	C6	Brown Street South	A6	Church Avenue South	E2	Cuckoo Lane	B4	Echlin Street
G4	Anglesea Street	B5	Bellevue	C2	Brunswick Street North	L1	Church Road	F6	Cuffe Lane	G3	Eden Quay
G5	Anne's Lane	H6	Bell's Lane	J1	Buckingham Street Lower	D3	Church Street	F6	Cuffe Street	C3	Ellis Quay
G5	Anne Street South	B3	Benburb Street	E5	Bull Alley Street	L2	Church Street East	G1	Cumberland Street North	H6	Ely Place
E2	Ann Street North	B1	Ben Edar Road	G3	Burgh Quay	J4	Church Street New	J4	Cumberland Street South	K2	Emerald Street
B2	Arbour Hill	H2	Beresford Place	H3	Butt Bridge	D3	Church Street Upper	H3	Custom House Quay	K4	Erne Place
C2	Arbour Place	D2	Beresford Street	L1	Caledon Road	J3	City Quay	F4	Dame Court	K4	Erne Place Lower
C5	Ardee Street	F6	Bishop Street	F6	Camden Place	L5	Clanwilliam Place	F4	Dame Lane	K4	Erne Street Lower
B2	Ard Right Road	C2	Blackhall Parade	F6	Camden Row	K4	Clarence Place Great	F4	Dame Street	K4	Erne Street Upper
A1	Arklow Street	C3	Blackhall Place	F6	Camden Street Lower	G5	Clarendon Street	G5	Dawson Street	E4	Essex Quay
D3	Arran Quay	C3	Blackhall Street	B6	Cameron Street	H5	Clare Street	D5	Dean Street	F4	Essex Street East
E3	Arran Street East	D6	Blackpitts	K1	Canon Lillis Avenue	F6	Clonmel Street	D5	Dean Swift Square	E4	Essex Street West
A1	Ashford Street	E2	Bolton Street	E3	Capel Street	K1	Coburg Place	J5	Denzille Lane	L6	Estate Cottages
D5	Ash Street	B5	Bond Street	K3	Cardiff Lane	G4	College Green	F5	Digges Lane	B6	Eugene Street
G3	Aston Quay	C4	Bonham Street	D5	Carman's Hall	G3	College Street	F6	Digges Street Upper	F4	Eustace Street
B1	Aughrim Lane	F5	Bow Lane East	A1	Carnew Street	J2	Commons Street	G3	D'Olier Street	A5	Ewington Lane
A1	Aughrim Place	A4	Bow Lane West	E4	Castle Street	E1	Constitution Hill	B6	Dolphin's Barn Street	E4	Exchange Street Lower
A1	Aughrim Street	D3	Bow Street	G1	Cathal Brugha Street	D4	Cook Street	F1	Dominick Place	F4	Exchequer Street
F5	Aungier Street	C5	Braithwaite Street	G2	Cathedral Street	E4	Cope Street	E1	Dominick Street Lower	F4	Fade Street
				C6	Chamber Street	E4	Copper Alley	E1	Dominick Street Upper	D3	Father Mathew Bridge
				G1	Champions Avenue	C6	Cork Street	B6	Donore Avenue	J5	Fenian Street
						D4	Cornmarket	E1	Dorset Street Upper	K1	Ferrymans Crossing

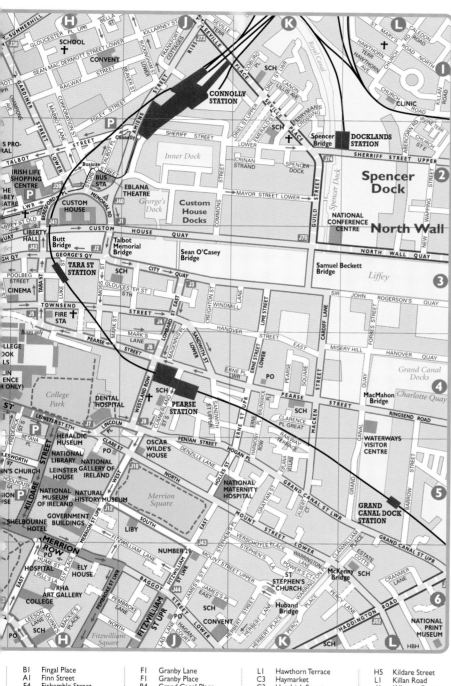

H1	Mabbot Lane	B5	Rainsford Street
K4	Macken Street	D2	Red Cow Lane
H6	Mackie's Place	F6	Redmond Hill
L4	MacMahon Bridge	C5	Reginald Street
J4	Magennis Place	A6	Reuben Street
B1	Malachi Road	L4	Ringsend Road
B2	Manor Place	B5	Robert Street South
B1	Manor Street	C3	Rory O'More Bridge
B5	Market Street South	B6	Rosary Road
D5	Marks Alley West	E5	Ross Road
J4	Mark's Lane	A1	Ross Street
H4	Mark Street	F1	Rutland Place
G2	Marlborough Street	G4	St Andrew Street
B6	Marrowbone Lane	A6	St Anthony's Road
E3	Mary's Abbey	D4	St Augustine Street
E3	Mary's Lane	A2	St Bricin's Park
F2	Mary Street	A6	St James's Walk
D3	May Lane	B1	St Joseph's Road
K2	Mayor Street Lower	L1	St Mary's Road North
A6	McCarthy Terrace	E3	St Michan's Street
K6	McKenny Bridge	E5	St Patrick's Close
C5	Meath Place	C2	St Paul Street
D5	Meath Street	H6	St Stephen's Green East
C3	Mellowes Bridge	G5	St Stephen's Green North
H2	Memorial Road	G6	St Stephen's Green South
F5	Mercer Street Lower	G5	St Stephen's Green West
F6	Mercer Street Upper	K3	Samuel Beckett Bridge
D4	Merchant's Quay	J4	Sandwith Street Lower
H6	Merrion Row	J4	Sandwith Street Upper
H5	Merrion Street Upper	G5	Schoolhouse Lane
F3	Millennium Bridge	C5	School Street
D6	Mill Street	A3	Sean Heuston Bridge
K4	Misery Hill	H1	Sean MacDermott Street Lower
B1	Moira Road	G1	Sean MacDermott Street Upper
G5	Molesworth Street	J1	Seville Place
F6	Montague Street	J1	Seville Terrace
A2	Montpelier Drive	J2	Sheriff Street Lower
A2	Montpelier Gardens	L2	Sherriff Street Upper
A3	Montpelier Hill	F5	Ship Street Great
A2	Montpelier Park	E4	Ship Street Little
F2	Moore Lane	B1	Sigurd Road
F2	Moore Street	L3	Sir John Rogerson's Quay
D2	Morning Star Avenue	B2	Sitric Road
B6	Morningstar Road	B2	Slade Row
H3	Moss Street	D3	Smithfield
A5	Mount Brown	F4	South Great George's Street
K5	Mount Street Lower	J5	South Merrion Square
J6	Mount Street Upper	K2	Spencer Bridge
B2	Mount Temple Road	K2	Spencer Dock
B2	Murtagh Road	A4	Steeven's Lane
G4	Nassau Street	K6	Stephen's Lane
E6	New Bride Street	J6	Stephen's Place
D6	Newmarket	F5	Stephen Street Lower
B5	Newport Street	F5	Stephen Street Upper
D6	New Row South	G6	Stokes Place
E6	New Street South	C2	Stoneybatter
L3	New Wapping Street	H2	Store Street
B1	Niall Street	F3	Strand Street Great
E5	Nicholas Street	G4	Suffolk Street
C2	Norseman Place	H1	Summerhill
A1	North Circular Road	C5	Summer Street South
G1	North Great George's Street	D5	Swift's Alley
C2	North King Street	A1	Swords Street
J5	North Merrion Square	F4	Sycamore Street
L3	North Wall Quay	H3	Talbot Memorial Bridge
G3	O'Connell Bridge	H2	Talbot Place
G2	O'Connell Street	G2	Talbot Street
A1	O'Devaney Gardens	H3	Tara Street
E3	O'Donovan Rossa Bridge	F3	Temple Bar
B2	Olaf Road	E1	Temple Cottages
C4	Oliver Bond Street	G1	Temple Lane North
K1	Oriel Street Lower	F4	Temple Lane South
K2	Oriel Street Upper	B3	Temple Street West
F3	Ormond Quay Lower	D5	The Coombe
E3	Ormond Quay Upper	C5	Thomas Court
C6	Ormond Street	G2	Thomas Lane
C6	Oscar Square	C4	Thomas Street
B1	Ostman Place	H3	Townsend Street
B6	Our Lady's Road	G4	Trinity Street
C3	Oxmantown Lane	C3	Usher's Island
A1	Oxmantown Road	D3	Usher's Quay
E1	Palmerston Place	C4	Usher Street
A3	Parkgate Street	K5	Verschoyle Place
F4	Parliament Street	D4	Vicar Street
F1	Parnell Square East	B3	Victoria Quay
F1	Parnell Square North	B2	Viking Place
F1	Parnell Square West	B2	Viking Road
E2	Parnell Street	D6	Ward's Hill
E5	Patrick Street	K6	Warrington Lane
K4	Pearse Square	K6	Warrington Place
H4	Pearse Street	B4	Watling Street
J6	Pembroke Lane	D5	Weaver's Street
H6	Pembroke Street Lower	F3	Wellington Quay
K6	Percy Lane	E4	Werburgh Street
K6	Percy Place	E1	Western Way
F5	Peter Row	J4	Westland Row
E5	Peter Street	H5	West Merrion Square
C5	Pimlico	G3	Westmorland Street
B5	Pim Street	F6	Wexford Street
H3	Poolbeg Street	G4	Wicklow Street
B5	Portland Street West	E6	Williams Place South
K6	Power's Court	F5	William Street South
D1	Prebend Street	J3	Windmill Lane
G2	Prince's Street North	E4	Winetavern Street
B2	Provost Row	B3	Wolfe Tone Quay
B1	Prussia Street	F2	Wolfe Tone Street
C3	Queen Street	E4	Wood Quay
H6	Quinn's Lane	F5	York Street
H1	Railway Street		
K5	Railway Terrace		

B1	Fingal Place	F1	Granby Lane	L1	Hawthorn Terrace	H5	Kildare Street
A1	Finn Street	F1	Granby Place	C3	Haymarket	L1	Killan Road
E4	Fishamble Street	B4	Grand Canal Place	C3	Hendrick Street	J1	Killarney Street
J6	Fitzwilliam Lane	L5	Grand Canal Quay	E1	Henrietta Lane	E2	King's Inns Street
H6	Fitzwilliam Square North	K5	Grand Canal Street Lower	E2	Henrietta Place	F5	King Street South
H6	Fitzwilliam Square West	L5	Grand Canal Street Upper	E1	Henrietta Street	C1	Kirwan Street
J6	Fitzwilliam Street Lower	C2	Grangegorman Lower	F2	Henry Street	C1	Kirwan Street Cottages
J6	Fitzwilliam Street Upper	E3	Grattan Bridge	K6	Herbert Lane	J6	Lad Lane
G3	Fleet Street	K5	Grattan Street	K6	Herbert Place	J6	Lad Lane Upper
H1	Foley Street	C5	Gray Street	K6	Herbert Street	D4	Lamb Alley
B5	Forbes Lane	E3	Greek Street	D4	High Street	H6	Leeson Lane
L4	Forbes Street	E2	Green Street	H6	Hogan Place	H4	Leinster Street South
C2	Fountain Place	K2	Guild Street	K5	Holles Street	F2	Liffey Street
F5	Francis Street	L6	Haddington Road	K6	Huband Bridge	F3	Liffey Street Lower
J1	Frankfort Cottages	J6	Hagan's Court	H6	Hume Street	F2	Liffey Street Upper
A3	Frank Sherwin Bridge	B1	Halliday Road	D3	Inns Quay	K3	Lime Street
H5	Frederick Street South	B2	Halliday Square	L2	Irvine Terrace	H4	Lincoln Place
E6	Fumbally Lane	E2	Halston Street	C3	Island Street	E2	Lisburn Street
D5	Garden Lane	D3	Hammond Lane	B2	Ivar Street	E3	Little Britain Street
H1	Gardiner Street Lower	C5	Hanbury Lane	C3	James Joyce Bridge	E2	Little Mary Street
G1	Gardiner Street Middle	E5	Hanover Lane	J6	James's Place East	E2	Loftus Lane
E3	George's Hill	L4	Hanover Quay	A4	James's Street	J3	Lombard Street East
H3	George's Quay	J3	Hanover Street East	J6	James's Street East	E6	Long Lane
F3	Gloucester Place Upper	F6	Harcourt Street	F2	Jervis Street	B5	Long's Place
H3	Gloucester Street South	K5	Harmony Row	E5	John Dillon Street	E4	Lord Edward Street
F5	Glovers Alley	B1	Harold Road	D4	John Street	B6	Loreto Road
E5	Golden Lane	G3	Hawkins Street	C5	John Street South	G3	Lotts
G4	Grafton Street	L1	Hawthorn Avenue	F6	Kevin Street Lower	A6	Lourdes Road
G5	Grafton Street			E6	Kevin Street Upper	H3	Luke Street

Galway

Galway is found on atlas page **34 C8**

C2	Abbey Gate Street	B3	Munster Avenue
A1	Ash Road	C3	New Dock Street
D2	Bótha Na Mban	B2	New Road
B2	Bóthar Einde	B1	Newcastle Avenue
D2	Bothar Irwin	B2	Newcastle Road
A1	Bóthar Phadraic Ui	C2	Newtown Smith
	Chonnaire	B2	Nun's Island Street
C3	Bridge Street	A1	O'Flaherty Road
B2	Canal Road Lower	A2	Palmyra Avenue
B1	Canal Road Upper	B2	Presentation Road
B3	Claddagh Quay	D2	Prospect Hill
A1	Colmcillie Road	C3	Quay Street
A1	Costello Road	D3	Queen Street
C3	Dock Road	A2	Raleigh Row
C3	Dock Street	C3	St Augustine Street
B3	Dominick Street	C2	St Brendan's Avenue
D1	Dyke Road	D1	St Bridget's Place
C2	Eglinton Street	C2	St Francis Street
D2	Eyre Square	B2	St Helen's Street
C2	Eyre Street	A2	St Mary's Park
B3	Father Burke Road	A2	St Mary's Road
A3	Father Griffin Avenue	C2	St Vincent's Avenue
A3	Father Griffin Road	A3	Sea Road
D2	Forster Street	A1	Shantalla Road
A1	Fursey Road	C2	Shop Street
D1	Headford Road	D2	Station Road
B2	Henry Street	A2	Taylor's Hill Road
C3	High Street	A3	The Crescent
D3	Lough Atalia Road	C3	The Long Walk
C2	Market Street	B1	University Road
A1	McDara Road	D1	Water Lane
C3	Merchants Road	C1	Waterside
C3	Middle Street	A3	Whitestrand Road
B2	Mill Street	C2	William Street
		B3	William Street West

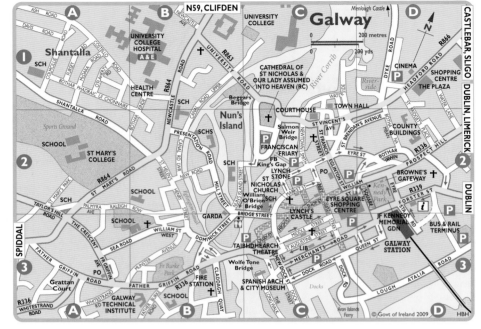

Kilkenny

Kilkenny is found on atlas page **21 N5**

A2	Abbey Street
B1	Ballybought Street
B1	Barrack Street
A2	Bateman's Quay
A2	Canal Square
B3	Castle Road
B1	Castlecomer Road
A3	College Road
A1	Dean Street
B2	Dublin Road
A2	Evan's Lane
B3	Father Hayden Road
A3	Friary Street
A3	Gaol Road
A1	Green Street
A1	Green's Hill
A1	Greensbridge Street
B1	Hebron Road
A2	High Street
A2	Irish Town
A2	James's Street
B2	John Street Lower
B2	John Street Upper
B2	John's Green
A2	John's Quay
A3	Lower New Street
B2	Maudlin Street
A2	Michael Street
A2	New Building Lane
A1	New Road
A3	Ormonde Street
A2	Parliament Street
A2	Parnell Street
A3	Patrick Street
A2	Rose Inn Street
A2	St Kiernan's Street
A3	The Parade
A2	Tilbury Place
A1	Vicar Street
A3	Walkin Street
B1	Wolfe Tone Street

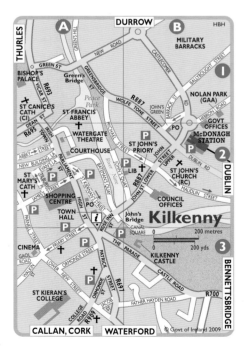

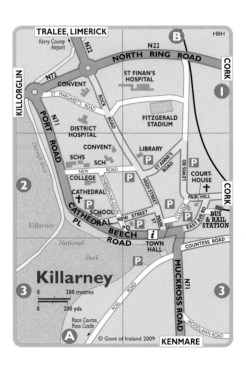

Killarney

Killarney is found on atlas page **10 B6**

A3	Beech Road	B3	Muckross Road
A2	Bohereen-na-Goun	A2	New Road
A2	Cathedral Place	B2	New Street
B2	College Street	A1	North Ring Road
B3	Countess Road	A1	Port Road
B2	East Avenue Road	A1	Rock Road
B2	Fair Hill	A3	Ross Road
B2	High Street	B2	St Anne's Road
B2	Lewis Road	A1	St Margaret's Road
B2	Main Street	B3	Woodlawn Road

Limerick

Limerick is found on atlas page **18 H3**

B3	Anne Street	C2	High Street
B2	Arthurs Quay	B2	Honans Quay
C1	Athlunkard Street	A2	Howley's Quay
B1	Bank Place	C2	John Square
B2	Bedford Row	C2	John's Street
A1	Belfield Gardens	D2	Keane Street
C1	Bishop's Street	D2	Keating Street
D3	Blackboy Road	C1	Lock Quay
C2	Brennans Row	A2	Lower Cecil Street
B1	Bridge Street	C3	Lower Gerald Griffin
C2	Broad Street		Street
B1	Castle Street	A3	Lower Mallow Street
C3	Cathedral Place	B3	Mallow Street
B3	Catherine Street	C2	Market Street
B3	Cecil Street	C1	Mary Street
C1	Charlotte's Quay	B2	Michael Street
B1	Clancy's Strand	C2	Milk Street
D2	Clare Street	A3	Mount Kennett Place
A1	Clareview Avenue	C3	Mulgrave Street
D1	Corbally Link Road	C2	Mungret Street
B3	Davis Street	C2	New Road
B2	Denmark Street	A3	Newenham Street
A3	Dock Road	B1	Nicholas Street
B3	Dominick Street	A2	North Circular Road
D2	Downey Street	D2	North Claughaun
B2	Ellen Street		Road
A1	Ennis Road	A2	O'Callaghan's Strand
A1	Farranshone Road	A3	O'Connell Street
D2	Flood Street	A3	O'Curry Street
B2	Francis Street	C2	Old Clare Street
C1	Gaol Lane	C2	Old Francis Street
D3	Garryowen	B3	Parnell Street
C1	George's Quay	B2	Patrick Street
D3	Geraldine Terrace	D2	Pennywell
A3	Glentworth Street	D2	Pennywell Lane
A1	Glenview Gardens	B3	Pery Square
C2	Grattan Street	B3	Pery Street
D3	Greenhill Road	D3	Pike Avenue
A3	Hartstonge Street	B1	Priory Park
A2	Harvey's Quay	B3	Roche's Street
A3	Henry Street	A1	Rockspring Gardens

C3	Rossa Avenue	C3	Sexton Street	C3	Summer Street	A3	Upper Henry Street
C3	Roxborough Avenue	B2	Shannon Street	A3	The Bishop's Quay	C3	Upper William Street
C3	Roxborough Road	D3	Singland Crescent	C1	The Island Road	D3	West Singland Road
B2	Rutland Street	C1	Sir Harry's Mall	A1	Thomond Row	B3	Wickham Street
B1	St Augustine Place	D3	South Claughaun Road	B2	Thomas Street	B2	William Street
D2	St Lelia Street	A3	Steamboat Quay	B3	Upper Gerald Griffin	A3	Windmill Street
B2	Sarsfield Street	A2	Strandville Gardens		Street		

Londonderry

Londonderry is found on atlas page **66 C9**

B1	Abbey Street	C2	Fountain Street
B3	Abercorn Road	C1	Foyle Embankment
A3	Anne Street	B3	Foyle Road
C2	Artillery Street	C2	Foyle Street
C1	Bank Place	B1	Francis Street
B3	Barrack Street	B1	Frederick Street
A1	Beechwood Avenue	B1	Great James Street
A2	Beechwood Street	B1	Harvey Street
D3	Benvarden Avenue	C2	Hawkin Street
B2	Bishop Street Within	D3	Hayesbank Park
A3	Bishop Street Without	B1	High Street
A2	Bligh's Lane	B3	Ivy Terrace
A1	Blucher Street	C3	John Street
A3	Bluebell Hill Gardens	D1	King Street
D2	Bond's Hill	D3	Knockdara Park
D1	Bond's Street	A3	Lecky Road
A3	Brandywell Road	D1	Limavady Road
C2	Bridge Street	A2	Limewood Street
B2	Butcher Street	C2	Linenhall Street
A2	Cable Street	B1	Lisfannon Park
C3	Carlisle Road	B1	Little Diamond
A3	Carrigans Lane	B1	Little James Street
C1	Castle Street	B2	London Street
B1	Chamberlain Street	A2	Lone Moor Road
D3	Chapel Road	B2	Long Tower Street
D2	Clooney Terrace	B3	Lower Bennett Street
B3	Cooke Street	B1	Lower Road
B1	Creggan Street	D2	Lower Violet Street
A2	Dove Gardens	B2	Magazine Street
D3	Duke Street	D3	Malvern Terrace
D3	Dunfield Terrace	D3	Margaret Street
D2	Dungiven Road	C2	Market Street
A1	Eastway	A1	Marlborough Road
B1	Eglinton Place	A1	Marlborough Street
A2	Elmwood Road	B3	Maureen Avenue
A2	Elmwood Street	B3	Miller Street
B3	Ewing Street	A2	Nualamont Drive
B1	Fahan Street	A1	Oakfield Crescent
B2	Fahan Street	A1	Oakfield Road
B3	Ferguson Street	C2	Orchard Street
D3	Fountain Hill	B2	Palace Street

D1	Pine Street	D2	Simpson's Brae	B3	Upper Bennett Street	B1	William Street
D2	Primrose Street	A3	Southend Park	C3	Wapping Lane		
C2	Pump Street	D3	Spencer Road	B1	Waterloo Street		
B2	Rossville Street	A2	Stanleys Walk	D2	Waterside Link		
B1	Sackville Street	B2	The Diamond	A1	Westland Avenue		
A3	St Columbas Walk	C1	Union Hall Place	A1	Westland Street		
C2	Shipquay Street	D2	Union Street	A1	Westland Terrace		

Sligo

Sligo is found on atlas page **52 C6**

C2	Abbey Street	C2	O'Connell Street
B2	Adelaide Street	C3	Old Market Street
B1	Ballast Quay	D3	Pearse Road
C1	Barrack Street	B1	Prin Mill Road
C1	Bridge Street	B1	Quay Street
C3	Burton Street	D2	Riverside
C2	Castle Street	D2	Saint Anne's Road
D3	Chapel Hill	C3	St Brigets Place
D2	Chapel Street	C1	Stephen Street
C2	Charles Street	C2	Teeling Street
A2	Church Hill	B2	Temple Street
B3	Circular Road	B2	The Lungy
C1	Connaughton Road	D1	The Mall
C3	Connolly Street	C2	Thomas Street
D2	Cranmore Mass Lane	B1	Union Place
A1	Finiskiln Road	B1	Union Street
C3	Gallows Hill	A2	Upper John Street
D2	Gaol Road	B1	Wine Street
C2	Grattan Street	B2	Wolfe Tone Street
C2	Harmony Hill		
C2	High Street		
C1	Holborn Hill		
C1	Holborn Street		
B1	Hughes Bridge		
A2	Jinks Avenue		
B2	John Street		
C2	Kennedy Parade		
A2	Knappagh Road		
B2	Lord Edward Street		
D2	Lower Abbey Street		
B1	Lower Quay Street		
B1	Lynn's Place		
C3	Mail Coach Road		
C2	Market Street		
C1	Markievicz Road		

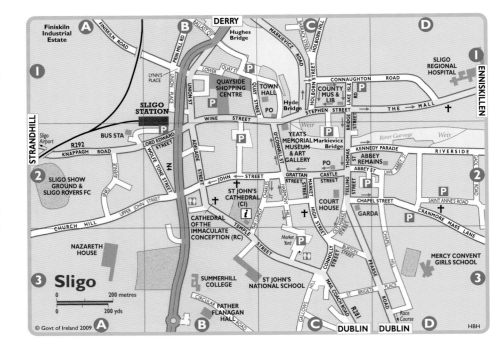

Waterford

Waterford is found on atlas page **14 E6**

D1	Abbey Road	B3	Manor Hill
D3	Adelphi Quay	B3	Manor Street
B1	Anne Street	A1	Mary Street
D1	Ard Mhuire	B3	Mayors Walk
B2	Barker Street	B1	Merchant's Quay
B3	Barrack Street	C3	Michael Street
C2	Barron Strand Street	A2	Military Road
C3	Beau Street	A2	Morgan Street
A3	Bernard Place	A3	Morrissons Avenue
A1	Bilberry Road	A3	Morrissons Road
C1	Bishopsgrove	A3	Mount Sion Avenue
B1	Bridge Street	B3	New Street
C2	Broad Street	B3	Newgate Street
D3	Canada Street	B2	Newports Square
A3	Cannon Street	B3	Newports Terrace
B3	Castle Street	A2	O'Connell Street
A2	Cathal Brugha Street	A2	Ozanam Street
C3	Catherine Street	C3	Parnell Street
B3	Convent Hill	B2	Patrick Street
C2	Custom House Quay	C2	Peter Street
B1	Dock Road	A2	Philip Street
A3	Doyle's Street	A1	Rockfield Park
A3	Emmett Place	D1	Rockshire Court
D1	Fountain Street	D1	Rockshire Road
B2	Francis Street	D3	Rose Lane
A1	Gracedieu Road	D3	Scotch Quay
A1	Grattan Quay	B3	Short Course
C2	Great Georges Street	A3	Slievekeale Road
B2	Green Street	C3	Spring Garden Alley
A3	Griffith Place	B3	Stephen Street
B3	Hennessy's Road	B1	Suir Street
C2	High Street	A2	Summer Hill
C3	John Street	A1	Summerhill Terrace
B3	Johns Lane	B2	The Glen
C3	Johnstown	C3	The Mall
C3	Lady Lane	B3	Thomas Hill
A3	Leamy Street	B2	Thomas Street
D3	Lombard Street	A2	Upper Yellow Road
A2	Lower Yellow Road	C3	Waterside
A3	Luke Wadding Street	D3	William Street

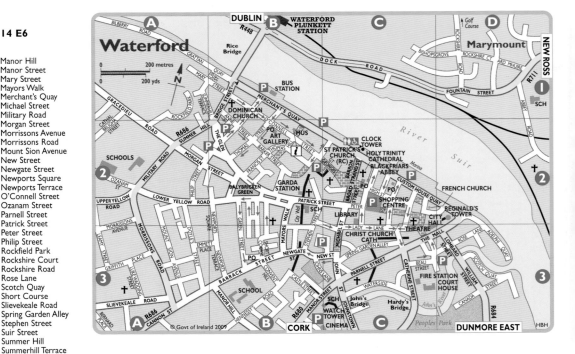

Motorways

The motorway maps on these pages consist of signposting panels, the layout of junctions, road numbers and exit destinations. To reflect the distances shown on the motorway signs, distances are given in miles in Northern Ireland and in kilometres in the Republic of Ireland.

Northern Ireland
M1	Belfast – Craigavon	78
M2, M22	Belfast – Randalstown	78
M1	Craigavon – Dungannon	79
M2	Ballymena Bypass	79

Republic of Ireland
M50	Dublin Ring Road	79
M1	Dublin – Dundalk	80
M2	Killshane – Ashbourne	81
M9	Knocktopher – Waterford	81
M4	Leixlip – McNeads Bridge	81
M6	M4 – Galway	82
M7	Naas – Limerick	83
M8	M7 – Cork	84
M11	Dublin – Rosslare	85
M18	Shannon – Ennis	86
M20	Limerick – Attyflin	86

Restricted Motorway Junctions

Northern Ireland

M1 BELFAST – DUNGANNON
Junction		
3	Westbound	No access, exit only.
	Eastbound	No exit, access only.
7	Westbound	No access, exit only.
	Eastbound	No restriction.

M2, M22 BELFAST – RANDALSTOWN
Junction		
2	Westbound	No restriction.
	Eastbound	No exit to M5.

Republic of Ireland

M1 DUBLIN – DUNDALK
Junction		
3	Northbound	No access, exit only.
	Southbound	No exit, access only.
8	Northbound	No access, exit only.
	Southbound	No exit, access only.
9	Northbound	No restriction.
	Southbound	No access, exit only.
11	Northbound	No exit, access only.
	Southbound	No access, exit only.
13	Northbound	No access, exit only.
	Southbound	No exit, access only.

M4 LEIXLIP – McNEADS BRIDGE
Junction		
10	Westbound	No access, exit only.
	Eastbound	No exit, access only.
11	Westbound	No access, exit only to M6 westbound.
	Eastbound	No exit. No access to M6.
12	Westbound	No exit, access only.
	Eastbound	No access, exit only.

M6 KINNEGAD – GALWAY
Junction		
1	Westbound	Exit only to M4 westbound.
	Eastbound	Access only from M4 eastbound.

M7 NAAS – LIMERICK
Junction		
11	Westbound	Exit only to M9 southbound.
	Eastbound	Access only from M9 northbound.
19	Westbound	Exit only to M8 southbound.
	Eastbound	Access only from M8 northbound.
20	Westbound	No access, exit only.
	Eastbound	No exit, access only.

M8 M7 – CORK
Junction		
1	Northbound	Exit only to M7 eastbound.
	Southbound	Access only from M7 westbound.
2	Northbound	No exit, access only.
	Southbound	No access, exit only.
5	Northbound	No access, exit only.
	Southbound	No exit, access only.
16	Northbound	No access, exit only.
	Southbound	No exit, access only.

M11 DUBLIN – ROSSLARE
Junction		
15	Northbound	No access, exit only.
	Southbound	No exit, access only.

M50 DUBLIN RING ROAD
Junction		
13	Northbound	No exit, access only.
	Southbound	No access, exit only.
17	Northbound	Access only from M11 northbound.
	Southbound	Exit only to M11 southbound.

Key to Motorway Maps

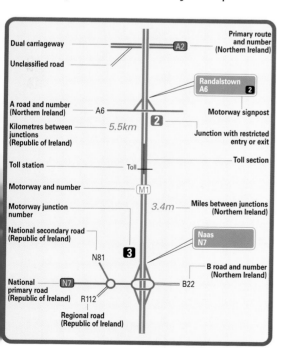

M1 Belfast – Craigavon

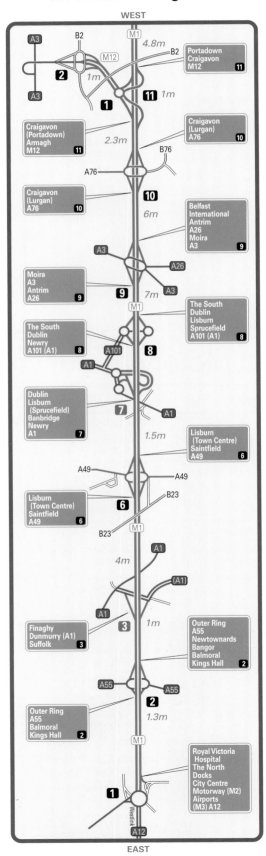

M2, M22 Belfast – Randalstown

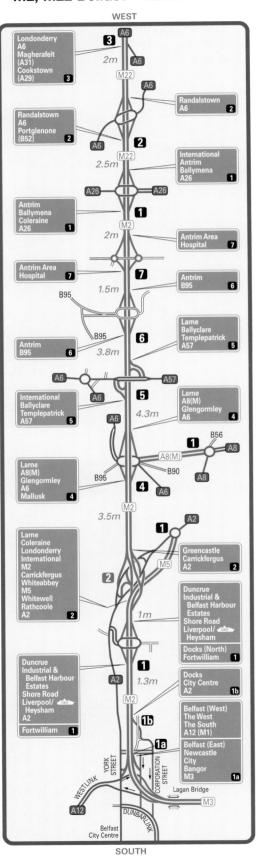

M1 Craigavon – Dungannon

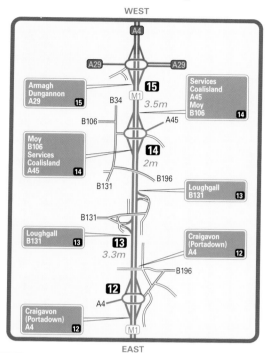

M2 Ballymena Bypass

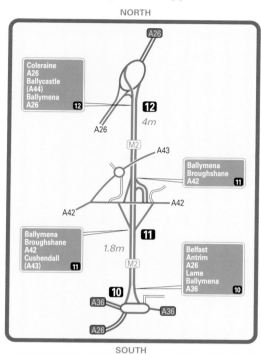

M50 Dublin Ring Road

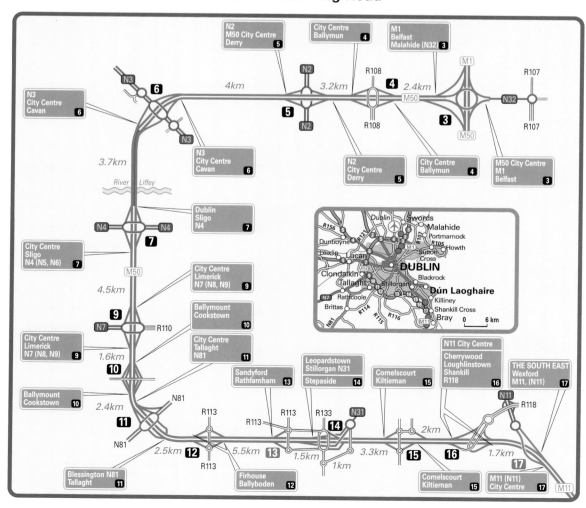

M1 Dublin – Drogheda

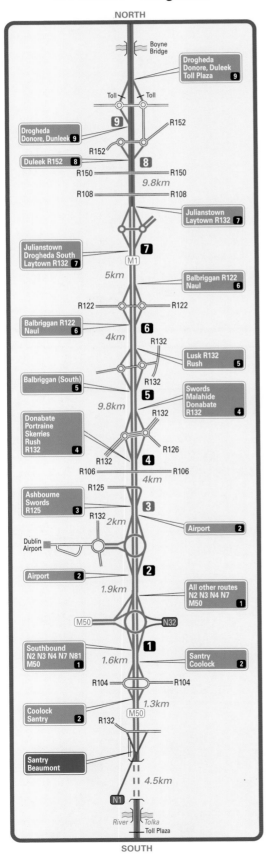

M1 Drogheda – Dundalk

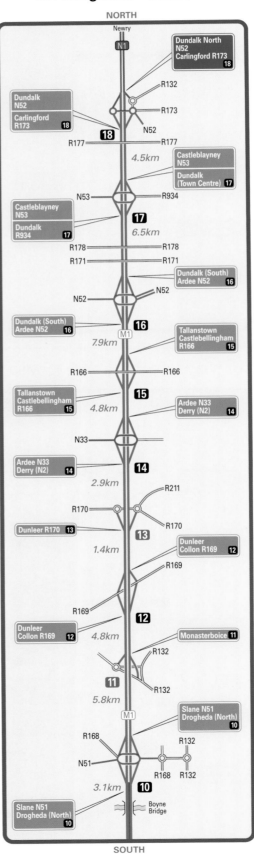

M2 Killshane – Ashbourne

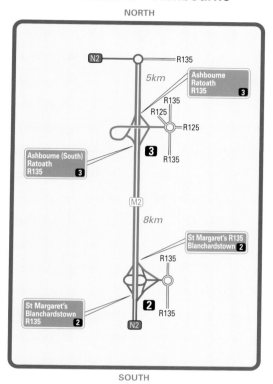

M9 Knocktopher – Waterford

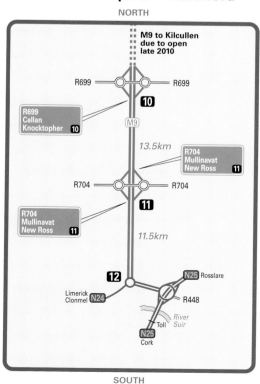

M4 Leixlip – McNeads Bridge

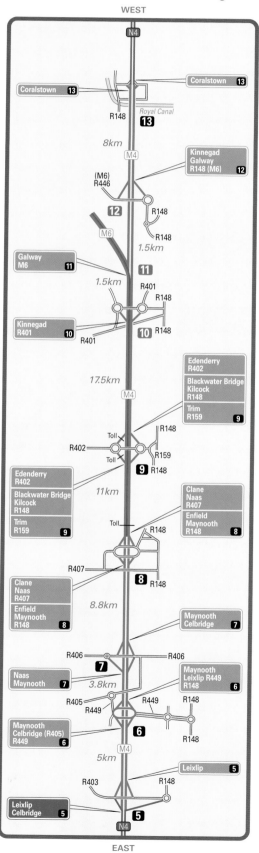

M6 M4 – Athlone

WEST

M6 1km

Athlone
Cavan
N55 10

N55

10

Athlone
Cavan
N55 10

1.5km

Athlone
R446 9

Athlone
R446 9

9

1.5km

Athlone
Birr
N62 8

Athlone (East)
Birr
N62 8

N62 8

8km

Moate
Clonmacnoise
R446 7

Moate
Clonmacnoise
R446 7

R446 7

6.5km

Moate
Horseleap
Clara
N80 6

Moate
Horseleap
Clara
N80 6

N80 6

R446

13.5km

M6

Tullamore
Kilbeggan
N52 5

N52 5

R446

Tullamore
Kilbeggan
N52 5

10km

Mullingar
Tyrellspass
N52 4

N52

R446

Mullingar
Tyrellspass
N52 4

4

5.5km

Rochfortbridge
Rhode
R400 3

R400 3

R446

Rochfortbridge
Rhode
R400 3

13km

Kinnegad
Milltownpass
R148 2

R446

Galway M6
Kinnegad
Milltownpass
R148 2

2

1km M4

1

M6

EAST

M6 Athlone – Galway

WEST

N6

N18 N18

19

8km

M6

Proposed
M18 Proposed
M17

18

3km

R348

Ballinasloe - Galway
Due to open Spring 2010

17

10km

N65

16

13.5km

Toll

12km

R446

R355

15

4.5km M6

Ballinasloe (East)
Shannonbridge
(R357) 14

R357

Ballinasloe (East)
Shannonbridge
(R357) 14

14

19km

Athlone (West)
Tuam
Athleague
Monksland
R362 13

R446 R362

Athlone (West)
Tuam
Athleague
Monksland
R362 13

R446

13

Roscommon
Sligo
N61 12

1.5km

Roscommon
Sligo
N61 12

N61

R446

12

2km

Athlone
Town Centre 11

Athlone
Town Centre 11

11

M6

EAST

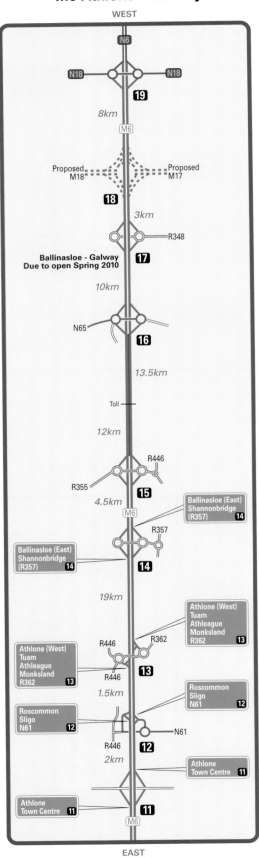

M7 Naas – M8

WEST

M8 (M7)	1.5km
M8 Cork 19	19
	11km
	Toll
R445	4km
	Portlaoise R445 18
Portlaoise R445 18	18 R445
	3.2km
	Cork N77 Carlow (N80) Tullamore Portlaoise 17
N77	17
Cork N77 Tipperary (N74) 17	
N80	N80
8km	
	Portarlington The Heath R419 16
R445	
Portlaoise R445 Carlow (N80) 16	R445 16
7.5km	
	Portarlington New Inn R445 15
Portarlington R445 15	15 R445
(M7)	R445
12.5km	
	Monasterevin Cherryville R445 14
Monasterevin Cherryville R445 14	14 R445
6.8km	
R415	Kildare R415 13
Kildare Nurney R415 13	13
Limerick Cork N8	6km R445
Newbridge The Curragh 12	R413 Newbridge Kilcullen The Curragh 12
N78	12 R445
N9 R413 M9	6km
R448	4.8km
Athy Kilcullen Castlecomer 11	11
Waterford Kilkenny Carlow M9 11	6km R445 Naas R445 10
Newbridge 10	10
	M7 6.5km Naas R445
R448	Dublin N7 9
Naas R445 9	9 N7

EAST

M7 Durrow – Limerick

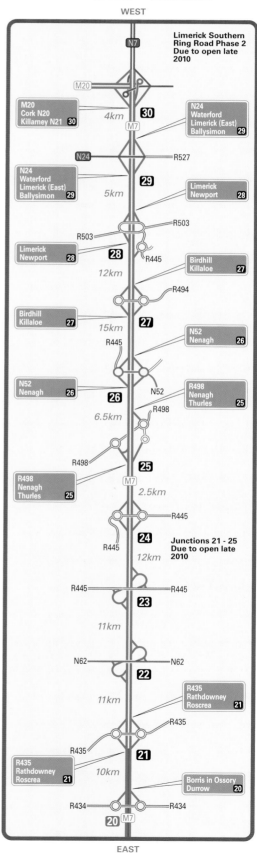

WEST

N7

Limerick Southern
Ring Road Phase 2
Due to open late
2010

M20 • 30 4km

M20 Cork N20 Killarney N21 30 • N24 Waterford Limerick (East) Ballysimon 29

N24 • M7 R527

N24 Waterford Limerick (East) Ballysimon 29 • 29 • Limerick Newport 28

5km

R503 • R503 • Limerick Newport 28 • 28 • R445 • Birdhill Killaloe 27

12km

Limerick Newport 28 • Birdhill Killaloe 27 • R494

Birdhill Killaloe 27 • 27 • N52 Nenagh 26

15km

R445 • N52 Nenagh 26 • 26 • N52 • R498 Nenagh Thurles 25

R498 Nenagh Thurles 25 • R498

6.5km

R498 • R498 Nenagh Thurles 25 • 25

M7 2.5km

R445

24 Junctions 21 - 25
Due to open late
2010

R445 • 12km • R445

R445 • R445

23

11km

N62 • N62

22

11km

R435 Rathdowney Roscrea 21

R435

R435 • 21

R435 Rathdowney Roscrea 21 • 10km • Borris in Ossory Durrow 20

R434 • R434

20 M7

EAST

M8 M7 – Cahir

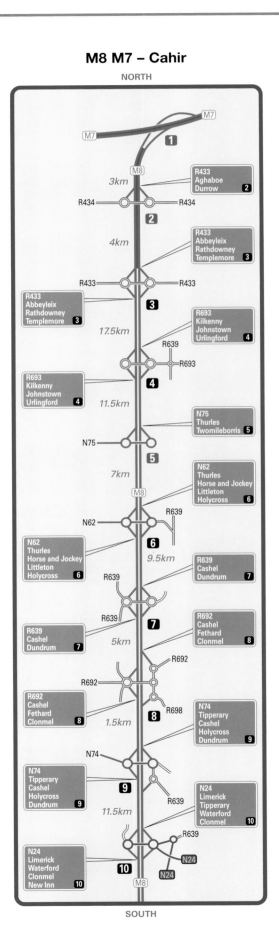

M8 Cahir – Cork

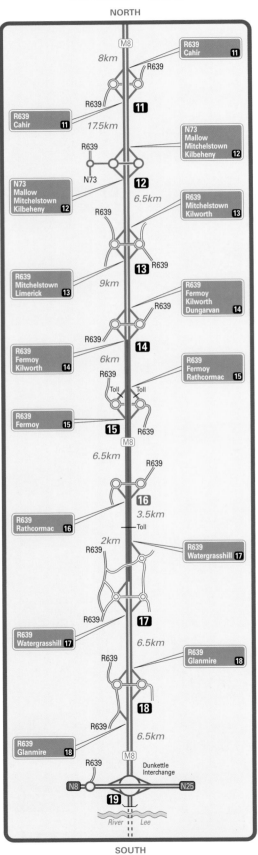

M11 Dublin – Rosslare

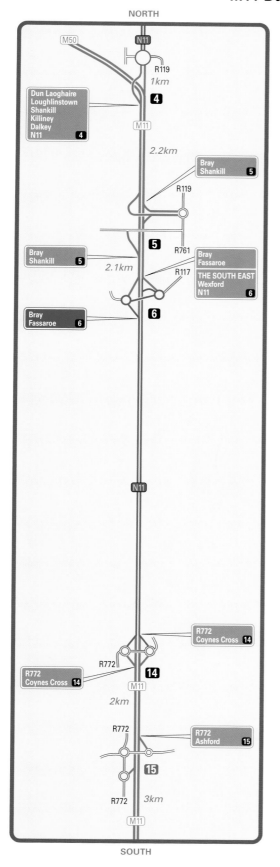

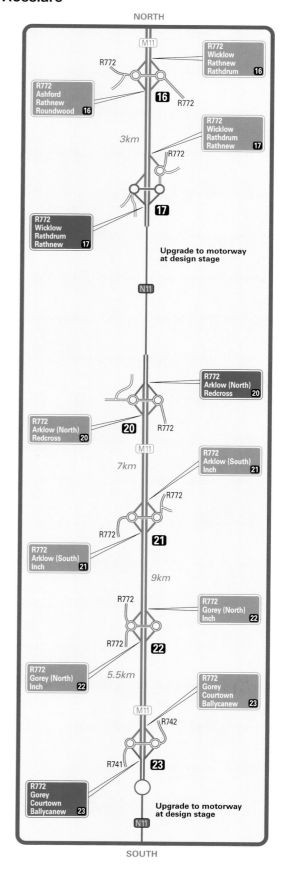

M18 Shannon – Ennis

M18 Gort – Crusheen
due to open Spring 2011

N18

R458
Ennis (North)
Barefield **14**

R458

14

3km

R458
Ennis (North)
Barefield **14**

R352
Scarriff
Tulla **13**

R352 — R352

13

R352
Scarriff
Tulla **13**

3km

N85
Ennis
Ennistymon
Kilrush **12**

N85

12

N85
Ennis
Ennistymon
Kilrush **12**

5km

R458
Quin
Dromoland
Ballygirreen **11**

R458

11 R458

R458
Quin
Dromoland
Ballygirreen **11**

5km

R472
Newmarket-on-Fergus
Carrigoran **10**

R472 R472

10

R472
Newmarket-on-Fergus
Carrigoran **10**

4km

N19
Shannon **9**

R458

N19

9

R458

N19
Shannon **9**

N18

M20 Limerick – Attyflin

M7 — M7

M20

1.5km

R926
Dooradoyle **2**

R926

2

R926
Dooradoyle **2**

3km

R510
Galway (M18)
Shannon
Foynes (N69)
Raheen **3**

R510

R510
Galway (M18)
Shannon
Foynes (N69)
Raheen **3**

3

3.5km

R526
Patrickswell **4**

R526

4

R526

R526
Patrickswell **4**

1.5km

Cork
Croom **5**

R526 — N20

Cork
Croom **5**

5

N21

Counties and administrative areas

The index lists places appearing in the main-map section of the atlas in alphabetical order. The reference before each name gives the atlas page number and grid reference of the square in which the place appears. The map shows counties and other internal administration areas in each country, together with a list of the abbreviated county name forms used in the index.

More than 50 top places of interest are indexed in red or green (if a World Heritage site). Airports appear in blue.

Northern Ireland

Antrim	Antrim
Armagh	Armagh
Belfast	Belfst
Down	Down
Fermanagh	Ferman
Londonderry	Lderry
Tyrone	Tyrone

Republic of Ireland

Carlow	Carlow	**Leitrim**	Leitrm
Cavan	Cavan	**Limerick**	Limrck
Clare	Clare	**Longford**	Longfd
Cork	Cork	**Louth**	Louth
Donegal	Donegl	**Mayo**	Mayo
Dublin	Dublin	**Meath**	Meath
Dublin City (1)	Dublin	**Monaghan**	Monhan
Dún Laoghaire-		**Offaly**	Offaly
Rathdown (2)	Dublin	**Roscommon**	Roscom
Fingal (3)	Dublin	**Sligo**	Sligo
South Dublin (4)	Dublin	**Tipperary North**	Tippry
Galway	Galway	**Tipperary South**	Tippry
Kerry	Kerry	**Waterford**	Watfd
Kildare	Kildre	**Westmeath**	Wmeath
Kilkenny	Kilken	**Wexford**	Wexfd
Laois	Laois	**Wicklow**	Wicklw

A

26 H3 **Abbey** Galway
34 G5 **Abbey** Galway
36 F1 **Abbeyderg Cross Roads** Longfd
16 F10 **Abbeydorney**/*Mainistir Ó dTorna* Kerry
17 L9 **Abbeyfeale**/*Mainistir na Féile* Limrck
45 K8 **Abbeylara**/*Mainistir Leathrátha* Longfd
29 K8 **Abbeyleix**/*Mainistir Laoise* Laois
36 G2 **Abbeyshrule**/*Mainistir Shruthla* Longfd
19 L4 **Abington** Limrck
48 E3 **Achadh**/*Aghadoon* Mayo
40 E4 **Achill Sound**/*Gob an Choire* Mayo
51 N8 **Achonry**/*Achadh Conaire* Sligo
51 K8 **Aclare**/*Áth an Chláir* Sligo
56 C5 **Acton** Armagh
15 K3 **Adamstown** Wexfd
18 F5 **Adare**/*Áth Dara* Limrck
42 D6 **Addergoole** Mayo
34 C7 **Addergoole**/*Eadargúil* Mayo
3 L4 **Adrigole**/*Eadargóil* Cork
28 H7 **Aghaboe** Laois
44 F7 **Aghaboy** Longfd
11 L9 **Aghabullogue** Cork
44 C1 **Aghacashel**/*Achadh an Chaisil* Leitrm
6 E7 **Aghada** Cork
42 G5 **Aghadiffin** Mayo
48 E3 **Aghadoon**/*Achadh* Mayo
67 M8 **Aghadowey** Lderry
4 B8 **Aghadown** Cork
62 E10 **Aghagallon** Antrim
41 L7 **Aghagower** Mayo
62 E10 **Aghalee** Antrim
44 C5 **Aghamore** Leitrm
42 F6 **Aghamore** Mayo
40 E7 **Aghany** Mayo
31 K7 **Aghavannagh** Wicklw
44 F3 **Aghavas** Leitrm
38 E4 **Agher Cross Roads** Meath
12 E8 **Aghern** Cork
48 D6 **Aghleam**/*An Eachléim* Mayo
44 H6 **Aghnacliff**/*Achadh na Cloiche* Longfd
8 F10 **Aghnagar Bridge** Kerry
5 L2 **Aghnamarroge Cross Roads** Cork
55 J10 **Aghnamullen** Monhan
67 M8 **Agivey Bridge** Lderry
27 M5 **Aglish** Tippry
13 K8 **Aglish** Watfd
8 G5 **Aglish**/*An Eaglais* Kerry
11 N7 **Ahadallane Cross Roads** Cork
16 F6 **Ahafona** Kerry
3 M7 **Ahakista** Cork
35 M6 **Ahascragh**/*Áth Eascrach* Galway
5 L1 **Aherla** Cork
12 E3 **Ahnaseed Bridge** Tippry
62 D2 **Ahoghill** Antrim
64 C9 **Ailt an Chorráin**/*Burtonport* Donegl
62 F7 **Aldergrove** Antrim
60 H2 **Alla Cross Roads** Lderry
38 D9 **Allen** Kildre
38 D8 **Allenwood**/*Fiodh Alúine* Kildre
2 F5 **Allihies**/*Na hAilichí* Cork
55 N4 **Allistragh** Armagh
35 K6 **Alloon Lower** Galway
22 F3 **Altamont Gardens** Carlow
59 N3 **Altnapaste** Donegl
64 D9 **Anagaire**/*Annagary* Donegl
8 H4 **Anascaul**/*Abhainn an Scáil* Kerry
2 E1 **An Baile Breac**/*Ballybrack* Kerry
8 E4 **An Baile Íochtarach**/*Ballyeightragh* Kerry
64 F3 **An Baile Thiar**/*West Town* Donegl
64 F3 **An Baile Thoir**/*East Town* Donegl
64 D6 **An Bun Beag**/*Bunbeg* Donegl
40 E3 **An Caiseal**/*Cashel* Mayo
65 M4 **An Caiseal**/*Cashel Glebe* Donegl
48 E4 **An Carn**/*Carn* Mayo

34 D8 **An Carn Mór**/*Carnmore* Galway
33 P7 **An Chaothach**/*Keeagh* Galway
58 C7 **An Charraig**/*Carrick* Donegl
33 J9 **An Cheathrú Rua**/*Carraroe* Galway
33 L2 **An Chloc Bhreac**/*Cloghbrack* Galway
40 E5 **An Chloich Mhór**/*Cloghmore* Mayo
59 L1 **An Cionn Garbh**/*Kingarrow* Donegl
8 G2 **An Clochán**/*Cloghane* Kerry
64 D10 **An Clochán Liath**/*Dunglow* Donegl
48 D6 **An Clochar**/*Clogher* Mayo
59 M3 **An Coimín**/*Commeen* Donegl
2 E1 **An Coireán**/*Waterville* Kerry
24 D4 **An Córa** Galway
40 E5 **An Corrán**/*Corraun* Mayo
8 E4 **An Daingean**/*Dingle* Kerry
40 E4 **An Doirín**/*Derreen* Mayo
8 G2 **An Drom**/*Drom* Kerry
59 J1 **An Dúchoraidh**/*Doocharry* Donegl
40 G5 **An Dumhach Bheag**/*Dooghbeg* Mayo
8 G5 **An Dún Meánach**/*Doonmanagh* Kerry
48 D6 **An Eachléim**/*Aghleam* Mayo
8 G5 **An Eaglais**/*Aglish* Kerry
64 G6 **An Fál Carrach**/*Falcarragh* Donegl
33 M2 **An Fhairche**/*Clonbur* Galway
8 D3 **An Fheothanach**/*Feohanagh* Kerry
48 D7 **An Fód Dubh**/*Blacksod* Mayo
48 E4 **An Geata Mór**/*Binghamstown* Mayo
8 D3 **An Ghlaise Bheag**/*Glashabeg* Kerry
19 N10 **Anglesborough** Limrck
19 P3 **Anglesey Bridge** Tippry
13 M9 **An Goirtín**/*Gorteen* Watfd
33 J6 **An Gort Mór**/*Gortmore* Galway
10 E10 **An Leaca Bhán**/*Lackabaun* Cork
64 B9 **An Leadhb Gharbh**/*Leabgarrow* Donegl
33 M9 **An Lochán Beag**/*Loughaunbeg* Galway
54 F8 **An Machaire**/*Maghery* Donegl
58 F1 **An Machaire**/*Maghery* Donegl
33 K3 **An Mám**/*Maum* Galway
40 D3 **An Mhaoilinn**/*Mweelin* Mayo
8 D3 **An Mhulríoch**/*Murreagh* Kerry
26 G9 **Annacarriga** Clare
19 Q5 **Annacarty** Tippry
56 E5 **Annaclone** Down
57 L4 **Annacloy** Down
19 J3 **Annacotty** Limrck
31 L9 **Annacurragh** Wicklw
8 H4 **Annagap** Kerry
64 D9 **Annagary**/*Anagaire* Donegl
47 K5 **Annagassan** Louth
19 K3 **Annagh** Limrck
43 K8 **Annagh** Roscom
24 F9 **Annagh Cross Roads** Clare
34 B6 **Annaghdown**/*Eanach Dhúin* Galway
26 D8 **Annaghneal** Clare
18 F1 **Annagore Bridge** Clare
56 G2 **Annahilt** Down
57 J10 **Annalong** Down
31 M5 **Annamoe**/*Áth na mBó* Wicklw
55 L9 **Annayalla** Monhan
11 J3 **Anne's Bridge** Cork
14 B9 **Annestown** Watfd
20 C4 **Annfield** Tippry
57 J6 **Annsborough** Down
13 N9 **An Rinn**/*Ringville* Watfd
33 N9 **An Spidéal**/*Spiddal* Galway
33 K4 **An Teach Dóite**/*Maam Cross* Galway
65 L8 **An Tearmann**/*Termon* Donegl
8 F10 **An tImleach Mór**/*Emlaghmore* Kerry

8 G2 **An Tír**/*Teer* Kerry
8 E10 **An Trian Iarach**/*Teeranearagh* Kerry
62 F5 **Antrim** Antrim
41 N9 **An tSraith**/*Srah* Mayo
48 F5 **An tSraith**/*Srah* Mayo
33 L9 **An Tulaigh**/*Tully* Galway
12 F5 **Araglin** Cork
12 E6 **Araglin Bridge** Cork
24 D2 **Aran Islands**/*Oileain Árann* Galway
45 P10 **Archerstown** Wmeath
46 E5 **Ardagh** Meath
17 P7 **Ardagh**/*Ardach* Limrck
44 G10 **Ardagh**/*Ardach* Longfd
43 M5 **Ardagh Cross Roads** Roscom
37 J8 **Ardan** Offaly
38 C4 **Ardanew** Meath
58 F4 **Ardara**/*Ard an Ratha* Donegl
22 F3 **Ardattin** Carlow
59 K5 **Ardbane** Donegl
62 B7 **Ardboe** Tyrone
2 E2 **Ard Caorach**/*Ardkearagh* Kerry
39 K1 **Ardcath** Meath
16 D10 **Ardconnell** Kerry
27 L7 **Ardcrony** Tippry
3 K2 **Ardea Bridge** Kerry
46 H5 **Ardee**/*Baile Átha Fhirdhia* Louth
16 D10 **Ardfert**/*Ard Fhearta* Kerry
5 J7 **Ardfield** Cork
13 J3 **Ardfinnan**/*Ard Fhionáin* Tippry
6 E3 **Ardglass** Cork
57 N6 **Ardglass** Down
2 H3 **Ardgroom**/*Dhá Dhrom* Cork
2 E2 **Ardkearagh**/*Ard Caorach* Kerry
57 P2 **Ardkeen** Down
34 B1 **Ardkill** Mayo
29 K6 **Ardlea** Laois
44 H1 **Ardlougher** Cavan
7 L4 **Ardmore**/*Aird Mhór* Watfd
37 K6 **Ardmorney** Wmeath
8 C3 **Ard na Caithne**/*Smerwick* Kerry
18 H2 **Ardnacrusha** Clare
34 F5 **Ardnasodan** Galway
19 J10 **Ardpatrick** Limrck
6 E7 **Ardra** Cork
3 Q5 **Ardrah** Cork
4 C4 **Ardrah** Cork
26 C2 **Ardrahan**/*Ard Raithin* Galway
55 P2 **Ardress** Armagh
30 C5 **Ardscull Cross Roads** Kildre
60 D5 **Ardstraw** Tyrone
61 Q7 **Ardtrea** Tyrone
4 H6 **Argideen Bridge** Cork
23 N2 **Arklow**/*An tInbhear Mór* Wicklw
29 Q8 **Arless** Laois
55 N4 **Armagh** Armagh
68 B6 **Armoy** Antrim
53 P6 **Arney** Ferman
17 P9 **Arranagh** Limrck
14 G6 **Arthurstown** Wexfd
67 K6 **Articlave** Lderry
60 E2 **Artigarvan** Tyrone
44 H4 **Arvagh**/*Armhach* Cavan
39 K3 **Ashbourne**/*Cill Dhéagláin* Meath
17 P10 **Ashford** Limrck
31 P5 **Ashford**/*Áth na Fuinseoige* Wicklw
20 E7 **Ashill** Tippry
23 J5 **Askamore** Wexfd
31 K8 **Askanagap** Wicklw
18 C4 **Askeaton**/*Eas Geitine* Limrck
16 G5 **Astee** Kerry
38 C1 **Athboy**/*Baile Átha Buí* Meath
17 L7 **Athea**/*Áth an tSléibhe* Limrck
34 G8 **Athenry**/*Baile Átha an Rí* Galway
30 E2 **Athgarvan** Kildre
18 H8 **Athlacca** Limrck
35 N2 **Athleague**/*Áth Liag* Roscom
36 C5 **Athlone**/*Baile Átha Luain* Wmeath
36 C5 **Athlone Castle** Wmeath
20 F4 **Athnid** Tippry
30 B6 **Athy**/*Baile Átha Í* Kildre
25 K9 **Attanagh** Laois
56 G10 **Attical** Down
35 N9 **Atticoffey** Galway
35 L6 **Attiregan** Galway

50 G8 **Attymass**/*Áit Tí an Mheasaigh* Mayo
34 H7 **Attymon**/*Áth Tiomáin* Galway
36 E3 **Auburn** Wmeath
34 D6 **Aucloggeen** Galway
9 J2 **Aughacasla** Kerry
54 G3 **Augher** Tyrone
15 L5 **Aughfad** Wexfd
9 L4 **Aughils** Kerry
62 B1 **Aughnacleagh** Antrim
55 J3 **Aughnacloy** Tyrone
20 B10 **Aughnagawer Cross Roads** Tippry
44 D1 **Aughnasheelan**/*Acadh na Sileann* Leitrm
25 N5 **Aughrim** Clare
35 M8 **Aughrim**/*Eachroim* Galway
31 L9 **Aughrim**/*Eachroim* Wicklw
31 N9 **Avoca**/*Abhóca* Wicklw

B

38 D5 **Baconstown** Meath
22 C4 **Bagenalstown**/*Muine Bheag* Carlow
8 D4 **Baile an Éanaigh**/*Ballineanig* Kerry
8 D4 **Baile an Fheirtéaraigh**/*Ballyferriter* Kerry
8 E3 **Baile an Lochaig**/*Ballinloghig* Kerry
8 E4 **Baile an Mhuilinn**/*Milltown* Kerry
8 D3 **Baile an Reannaigh**/*Ballinrannig* Kerry
2 C1 **Baile an Sceilg**/*Ballinskelligs* Kerry
24 D4 **Baile an Teampall** Galway
10 F9 **Baile Bhuirne**/*Ballyvourney* Cork
34 D7 **Baile Chláir**/*Claregalway* Galway
46 E9 **Baile Ghib**/*Gibstown* Meath
3 N10 **Baile Iarthach**/*Ballyieragh* Cork
10 G9 **Baile Mhic Íre**/*Ballymakeery* Cork
59 K2 **Baile na Finne**/*Fintown* Donegl
2 B1 **Baile na hAbhann**/*Ballynahow* Kerry
33 K9 **Baile na hAbhann**/*Ballynahown* Galway
8 D4 **Baile na nÁith**/*Ballynana* Kerry
8 D3 **Baile na nGall**/*Ballynagall* Kerry
13 N9 **Baile na nGall**/*Ballynagaul* Watfd
46 E8 **Baile Órthaí**/*Oristown* Meath
8 E2 **Baile Reo**/*Ballyroe* Kerry
8 G2 **Baile Uí Dhuinn**/*Ballyquin* Kerry
56 H2 **Baileysmill** Down
46 B4 **Bailieborough**/*Coill an Choillaigh* Cavan
39 N1 **Balbriggan**/*Baile Brigin* Dublin
51 P1 **Balinfull** Sligo
42 B7 **Balla** Mayo
26 C4 **Ballady** Cork
9 Q3 **Ballady** Cork
34 F1 **Ballagh** Galway
17 P9 **Ballagh** Limrck
35 Q3 **Ballagh** Roscom
43 Q9 **Ballagh** Roscom
20 C7 **Ballagh** Tippry
15 J3 **Ballagh** Wexfd
43 J5 **Ballaghaderreen**/*Bealach an Doirin* Roscom
17 L9 **Ballaghboy** Limrck
20 F8 **Ballaghboy** Tippry
23 K9 **Ballaghkeen** Wexfd
28 F6 **Ballaghmore** Laois
52 D3 **Ballaghnatrillick** Sligo
62 H10 **Ballantine Garden Village** Down
37 J9 **Ballard** Offaly
22 H3 **Ballard Cross Roads** Wicklw
26 C4 **Ballardiggan** Galway
15 Q7 **Ballare** Wexfd
21 K3 **Balleen** Kildre
29 Q8 **Ballickmoyler** Laois
22 B10 **Ballilogue** Kilken
26 H10 **Ballina** Clare
37 K3 **Ballina** Wmeath
50 F7 **Ballina**/*Béal an Átha* Mayo

5 P2 **Ballinaboy** Cork
32 G5 **Ballinaboy** Galway
37 P5 **Ballinabrackey** Meath
22 B2 **Ballinabranagh** Carlow
31 M8 **Ballinaclash** Wicklw
5 N4 **Ballinadee** Cork
43 M2 **Ballinafad**/*Béal an Átha Fada* Sligo
37 L9 **Ballinagar** Offaly
45 K4 **Ballinagh**/*Béal Átha na nEach* Cavan
53 J9 **Ballinagleragh** Leitrm
19 L1 **Ballinahinch** Tippry
29 L8 **Ballinakill**/*Baile na Coille* Laois
37 K1 **Ballinalack** Wmeath
44 G7 **Ballinalee**/*Béal Átha na Lao* Longfd
53 Q3 **Ballinamallard** Ferman
21 L5 **Ballinamara Cross Roads** Kilken
43 N5 **Ballinameen** Roscom
44 E1 **Ballinamore**/*Béal an Átha Móir* Leitrm
35 M4 **Ballinamore Bridge** Galway
5 K5 **Ballinascarty** Cork
35 P7 **Ballinasloe**/*Béal Átha na Sluaighe* Galway
12 H7 **Ballinaspick** Watfd
5 Q4 **Ballinclashet** Cork
15 L3 **Ballinclay** Wexfd
16 F9 **Ballincloher Cross Roads** Kerry
11 P10 **Ballincollig**/*Baile an Chollaigh* Cork
27 M3 **Ballincor** Tippry
14 E5 **Ballincrea** Kilken
6 D3 **Ballincurrig** Cork
22 F7 **Ballindaggan** Wexfd
12 C5 **Ballindangan** Cork
25 N1 **Ballinderreen**/*Baile an Dorín* Galway
27 L5 **Ballinderry** Tippry
42 D10 **Ballindine**/*Baile an Daighin* Mayo
52 E10 **Ballindoon** Sligo
60 D3 **Ballindrait**/*Baile an Droichid* Donegl
8 D4 **Ballineanig**/*Baile an Éanaigh* Kerry
4 H4 **Ballineen**/*Béal Átha Fhinin* Cork
18 D6 **Ballingarrane** Limrck
27 N5 **Ballingarry** Tippry
18 E7 **Ballingarry**/*Baile an Gharraí* Limrck
21 J7 **Ballingarry**/*Baile an Gharraí* Tippry
4 E1 **Ballingeary**/*Béal Átha an Ghaorthaidh* Cork
31 K9 **Ballinglen** Wicklw
4 G5 **Ballingurteen** Cork
5 P2 **Ballinhassig** Cork
34 E9 **Ballinillaun** Galway
22 C5 **Ballinkillin** Carlow
18 F8 **Ballinleeny** Limrck
8 E3 **Ballinloghig**/*Baile an Lochaig* Kerry
45 Q8 **Ballinlough** Meath
42 H8 **Ballinlough**/*Baile an Locha* Roscom
6 C8 **Ballinluska** Cork
44 F5 **Ballinmuck** Longfd
5 K6 **Ballinoroher** Cork
56 H10 **Ballinran** Down
8 D3 **Ballinrannig**/*Baile an Reannaigh* Kerry
6 B7 **Ballinreeshig** Cork
33 P1 **Ballinrobe**/*Baile an Róba* Mayo
25 P7 **Ballinruan** Clare
2 C1 **Ballinskelligs**/*Baile an Sceilg* Kerry
5 N5 **Ballinspittle**/*Béal Átha an Spidéil* Cork
43 L9 **Ballintober** Roscom
52 E8 **Ballintogher**/*Baile an Tóchair* Sligo
67 Q4 **Ballintoy** Antrim
59 K9 **Ballintra**/*Baile an tSratha* Donegl
41 N8 **Ballintubber** Mayo
29 P6 **Ballintubbert** Laois
20 G7 **Ballinunty** Tippry
20 F7 **Ballinure** Tippry
13 Q1 **Ballinurra** Tippry
22 C9 **Ballinvarry** Kilken
20 C2 **Ballinveny** Tippry
5 J2 **Ballinvoher** Cork
5 N5 **Ballinvronig** Cork
30 D5 **Ballitore**/*Béal Átha an Tuair* Kildre
38 B3 **Ballivor**/*Baile Íomhair* Meath
22 E3 **Ballon**/*Balana* Carlow
57 L1 **Balloo** Down
52 E3 **Balloor** Leitrm

46 H1 **Ballsmill** Armagh
57 N4 **Balltculter** Down
58 H10 **Ballure** Donegl
18 E6 **Ballvea** Limrck
12 D4 **Ballyaghaderg Bridge** Cork
18 F9 **Ballyagran** Limrck
18 D7 **Ballyallinan** Limrck
46 H5 **Ballybailie Cross Roads** Louth
35 L5 **Ballybaun** Galway
55 K9 **Ballybay/Béal Átha Beithe** Monhan
46 E2 **Ballybay Cross Roads** Monhan
13 K3 **Ballybeg** Tippry
27 P9 **Ballybeg** Tippry
39 L8 **Ballyboden** Dublin
59 P4 **Ballybofey/Bealach Feich** Donegl
37 Q5 **Ballyboggan** Meath
39 M3 **Ballyboghil/Baile Bachaille** Dublin
67 N6 **Ballybogy** Antrim
36 E5 **Ballybornia** Wmeath
28 F2 **Ballyboy** Offaly
3 M9 **Ballybrack** Cork
38 F6 **Ballybrack** Kildre
7 J2 **Ballybrack** Watfd
2 E1 **Ballybrack/An Baile Breac** Kerry
20 E3 **Ballybristy** Tippry
29 N3 **Ballybrittas** Laois
16 E10 **Ballybroman** Kerry
19 K5 **Ballybrood** Limrck
28 G8 **Ballybrophy/Baile Uí Bhróithe** Laois
18 F2 **Ballybroughan** Clare
37 P6 **Ballybryan** Offaly
16 F6 **Ballybunion/Baile an Bhuinnéanaigh** Kerry
30 D8 **Ballyburn** Kildre
19 M1 **Ballycahane** Tippry
20 D5 **Ballycahill** Tippry
21 L6 **Ballycallan** Kilken
23 L6 **Ballycanew/Baile Uí Chonnmhaí** Wexfd
18 H2 **Ballycar** Clare
22 H7 **Ballycarney** Wexfd
63 L4 **Ballycarry** Antrim
14 D7 **Ballycashin** Watfd
68 C4 **Ballycastle** Antrim
50 D3 **Ballycastle/Baile an Chaisil** Mayo
62 H4 **Ballyclare** Antrim
44 B10 **Ballyclare** Roscom
13 L1 **Ballyclerahan** Tippry
11 M4 **Ballyclogh/Baile Cloch** Cork
15 N6 **Ballycogly** Wexfd
29 J8 **Ballycolla** Laois
3 P6 **Ballycommane** Cork
27 K8 **Ballycommon** Tippry
21 N2 **Ballycomy** Kilken
32 C5 **Ballyconneely/Baile Conaola** Galway
53 Q10 **Ballyconnell/Béal Átha Conaill** Cavan
17 P1 **Ballycorick Bridge** Clare
6 G7 **Ballycotton/Baile Choitín** Cork
27 L2 **Ballycrossaun** Galway
48 H8 **Ballycroy/Baile Chruaich** Mayo
13 M8 **Ballycullane** Watfd
14 H6 **Ballycullane/Baile Uí Choileáin** Wexfd
36 G7 **Ballycumber/Béal Átha Chomair** Offaly
7 L2 **Ballycurrane** Watfd
12 A7 **Ballydague** Cork
10 G6 **Ballydaly** Cork
35 Q7 **Ballydangan** Roscom
6 F7 **Ballydavid** Cork
26 G1 **Ballydavid** Galway
3 P7 **Ballydehob/Béal an Dá Chab** Cork
12 C5 **Ballydeloughy** Cork
10 F4 **Ballydesmond/Baile Deasumhan** Cork
2 F6 **Ballydonegan** Cork
26 G1 **Ballydoogan** Galway
12 A6 **Ballydoyle** Cork
14 C7 **Ballyduff** Watfd
23 J6 **Ballyduff** Wexfd
16 F8 **Ballyduff/An Baile Dubh** Kerry
12 G7 **Ballyduff/An Baile Dubh** Watfd
31 N4 **Ballyduff Cross Roads** Wicklw
12 G5 **Ballyeafy** Watfd
62 H4 **Ballyeaston** Antrim
35 M8 **Ballyeighter** Galway
8 E4 **Ballyeightragh/An Baile Íochtarach** Kerry
23 M3 **Ballyfad** Wexfd

42 D7 **Ballyfarnagh** Mayo
43 P1 **Ballyfarnan/Baile Átha Fearnáin** Roscom
14 E3 **Ballyfasy** Kilken
6 B8 **Ballyfeard** Cork
8 D4 **Ballyferriter/Baile an Fheirtéaraigh** Kerry
23 L6 **Ballyfin** Wexfd
29 J4 **Ballyfin/An Baile Fionn** Laois
35 N4 **Ballyforan/Béal Átha Feorainne** Roscom
37 P7 **Ballyfore** Offaly
21 N4 **Ballyfoyle** Kilken
28 D5 **Ballygaddy Cross Roads** Offaly
63 K1 **Ballygalley** Antrim
35 M3 **Ballygar/Béal Átha Ghártha** Galway
13 R7 **Ballygarran** Watfd
14 B7 **Ballygarran** Watfd
23 N7 **Ballygarrett** Wexfd
41 Q9 **Ballygarries** Mayo
5 Q2 **Ballygarvan** Cork
54 H2 **Ballygawley** Tyrone
52 D8 **Ballygawley/Baile Uí Dhálaigh** Sligo
62 F2 **Ballygelly** Antrim
41 Q8 **Ballyglass** Mayo
42 H5 **Ballyglass** Mayo
50 D4 **Ballyglass** Mayo
14 C6 **Ballygorey** Kilken
66 C1 **Ballygorman** Donegl
23 L8 **Ballygortin** Wexfd
63 L10 **Ballygowan** Down
11 L3 **Ballygrady** Cork
20 C8 **Ballygriffin** Tippry
22 B9 **Ballygub** Kilken
18 H9 **Ballygubba** Limrck
14 G6 **Ballyhack** Wexfd
30 E9 **Ballyhacket Cross Roads** Carlow
18 H10 **Ballyhaght** Limrck
17 M5 **Ballyhahill** Limrck
45 L1 **Ballyhaise/Béal Átha hÉis** Cavan
63 Q10 **Ballyhalbert** Down
33 Q5 **Ballyhale** Galway
21 N9 **Ballyhale/Baile Héil** Kilken
19 Q1 **Ballyhane Cross Roads** Tippry
5 N1 **Ballyhank** Cork
9 Q5 **Ballyhar** Kerry
42 F8 **Ballyhaunis/Béal Átha hAmhnais** Mayo
41 N7 **Ballyhean** Mayo
34 D2 **Ballyhear** Galway
45 L6 **Ballyheelan** Cavan
16 D9 **Ballyheige/Baile Uí Thaidhg** Kerry
34 B2 **Ballyhenry** Mayo
25 P9 **Ballyhickey** Clare
22 H10 **Ballyhoge** Wexfd
14 E4 **Ballyhomuck** Kilken
11 J4 **Ballyhoolahan** Cork
12 B7 **Ballyhooly/Baile Átha hÚlla** Cork
57 N5 **Ballyhornan** Down
54 B10 **Ballyhugh** Cavan
37 N8 **Ballyhugh** Offaly
3 N10 **Ballyieragh/Baile Iarthach** Cork
45 N5 **Ballyjamesduff/Baile Shéamais Dhuibh** Cavan
37 M9 **Ballykean** Offaly
21 L6 **Ballykeefe Cross Roads** Kilken
56 G3 **Ballykeel** Down
36 D5 **Ballykeeran** Wmeath
66 G8 **Ballykelly** Lderry
37 Q8 **Ballykilleen** Offaly
6 H4 **Ballykilty** Cork
57 K6 **Ballykinler** Down
14 E7 **Ballykinsella** Watfd
31 J3 **Ballyknockan** Wicklw
6 F7 **Ballylanders** Cork
19 M10 **Ballylanders/Baile an Londraigh** Limrck
13 R6 **Ballylaneen** Watfd
5 M3 **Ballylangley** Cork
14 B8 **Ballyleen** Watfd
55 Q4 **Ballyleny** Armagh
63 J9 **Ballylesson** Down
3 Q4 **Ballylickey** Cork
66 B3 **Ballyliffin/Baile Lifín** Donegl
21 K7 **Ballyline** Kilken
29 M9 **Ballylinnen** Kilken
67 M7 **Ballylintagh** Lderry
16 H6 **Ballylongford/Béal Átha Longfoirt** Kerry
19 M8 **Ballylooby** Limrck
12 H3 **Ballylooby** Tippry
23 K10 **Ballylucas** Wexfd
63 L2 **Ballylumford** Antrim

29 P7 **Ballylynan/Baile Uí Laigheanáin** Laois
13 L4 **Ballymacarbry/Baile Mhac Cairbre** Watfd
14 E9 **Ballymacaw** Watfd
9 Q2 **Ballymacelligott** Kerry
45 L6 **Ballymachugh** Cavan
27 M8 **Ballymackey** Tippry
13 M7 **Ballymacmague** Watfd
6 H5 **Ballymacoda** Cork
26 C3 **Ballymacquiff** Galway
43 N9 **Ballymacurly** Roscom
35 K6 **Ballymacward** Galway
7 J5 **Ballymadog** Cork
66 B6 **Ballymagan** Donegl
66 G3 **Ballymagaraghy** Donegl
60 E2 **Ballymagorry** Tyrone
36 F2 **Ballymahon/Baile Uí Mhathain** Longfd
10 G9 **Ballymakeery/Baile Mhic Íre** Cork
47 K7 **Ballymakenny** Louth
45 M8 **Ballymanus** Wmeath
56 H10 **Ballymartin** Down
5 P3 **Ballymartle** Cork
62 E2 **Ballymena** Antrim
43 K9 **Ballymoe/Béal Átha Mó** Galway
67 N7 **Ballymoney** Antrim
23 N4 **Ballymoney Cross Roads** Wexfd
6 D6 **Ballymore** Cork
65 J6 **Ballymore** Donegl
36 G4 **Ballymore/An Baile Mór** Wmeath
30 G2 **Ballymore Eustace/An Baile Mór** Kildre
14 C8 **Ballymorris** Watfd
52 C10 **Ballymote/Baile an Mhóta** Sligo
30 E4 **Ballymount** Kildre
23 J10 **Ballymurn** Wexfd
22 D7 **Ballymurphy** Carlow
17 N9 **Ballymurragh** Limrck
35 Q1 **Ballymurray** Roscom
14 H4 **Ballynabola** Wexfd
34 E10 **Ballynabucky** Galway
2 D6 **Ballynacallagh** Cork
17 P2 **Ballynacally** Clare
4 G4 **Ballynacarriga** Cork
37 J2 **Ballynacarrigy/Baile na Carraige** Wmeath
51 P6 **Ballynacarrow** Sligo
27 M10 **Ballynaclogh** Tippry
6 F4 **Ballynacole** Cork
6 E5 **Ballynacorra** Cork
5 Q3 **Ballynacourty** Cork
13 N8 **Ballynacourty** Watfd
45 N7 **Ballynacree** Meath
37 L1 **Ballynafid** Wmeath
8 D3 **Ballynagall/Baile na nGall** Kerry
6 C4 **Ballynagaul** Cork
13 N9 **Ballynagaul/Baile na nGall** Watfd
6 A2 **Ballynaglogh West** Cork
37 K6 **Ballynagore** Wmeath
11 K8 **Ballynagree** Cork
5 P2 **Ballynagrumoolia** Cork
11 L6 **Ballynaguilkee** Watfd
57 J3 **Ballynahinch** Down
2 B1 **Ballynahow/Baile na hAbhann** Cork
36 E7 **Ballynahown** Wmeath
33 K9 **Ballynahown/Baile na hAbhann** Galway
50 E6 **Ballynahowna** Mayo
10 E4 **Ballynahulla** Kerry
37 M9 **Ballynakill** Offaly
36 D4 **Ballynakill** Wmeath
3 J6 **Ballynakilla** Cork
60 G3 **Ballynamallaght** Tyrone
5 P3 **Ballynamaul** Cork
11 P6 **Ballynamona** Cork
15 J5 **Ballynamona** Wexfd
47 N2 **Ballynamoy** Louth
12 B7 **Ballynamuddagh** Cork
13 L5 **Ballynamult** Watfd
8 D4 **Ballynana/Baile na nÁith** Kerry
38 G5 **Ballynare Cross Roads** Meath
45 L6 **Ballynarry** Cavan
16 E8 **Ballynaskreena** Kerry
42 C8 **Ballynastangford** Mayo
60 H2 **Ballyneaner** Tyrone
19 J5 **Ballyneety** Limrck
13 Q2 **Ballyneil** Tippry
12 F9 **Ballynennan** Tippry
12 F9 **Ballynoe/An Baile Nua** Cork
18 D8 **Ballynoe Bridge** Limrck
63 J4 **Ballynure** Antrim
12 A3 **Ballyorgan** Limrck
23 L6 **Ballyoughter** Wexfd
4 C6 **Ballyourane** Cork
13 P1 **Ballypatrick** Tippry

13 J9 **Ballyphilip** Watfd
12 F4 **Ballyporeen/Béal Átha Póirín** Tippry
13 R3 **Ballyquin** Watfd
8 G2 **Ballyquin/Baile Uí Dhuinn** Kerry
21 L2 **Ballyragget/Béal Átha Ragad** Kilken
67 M6 **Ballyrashane** Lderry
6 G3 **Ballyree** Cork
55 J2 **Ballyreagh** Tyrone
5 P4 **Ballyregan** Cork
29 L7 **Ballyroan/Baile Átha an Róine** Laois
43 N6 **Ballyroddy** Roscom
8 E2 **Ballyroe/Baile Reo** Kerry
22 H5 **Ballyroebuck** Wexfd
62 A5 **Ballyronan** Lderry
56 F6 **Ballyroney** Down
3 K7 **Ballyroon** Cork
22 C3 **Ballyryan** Carlow
52 C8 **Ballysadare/Baile Easa Dara** Sligo
52 G1 **Ballyshannon/Béal Átha Seanaiah** Donegl
16 E10 **Ballysheen** Kerry
14 E8 **Ballyshoneen** Watfd
27 J3 **Ballyshrule** Galway
11 N6 **Ballysimon Cross Roads** Cork
20 H6 **Ballysloe** Tippry
20 F2 **Ballysorrell** Tippry
18 D3 **Ballysteen** Limrck
40 D6 **Ballytoohy** Mayo
23 M9 **Ballyvaldon** Wexfd
19 N6 **Ballyvalode** Limrck
11 P8 **Ballyvaloon** Cork
25 K3 **Ballyvaughan/Baile Uí Bheacháin** Clare
22 E3 **Ballyveal** Carlow
13 J3 **Ballyveera** Tippry
4 G7 **Ballyvireen Bridge** Cork
12 A4 **Ballyvisteen** Cork
3 K9 **Ballyvoge** Cork
35 M5 **Ballyvoneen** Galway
25 N10 **Ballyvonnavaun** Clare
6 B9 **Ballyvorane** Cork
10 F9 **Ballyvourney/Baile Bhuirne** Cork
68 D4 **Ballyvoy** Antrim
13 P7 **Ballyvoyle Cross Roads** Watfd
63 Q9 **Ballywalter** Down
56 G6 **Ballyward** Down
12 A5 **Ballywater** Cork
67 K6 **Ballywildrick** Lderry
5 N4 **Ballywilliam** Cork
22 D10 **Ballywilliam** Wexfd
67 N7 **Balnamore** Antrim
39 J1 **Balrath** Meath
37 Q1 **Balrath Cross Roads** Wmeath
39 N1 **Balrothery** Dublin
39 M1 **Balscaddan** Dublin
4 B9 **Baltimore/Dún na Séad** Cork
30 F7 **Baltinglass/Bealach Conglais** Wicklw
16 E9 **Baltovin** Kerry
47 L8 **Baltray/Baile Trá** Louth
51 L9 **Banada** Sligo
27 P1 **Banagher/Beannchar** Offaly
56 D4 **Banbridge** Down
5 L3 **Bandon/Droichead na Bandan** Cork
16 G9 **Banemore** Kerry
63 N6 **Bangor** Down
49 J6 **Bangor Erris/Beanncho** Mayo
16 D10 **Banna** Kerry
11 L4 **Bannagh Cross Roads** Cork
62 B10 **Bannfoot** Armagh
25 L10 **Bansha** Clare
20 B10 **Bansha/An Bháinseach** Tippry
11 K5 **Banteer/Bántir** Cork
3 P5 **Bantry/Beanntraí** Cork
3 P5 **Bantry Gardens** Cork
66 G9 **Baranailt** Lderry
25 N8 **Barefield** Clare
4 C9 **Barloge** Cork
19 M6 **Barna** Limrck
27 P7 **Barna** Offaly
33 Q9 **Barna/Bearna** Galway
42 E4 **Barnacahoge** Mayo
43 K6 **Barnacawley** Roscom
34 G2 **Barnaderg** Galway
3 P6 **Barnaghgeehy** Cork
4 D4 **Barnagowlane** Cork
20 F3 **Barnalisheen** Tippry
42 E4 **Barnalyra** Mayo
10 C10 **Barnastooka** Kerry
48 G4 **Barnatra/Barr na Trá** Mayo
59 M6 **Barnesmore** Donegl
42 D8 **Barnycarroll** Mayo

3 N3 **Barony Bridge** Cork
11 L1 **Barrack Cross Roads** Cork
10 D6 **Barraduff** Kerry
26 G3 **Barratoor** Galway
4 C8 **Barrboy** Cork
21 N9 **Barrettstown** Kilken
17 P4 **Barrigone** Limrck
19 K4 **Barringtonsbridge** Limrck
48 G4 **Barr na Trá/Barnatra** Mayo
9 L1 **Barrow** Kerry
36 F1 **Barry** Longfd
12 D9 **Bartlemy** Cork
15 M8 **Bastardstown** Wexfd
17 K10 **Bateman's Bridge** Kerry
38 H4 **Batterstown** Meath
62 G3 **Battery Bridge** Antrim
37 L5 **Baughna** Wmeath
4 H2 **Baulbrack** Cork
21 P9 **Baunskeha** Kilken
25 J8 **Bauntlieve** Clare
10 H4 **Bawnaneel** Cork
4 C5 **Bawnboy** Cork
53 P10 **Bawnboy/An Bábhún Buí** Cavan
11 K3 **Bawn Cross Roads** Cork
44 F10 **Bawn Cross Roads** Longfd
13 L3 **Bawnfune** Watfd
4 D9 **Bawnlahan** Cork
34 F2 **Beagh** Galway
16 F5 **Beal** Kerry
25 L3 **Bealaclugga** Clare
33 J7 **Bealadangan/Béal an Daingin** Galway
16 G2 **Bealaha** Clare
9 L8 **Bealalaw Bridge** Kerry
59 L2 **Béal an Átha Móir/Bellanamore** Donegl
33 J7 **Béal an Daingin/Bealadangan** Galway
48 F4 **Béal an Mhuirthead/Belmullet** Mayo
4 E1 **Béal Átha an Ghaorthaidh/Ballingeary** Cork
49 L3 **Béal Deirg/Belderg** Mayo
36 E5 **Bealin** Wmeath
5 K2 **Bealnablath** Cork
11 L9 **Bealnamorive** Cork
33 Q9 **Bearna/Barna** Galway
9 P6 **Beaufort** Kerry
38 F2 **Bective** Meath
12 B9 **Behernagh** Cork
50 G7 **Behy Bridge** Mayo
42 E8 **Bekan** Mayo
41 P7 **Belcarra** Mayo
34 D4 **Belclare** Galway
53 L6 **Belcoo** Ferman
49 L3 **Belderg/Béal Deirg** Mayo
63 J8 **Belfast** Belfst
62 E7 **Belfast International** Antrim
5 Q4 **Belgooly** Cork
49 L6 **Bellacorrick/Béal Átha Chomhraic** Mayo
52 C8 **Belladrihid** Sligo
40 G2 **Bellagarvaun** Mayo
62 B3 **Bellaghy** Lderry
35 N7 **Bellagill Bridge** Galway
42 F3 **Bellahy** Sligo
49 J4 **Bellanaboy Bridge/Droichead Bhéal an Átha Buí** Mayo
43 L6 **Bellanagare/Béal Átha na gCarr** Roscom
53 P6 **Bellanaleck** Ferman
59 L2 **Bellanamore/Béal an Átha Móir** Donegl
36 B5 **Bellanamullia** Roscom
45 M1 **Bellancargy** Cavan
35 Q6 **Bellaneeny** Roscom
54 H6 **Bellanode** Monhan
41 Q5 **Bellavary/Béal Átha Bhearaigh** Mayo
55 Q8 **Belleek** Armagh
52 H2 **Belleek** Ferman
50 F6 **Belleek** Mayo
52 H2 **Belleek Pottery** Ferman
47 K10 **Bellewstown** Meath
37 N7 **Bellmount** Offaly
48 F4 **Belmullet/Béal an Mhuirthead** Mayo
63 L4 **Beltoy** Antrim
41 M3 **Beltra** Mayo
51 N4 **Beltra/Béal Trá** Sligo
54 C10 **Belturbet/Béal Tairbirt** Cavan
6 C5 **Belvelly** Cork
55 M3 **Benburb** Tyrone
47 J9 **Bend of the Boyne** Meath
67 N8 **Bendooragh** Antrim

30 D9 **Bennekerry** Carlow
21 P7 **Bennettsbridge/** *Droichead Binéid* Kilken
67 J5 **Benone** Lderry
60 H9 **Beragh** Tyrone
11 M8 **Bernard Cross Roads** Cork
11 N9 **Berrings** Cork
56 N8 **Bessbrook** Armagh
47 M9 **Bettystown/** *Baile an Bhiataigh* Meath
59 N6 **Big Bridge** Tyrone
62 G3 **Big Collin** Antrim
21 Q2 **Bilboa** Laois
48 E4 **Binghamstown/** *An Geata Mór* Mayo
19 L1 **Birdhill** Tippry
28 C3 **Birr/** *Biorra* Offaly
28 C4 **Birr Castle Demesne** Offaly
57 N5 **Bishops Court** Down
14 D5 **Bishopshall** Kilken
12 F6 **Black** Watfd
20 E10 **Blackcastle** Tippry
15 L3 **Blackhall** Wexfd
53 L6 **Blacklion** Cavan
36 H10 **Black Lion** Offaly
6 B5 **Blackrock** Cork
39 N8 **Blackrock** Dublin
47 K3 **Blackrock/** *Na Creagacha Dubha* Louth
48 D7 **Blacksod/** *An Fód Dubh* Mayo
9 L7 **Blackstones Bridge** Kerry
23 L10 **Blackwater/** *An Abhainn Dubh* Wexfd
3 K1 **Blackwater Bridge** Kerry
38 C5 **Blackwater Bridge** Kildre
55 M3 **Blackwatertown** Armagh
38 D8 **Blackwood/** *Coil Dubh* Kildre
67 M5 **Blagh** Lderry
39 K6 **Blanchardstown** Dublin
17 L7 **Blane Bridge** Limrck
11 Q9 **Blarney/** *An Bhlarna* Cork
11 Q9 **Blarney Castle** Cork
56 C3 **Bleary** Down
9 N2 **Blennerville** Kerry
30 H2 **Blessington/** *Baile Coimín* Wicklw
36 H10 **Blue Ball** Offaly
10 H3 **Blueford** Cork
6 B8 **Boardee** Cork
57 J2 **Boardmills** Down
43 J4 **Bockagh** Roscom
26 E8 **Bodyke** Clare
41 N3 **Bofeenaun** Mayo
21 J5 **Boggan** Mayo
46 C6 **Boggan Cross Roads** Meath
28 E9 **Boggaun** Tippry
39 M1 **Bog of The Ring** Dublin
4 F1 **Bohane's Cross Roads** Cork
9 L8 **Boheeshil** Kerry
19 K4 **Boher** Limrck
28 E5 **Boheraphuca** Offaly
13 K7 **Boheravaghera Cross Roads** Watfd
11 P3 **Boherboy Cross Roads** Cork
10 H4 **Boherbue** Cork
19 J4 **Bohereen** Limrck
38 F7 **Boherhole Cross Roads** Kildre
20 D7 **Boherlahan** Tippry
46 E10 **Bohermeen/** *An Bóthar Mín* Meath
12 G2 **Bohernarnane** Tippry
45 K9 **Boherquill** Wmeath
19 L6 **Boherroe** Limrck
42 C4 **Bohola/** *Both Chomhla* Mayo
67 J7 **Bolea** Lderry
67 L9 **Boleran** Lderry
29 P7 **Boley** Laois
22 H3 **Boley** Wicklw
30 G3 **Boleybeg Cross Roads** Kildre
30 C4 **Boley Cross Roads** Kildre
23 K7 **Boleyvogue** Wexfd
40 E5 **Bolinglanna/** *Buaile an Ghleanna* Mayo
17 J8 **Bolton's Cross Roads** Kerry
7 J3 **Boola** Watfd
12 G2 **Boolakennedy** Tippry
22 C6 **Borris/** *An Bhuiríos* Carlow
28 F7 **Borris in Ossory/** *Buiríos Mór Osraí* Laois
27 M6 **Borrisokane/** *Buiríos Uí Chéin* Tippry

20 C3 **Borrisoleigh/** *Buiríos Ó Luigheach* Tippry
25 N5 **Boston** Clare
19 K8 **Bottomstown** Limrck
45 K10 **Bottomy** Wmeath
20 D4 **Bouladuff** Tippry
67 M10 **Bovedy** Lderry
66 H10 **Bovevagh** Lderry
43 N3 **Boyle/** *Mainistir na Búille* Roscom
34 H1 **Boyounagh** Galway
37 N9 **Brackagh** Offaly
12 E3 **Brackbaun Bridge** Limrck
3 J1 **Brackloon** Kerry
43 L7 **Brackloon** Roscom
43 M6 **Brackloon Cross Roads** Roscom
37 P2 **Bracklyn** Wmeath
37 Q10 **Bracknagh** Offaly
36 B1 **Bracknagh** Roscom
36 E10 **Brackny** Offaly
50 F8 **Brackwanshagh** Mayo
3 N6 **Brahalish** Cork
8 G2 **Brandon/** *Cé Bhréanainn* Kerry
8 F2 **Brandon Mountain/** *Cnoc Bréanainn* Kerry
54 H7 **Brandrum** Monhan
30 F3 **Brannockstown** Kildre
39 P10 **Bray/** *Bré* Wicklw
60 E1 **Bready** Tyrone
5 J4 **Breaghna** Cork
16 E4 **Breaghva** Clare
41 P6 **Breaghwy** Mayo
22 G10 **Bree** Wexfd
6 H2 **Breeda** Cork
42 E8 **Brickeens** Mayo
12 D8 **Bridebridge** Cork
35 Q5 **Brideswell** Roscom
66 B8 **Bridge End** Donegl
23 J2 **Bridgeland** Wicklw
59 K8 **Bridgetown** Donegl
19 J1 **Bridgetown/** *Baile an Droichid* Clare
15 M7 **Bridgetown/** *Baile an Droichid* Wexfd
61 Q8 **Brigh** Tyrone
64 E6 **Brinlack/** *Bun na Leaca* Donegl
13 P6 **Briska** Watfd
39 J9 **Brittas** Dublin
12 E9 **Britway** Cork
38 B5 **Broadford** Kildre
18 C10 **Broadford** Limrck
26 E10 **Broadford/** *Áth Leathan* Clare
15 Q7 **Broadway** Wexfd
67 K10 **Brockagh** Lderry
18 D9 **Broken Bridge** Limrck
54 C5 **Brookeborough** Ferman
19 P8 **Brookville Bridge** Tippry
46 E1 **Broomfield** Monhan
10 E1 **Brosna** Kerry
28 C6 **Brosna** Offaly
28 E1 **Broughal** Offaly
11 Q3 **Brough Cross Roads** Cork
62 F1 **Broughshane** Antrim
45 J8 **Browne's Cross Roads** Longfd
7 J2 **Brown's Cross Roads** Watfd
66 F6 **Brown Shoulder** Donegl
46 G10 **Brownstown** Meath
14 E9 **Brownstown** Watfd
30 D3 **Brownstown Cross Roads** Kildre
20 E4 **Brownstown Cross Roads** Tippry
20 G3 **Bruckana** Kilken
58 F7 **Bruckles** Donegl
19 J7 **Bruff/** *An Brú* Limrck
42 E6 **Bruff Cross Roads** Mayo
18 H8 **Bruree/** *Brú Rí* Limrck
56 H7 **Bryansford** Down
40 E5 **Buaile an Ghleanna/** *Bolinglanna* Mayo
62 G1 **Buckna** Antrim
52 G3 **Buckode** Leitrm
14 B7 **Buck's Cross Roads** Watfd
19 J9 **Bulgaden** Limrck
35 J9 **Bullaun** Galway
40 D3 **Bunacurry/** *Bun an Churraigh* Mayo
40 D3 **Bun an Churraigh/** *Bunacurry* Mayo
3 N2 **Bunane** Kerry
3 K2 **Bunaw** Kerry
64 E8 **Bunbeg/** *An Bun Beag* Donegl
37 K1 **Bunbrosna** Wmeath
22 G5 **Bunclody/** *Bun Clóidí* Wexfd
65 Q6 **Buncrana/** *Bun Cranncha* Donegl

52 F2 **Bundoran/** *Bun Dobhrain* Donegl
9 K7 **Bunglasha** Kerry
58 F6 **Bungosteen Bridge** Donegl
44 H7 **Bunlahy** Longfd
14 A9 **Bunmahon/** *Bun Machan* Watfd
33 Q3 **Bunnafollistran** Mayo
32 G5 **Bun na hAbhann/** *Bunnahown* Galway
48 G5 **Bun na hAbhna/** *Bunnahowen* Mayo
48 G5 **Bunnahowen/** *Bun na hAbhna* Mayo
32 G5 **Bunnahown/** *Bun na hAbhann* Galway
64 E6 **Bun na Leaca/** *Brinlack* Donegl
51 P8 **Bunnanaddan** Sligo
50 H7 **Bunnyconnellan** Mayo
18 F2 **Bunratty** Clare
18 F2 **Bunratty Castle and Folk Park** Clare
21 M7 **Burnchurch** Kilken
12 F3 **Burncourt** Tippry
66 B8 **Burnfoot/** *Bun na hAbhann* Donegl
11 P6 **Burnfort** Cork
17 N2 **Burren** Clare
56 D9 **Burren** Down
25 L2 **Burren/** *Boirinn* Clare
17 M2 **Burrenfadda** Clare
66 B8 **Burt** Donegl
64 C9 **Burtonport/** *Ailt an Chorráin* Donegl
30 C6 **Burtown Cross Roads** Kildre
67 N4 **Bushmills** Antrim
45 L1 **Butlers Bridge/** *Droichead an Bhuitléaraigh* Cavan
5 L7 **Butlerstown** Cork
11 N3 **Buttevant/** *Cill na Mallach* Cork
11 N7 **Bweeng** Cork

C

55 K1 **Cabragh** Tyrone
38 C6 **Cadamstown** Kildre
28 F3 **Cadamstown** Offaly
62 D4 **Caddy** Antrim
67 M9 **Caheny Bridge** Lderry
26 E6 **Caher** Clare
3 K7 **Caher** Cork
9 K4 **Caheracruttera** Kerry
34 D9 **Caheradrine** Galway
4 C6 **Caheragh** Cork
35 L9 **Caherakillen** Galway
2 E1 **Caherbarnagh** Kerry
19 K5 **Caherconlish/** *Cathair Chinn Lis* Limrck
2 F3 **Caherdaniel/** *Cathair Dónall* Kerry
17 P1 **Caherea** Clare
17 L10 **Caher Hill** Limrck
34 F7 **Caherlea** Galway
34 C3 **Caherlistrane** Galway
2 F6 **Cahermore** Cork
25 P3 **Cahermore** Galway
4 C3 **Cahermuckee** Cork
17 K1 **Cahermurphy** Clare
24 G9 **Caherogan** Clare
34 F5 **Caherphuca** Galway
25 J7 **Cahersherkin** Clare
8 F9 **Cahersiveen/** *Cathair Saidhbhín* Kerry
13 J2 **Cahir/** *An Chathair* Tippry
13 J2 **Cahir Castle** Tippry
22 G8 **Caim** Wexfd
43 N5 **Caldragh Cross Roads** Roscom
55 L4 **Caledon** Tyrone
21 L8 **Callan/** *Callain* Kilken
42 C3 **Callow** Mayo
43 L4 **Callow** Roscom
35 L5 **Caltra** Galway
35 M7 **Caltraghlea** Galway
30 E4 **Calverstown** Kildre
33 K6 **Camas/** *Camas* Galway
56 B8 **Camlough** Armagh
23 K6 **Camolin/** *Cam Eolaing* Wexfd
9 K3 **Camp** Kerry
14 G5 **Campile/** *Ceann Poill* Wexfd
28 G6 **Camross/** *Camros* Laois
33 K6 **Camus/** *Camas* Galway
45 Q3 **Canningstown** Cavan
4 E2 **Caolmhagh/** *Kealvaugh* Cork
68 B5 **Cape Castle** Antrim
4 C2 **Cappaboy Beg** Cork
12 C7 **Cappagh** Cork

18 D5 **Cappagh** Limrck
61 L9 **Cappagh** Tyrone
25 M3 **Cappaghmore** Galway
19 P5 **Cappagh White /** *An Cheapach* Tippry
28 F2 **Cappagowlan** Offaly
28 F9 **Cappalinnan** Laois
19 M4 **Cappamore/** *An Cheapach Mhór* Limrck
35 L8 **Cappataggle** Galway
13 K7 **Cappoquin/** *Ceapach Choinn* Watfd
9 K6 **Caragh Bridge** Kerry
43 M8 **Caran** Roscom
38 B7 **Carbury** Kildre
10 D4 **Carker** Kerry
61 N9 **Carland** Tyrone
46 D8 **Carlanstown/** *Droichead Chearbhalláin* Meath
47 M1 **Carlingford/** *Cairlinn* Louth
30 C9 **Carlow/** *Ceatharlach* Carlow
61 M1 **Carn** Lderry
36 H4 **Carn** Wmeath
48 E4 **Carn/** *An Carn* Mayo
32 F7 **Carna/** *Carna* Galway
62 H1 **Carnalbanagh Sheddings** Antrim
61 J2 **Carnanreagh** Lderry
46 B8 **Carnaross/** *Carn na Ros* Meath
63 K1 **Carncastle** Antrim
66 D3 **Carndonagh/** *Carn Domhnach* Donegl
23 J4 **Carnew/** *Carn an Bhua* Wicklw
52 C5 **Carney** Sligo
27 L6 **Carney** Tippry
68 F9 **Carnlough** Antrim
63 J6 **Carnmoney** Antrim
34 D8 **Carnmore/** *An Carn Mór* Galway
34 E6 **Carnoneen** Galway
55 J3 **Carnteel** Tyrone
42 G3 **Carracastle** Mayo
38 E9 **Carragh** Kildre
43 J8 **Carraghs** Roscom
41 K6 **Carraholly** Mayo
65 L5 **Carraig Airt/** *Carrickart* Donegl
25 L5 **Carran** Clare
21 P6 **Carran** Kilken
33 J9 **Carraroe/** *An Cheathrú Rua* Galway
9 N8 **Carrauntoohil** Kerry
15 K6 **Carrick** Wexfd
58 C7 **Carrick/** *An Charraig* Donegl
45 L4 **Carrickaboy** Cavan
68 B4 **Carrick-a-Rede Rope Bridge** Antrim
65 L5 **Carrickart/** *Carraig Airt* Donegl
46 E4 **Carrickashedoge** Monhan
36 G1 **Carrickboy/** *An Charraig Bhuí* Longfd
63 L5 **Carrickfergus** Antrim
46 E3 **Carrickmacross/** *Carraig Mhachaire Rois* Monhan
39 N9 **Carrickmines** Dublin
61 K8 **Carrickmore or Termon Rock** Tyrone
43 Q4 **Carrick-on-Shannon/** *Cora Droma Rúisc* Leitrm
13 R2 **Carrick-on-Suir/** *Carraig na Siúire* Tippry
54 H4 **Carrickroe** Monhan
27 P4 **Carrig** Tippry
30 H2 **Carrig** Wicklw
9 J2 **Carrigacappul** Kerry
11 L10 **Carrigadrohid** Cork
11 K8 **Carrigagulla** Cork
16 E4 **Carrigaholt/** *Carrig an chabhaltaigh* Clare
27 M4 **Carrigahorig** Tippry
6 B7 **Carrigaline/** *Carraig Uí Leighin* Cork
44 G3 **Carrigallen/** *Carraig Álainn* Leitrm
45 K5 **Carrigan** Cavan
10 H8 **Carriganimmy** Cork
12 F3 **Carriganroe** Tippry
66 B10 **Carrigans/** *An Carraigín* Donegl
27 K9 **Carrigatogher** Tippry
4 E6 **Carrigbaun Cross Roads** Cork
4 E6 **Carrigeeny** Cork
31 N3 **Carriggower** Wicklw
17 N7 **Carrigkerry** Limrck
11 R8 **Carrignavar** Cork
6 D5 **Carrigtohill/** *Carrig Thuathail* Cork
14 B7 **Carroll's Cross Roads** Watfd

20 B7 **Carrow** Tippry
63 P8 **Carrowdore** Down
24 G6 **Carrowduff** Clare
43 M9 **Carrowduff** Roscom
51 M6 **Carroweden** Sligo
26 C2 **Carrowkeel** Galway
33 Q1 **Carrowkeel** Mayo
65 N6 **Carrowkeel/** *An Cheathrú Chaol* Donegl
34 G1 **Carrowkeelanahglass** Galway
41 K9 **Carrowkennedy** Mayo
66 F3 **Carrowmenagh** Donegl
34 D10 **Carrowmore** Galway
34 C1 **Carrowmore** Mayo
34 C4 **Carrowmore** Mayo
50 E4 **Carrowmore** Mayo
51 M7 **Carrowmore** Sligo
33 Q5 **Carrowmoreknock** Galway
52 C7 **Carrowmore Megalithic Cemetery** Sligo
41 P8 **Carrownacon** Mayo
50 H3 **Carrowpadeen** Sligo
35 P6 **Carrowreagh** Roscom
36 C2 **Carrowrory** Longfd
48 H2 **Carrowteige/** *Ceathrú Thaidhg* Mayo
53 Q6 **Carry Bridge** Ferman
63 K9 **Carryduff** Down
26 E1 **Cartron** Galway
22 D6 **Cashel** Carlow
29 L6 **Cashel** Laois
32 G5 **Cashel/** *An Caiseal* Galway
40 E3 **Cashel/** *An Caiseal* Mayo
20 D8 **Cashel/** *Caiseal* Tippry
52 C4 **Cashelgarran** Sligo
65 M4 **Cashel Glebe/** *An Caiseal* Donegl
34 E8 **Cashla** Galway
32 D1 **Cashleen** Galway
33 K8 **Casla/** *Costelloe* Galway
14 H4 **Cassagh** Wexfd
48 M1 **Castlebaldwin/** *Béal Átha na gCarraigíní* Sligo
41 N5 **Castlebar/** *Caislean an Bharraigh* Mayo
47 K4 **Castlebellingham/** *Baile an Ghearlánaigh* Louth
12 B7 **Castleblagh** Cork
35 K5 **Castleblakeney** Galway
55 M10 **Castleblaney/** *Baile na Lorgan* Monhan
15 P3 **Castlebridge/** *Droichead an Chaisleáin* Wexfd
67 P5 **Castlecat** Antrim
61 N10 **Castlecaulfield** Tyrone
21 N2 **Castlecomer/** *Caisleán an Chomair* Kilken
19 K2 **Castleconnell/** *Caisleán Uí Chonnaill* Limrck
50 G6 **Castleconor** Sligo
53 Q5 **Castle Coole** Ferman
35 N1 **Castlecoote** Roscom
11 M3 **Castlecor** Cork
2 F2 **Castle Cove** Kerry
28 G2 **Castlecuffe Cross Roads** Laois
62 A4 **Castledawson** Lderry
60 C6 **Castlederg** Tyrone
30 D7 **Castledermot/** *Diseart Diarmada* Kildre
22 G7 **Castledockerell** Wexfd
60 C3 **Castlefinn/** *Caisleán na Finne* Donegl
4 H7 **Castlefreke** Cork
52 D2 **Castlegal** Sligo
9 J2 **Castlegregory/** *Caisleán Ghriaire* Kerry
40 G2 **Castlehill** Mayo
50 D8 **Castlehill** Mayo
10 C3 **Castleisland/** *Oileán Ciarraí* Kerry
37 P6 **Castlejordan** Meath
39 K6 **Castleknock** Dublin
20 E2 **Castleleiny** Tippry
23 K9 **Castlellis** Wexfd
12 D8 **Castlelyons/** *Caisleán Ó Liatháin* Cork
9 N4 **Castlemaine/** *Caisleán na Mainge* Kerry
6 G5 **Castlemartyr/** *Baile na Martra* Cork
43 M8 **Castleplunket** Roscom
45 M9 **Castlepollard/** *Baile na gCros* Wmeath
34 C6 **Castlequarter/** *Ceathrú an Chaisleáin* Galway
45 N6 **Castlerahan** Cavan
43 K7 **Castlerea/** *An Caisleán Riabhach* Roscom
67 K5 **Castlerock** Lderry
55 K7 **Castleshane** Monhan
25 L5 **Castletown** Clare
4 H3 **Castletown** Cork
18 E8 **Castletown** Limrck
46 E7 **Castletown** Meath
23 N4 **Castletown** Wexfd

Castletown – Croghan 91

45 L8 Castletown Wmeath
28 H6 Castletown/*Baile an Chaisleáin* Laois
2 H5 Castletown Bearhaven/*Baile Chaisleáin Bhéarra* Cork
37 J5 Castletown Geoghegan Wmeath
38 H7 Castletown House Kildre
12 A6 Castletownroche/*Baile Chaisleáin an Róistigh* Cork
4 E8 Castletownshend/*Baile an Chaisleáin* Cork
21 Q4 Castlewarren Kilken
56 H6 Castlewellan Down
2 F3 Cathair Dónall/*Caherdaniel* Kerry
16 E8 Causeway/*An Tóchar* Kerry
45 L2 Cavan/*An Cabhán* Cavan
55 J8 Cavanagarvan Monhan
59 K10 Cavangarden Donegl
4 D5 Ceancullig Cork
8 D4 Ceann Trá/*Ventry* Kerry
34 C6 Ceathrú an Chaisleáin/*Castlequarter* Galway
48 H2 Ceathrú Thaidhg/*Carrowteige* Mayo
8 G2 Cé Bhréanainn/*Brandon* Kerry
11 M4 Cecilstown Cork
49 M2 Céide Fields Mayo
38 H7 Celbridge/*Cill Droichid* Kildre
46 H3 Chanonrock Louth
57 N6 Chapeltown Down
8 D9 Chapeltown Kerry
22 F10 Chapel Village Wexfd
55 N2 Charlemont Armagh
42 F3 Charlestown/*Baile Chathail* Mayo
18 G10 Charleville/*An Ráth* Cork
14 F6 Cheekpoint Watfd
30 B2 Cherryville Kildre
62 C3 Chesney's Corner Antrim
6 D7 Church Bay Cork
35 Q2 Churchboro Cross Roscom
4 C8 Church Cross Cork
41 M10 Churchfield/*Páirc an Teampaill* Mayo
9 M1 Church Hill Kerry
65 K9 Church Hill/*Mín an Lábain* Donegl
43 L5 Churchstreet Roscom
6 F7 Churchtown Cork
65 Q10 Church Town Donegl
14 G9 Churchtown Watfd
15 Q7 Churchtown Wexfd
11 N2 Churchtown/*Baile an Teampail* Cork
38 D1 Cill Bhríde/*Kilbride* Meath
33 J6 Cill Bhriocáin/*Kilbrickan* Galway
58 D7 Cill Charthaigh/*Kilcar* Donegl
32 G7 Cill Chiaráin/*Kilkieran* Galway
7 M3 Cill Cholmáin/*Kilcolman* Watfd
8 E3 Cill Chuáin/*Kilquane* Kerry
24 C3 Cill Éinne/*Killeany* Galway
8 H10 Cillín Liath/*Killeenleagh* Kerry
24 B2 Cill Mhuirbhigh/*Kilmurvy* Galway
10 H10 Cill na Martra/*Killnamartery* Cork
8 E10 Cill Ó Luaigh/*Killoluaig* Kerry
24 C3 Cill Rónáin/*Kilronan* Galway
8 D4 Cill Ura/*Kildurrihy* Kerry
2 C1 Cill Urlaí/*Killurly* Kerry
33 K7 Cinn Mhara/*Kinvarra* Galway
64 C9 Cionn Caslach/*Kincaslough* Donegl
63 K8 City of Belfast Crematorium Down
66 E8 City of Derry Lderry
54 D3 Clabby Ferman
32 B2 Claddaghduff Galway
62 B2 Clady Lderry
60 C4 Clady Tyrone
55 Q6 Cladymilltown Armagh
40 F3 Claggan Mayo
10 F3 Clamper Bridge Cork
38 F8 Clane/*Claonadh* Kildre
36 H7 Clara/*Clóirtheach* Offaly
29 J2 Clarahill Laois
56 B5 Clare Armagh
25 M10 Clarecastle/*Droichead an Chláir* Clare
28 D4 Clareen Offaly
18 C1 Clareen Bridge Clare
34 D7 Claregalway/*Baile Chláir* Galway
42 C9 Claremorris/*Clár Chlainne Mhuiris* Mayo
18 G4 Clarina Limrck
34 E9 Clarinbridge/*Droichead an Chláirín* Galway
37 K2 Clark's Cross Roads Wmeath
27 N8 Clash Tippry
19 M7 Clashdrumsmith Tippry
7 K3 Clashmore/*Clais Mhór* Watfd
17 M8 Clash North Limrck
14 B5 Clashroe Watfd
17 M8 Clash South Limrck
60 H1 Claudy Lderry
32 C2 Cleggan/*An Cloigeann* Galway
18 D2 Clenagh Clare
15 M6 Cleristown Wexfd
43 K6 Clerragh Roscom
32 D3 Clifden/*An Clochán* Galway
45 N3 Clifferna Cavan
52 D3 Cliffony/*Cliafuine* Sligo
24 F6 Cliffs of Moher Clare
37 P4 Clocrave Wmeath
61 K9 Clogfin Tyrone
14 C5 Clogga Kilken
23 P3 Clogga Wicklw
68 B10 Clogh Antrim
28 H8 Clogh Laois
23 L5 Clogh Wexfd
29 N9 Clogh/*An Chloch* Kilken
37 N2 Cloghan Wmeath
59 M3 Cloghan/*An Clochan* Donegl
36 D10 Cloghan/*An Clochán* Offaly
3 J10 Cloghane Cork
8 G2 Cloghane/*An Clochán* Kerry
34 C1 Cloghans Hill Mayo
38 B6 Clogharinka Kildre
21 P3 Clogharinka Kilken
17 K1 Cloghaun Clare
34 D6 Cloghaun Galway
26 E8 Cloghaun Bridge Clare
51 P2 Cloghboley Sligo
17 J10 Cloghboola Kerry
33 L2 Cloghbrack/*An Chloc Bhreac* Galway
38 B2 Cloghbrack Bridge Meath
60 E2 Cloghcor Tyrone
13 L4 Clogheen Watfd
12 H4 Clogheen/*An Chloichín* Tippry
41 L6 Clogher Mayo
41 P8 Clogher Mayo
44 B5 Clogher Roscom
54 F3 Clogher Tyrone
48 D6 Clogher/*An Clochar* Mayo
18 H1 Cloghera Clare
47 M7 Clogherhead/*Ceann Chlochair* Louth
68 B9 Clogh Mills Antrim
40 E5 Cloghmore/*An Chloich Mhór* Mayo
21 P3 Cloghpook Kilken
39 M5 Cloghran Dublin
11 P10 Cloghroe Cork
10 F2 Cloghvoula Cork
18 D6 Clogh West Limrck
57 P2 Cloghy Down
22 G6 Clohamon/*Cloch Ámainn* Wexfd
14 E8 Clohernagh Watfd
23 K6 Clologe Wexfd
28 D8 Clonakenny Tippry
5 J6 Clonakilty/*Cloich na Coillte* Cork
39 K1 Clonalvy Meath
7 J5 Clonard Cork
38 B4 Clonard Meath
15 N4 Clonard Wexfd
28 H2 Clonaslee/*Cluain na Slí* Laois
37 P9 Clonavoe Offaly
34 H2 Clonbern Galway
37 Q9 Clonbullogue/*Cluain Bolg* Offaly
33 M2 Clonbur/*An Fhairche* Galway
37 P9 Cloncreen Offaly
36 F3 Cloncullen Wmeath
28 F6 Clonculty Laois
38 E5 Cloncurry Kildre
39 K7 Clondalkin Dublin
10 H9 Clondrohid Cork
12 E7 Clondulane Cork
13 Q4 Clonea Watfd
39 J5 Clonee Meath
37 L7 Cloneen Offaly
20 H9 Cloneen Tippry
22 G4 Clonegall/*Cluain na nGall* Carlow
59 P9 Clonelly Ferman
54 F8 Clones/*Cluain Eois* Monhan
23 M7 Clonevin Cross Roads Wexfd
36 B9 Clonfert/*Cluain Fearta* Galway
36 B10 Clonfert Cross Roads Galway
15 J5 Clongeen Wexfd
28 H6 Clonincurragh Laois
10 D8 Clonkeen Kerry
29 K5 Clonkeen Laois
35 J6 Clonkeenkerrill Galway
19 J2 Clonlara/*Cluain Lára* Clare
37 Q1 Clonleame Cross Roads Wmeath
37 N2 Clonlost Wmeath
36 C7 Clonmacnoise/*Cluain Mhic Nóis* Offaly
21 K4 Clonmantagh Kilken
66 B3 Clonmany/*Cluain Maine* Donegl
20 G2 Clonmeen Laois
13 M2 Clonmel/*Cluain Meala* Tippry
45 Q10 Clonmellon Wmeath
30 H9 Clonmore Carlow
47 L6 Clonmore Louth
28 E9 Clonmore Tippry
6 F3 Clonmult Cork
36 D9 Clonony Offaly
20 C6 Clonoulty Tippry
22 F10 Clonroche/*Cluain an Róistigh* Wexfd
23 L3 Clonroe Cross Roads Wexfd
39 K6 Clonsilla Dublin
39 N6 Clontarf Dublin
55 L8 Clontibret Monhan
21 L3 Clontubbrid Kilken
38 B3 Clonycavan Meath
29 L1 Clonygowan/*Cluain na nGamhan* Offaly
29 L2 Clonyquin Offaly
34 C7 Cloonacauneen/*Cluain Mhic Cáinín* Galway
51 L7 Cloonacool Sligo
45 J6 Cloonagh Longfd
34 C6 Cloonboo/*Cluain Bú* Galway
36 B1 Clooncah Roscom
41 M4 Cloondaff Mayo
44 D8 Cloondara Longfd
44 E4 Cloone/*An Chluain* Leitrm
44 D6 Clooneagh Leitrm
45 J6 Clooneen Longfd
58 F3 Clooney Donegl
35 Q8 Cloonfad Roscom
42 G9 Cloonfad Roscom
43 K5 Cloonfad Cross Roads Roscom
42 D6 Cloonfallagh Mayo
25 L9 Cloonfeagh Clare
42 E3 Cloonfinish Mayo
43 J7 Cloonfower Roscom
50 J6 Cloonkeelaun Sligo
42 H10 Cloonkeen Galway
41 N6 Cloonkeen Mayo
43 J8 Cloonkeen Roscom
51 P7 Cloonkeevy Sligo
42 D7 Cloonlee Mayo
19 N5 Cloonlusk Limrck
42 G3 Cloonmore Cross Roads Mayo
43 P8 Cloonmurray Roscom
34 H1 Cloonnacat Galway
8 G2 Cloonsharragh/*Cluain Searrach* Kerry
43 K6 Cloonsheever Roscom
42 H3 Cloontia Mayo
26 F7 Cloonusker Clare
35 K8 Cloonymorris Galway
43 P8 Cloonyogan Roscom
43 N7 Cloonyquin Roscom
46 B10 Cloran Cross Roads Wmeath
57 K5 Clough Down
5 L1 Cloughduv Cork
27 N7 Cloughjordan/*Cloch Shiurdáin* Tippry
18 D8 Clouncagh Limrck
45 L1 Cloverhill Cavan
6 F6 Cloyne/*Cluain* Cork
34 C6 Cluain Bú/*Cloonboo* Galway
34 C7 Cluain Mhic Cáinín/*Cloonacauneen* Galway
8 G2 Cluain Searrach/*Cloonsharragh* Kerry
4 G5 Clubhouse Cross Roads Cork
17 L10 Clydagh Bridge Kerry
8 E4 Cnoc an Bhróigín/*Knockavrogeen* Kerry
48 G3 Cnocán na Líne/*Knocknalina* Mayo
48 G4 Cnoc na Lobhar/*Knocknalower* Mayo
9 J9 Cnocrua/*Knockroe* Kerry
11 M10 Coachford/*Áth an Choiste* Cork
61 Q7 Coagh Tyrone
20 H6 Coalbrook Tippry
61 P9 Coalisland Tyrone
21 P2 Coan Kilken
6 C6 Cobh/*An Cóbh* Cork
33 L1 Coill an tSiáin/*Killateeaun* Mayo
32 H7 Coill Sáile/*Kylesalia* Galway
34 C8 Coill Uachtar/*Kilroghter* Galway
30 E5 Colbinstown Wicklw
36 G1 Colehill Longfd
67 L6 Coleraine Lderry
15 N4 Colestown Wexfd
13 M7 Colligan Bridge Watfd
45 N10 Collinstown/*Baile na gCailleach* Wmeath
46 H7 Collon/*Collann* Louth
52 C8 Collooney/*Cúil Mhuine* Sligo
3 J3 Collorus Kerry
20 F10 Colman Tippry
34 H6 Colmanstown Galway
47 L9 Colp Meath
63 M9 Comber Down
19 Q1 Commaun More Tippry
59 M3 Commeen/*An Coimín* Donegl
58 F5 Common Bridge Donegl
5 K2 Commons Cork
21 J6 Commons Tippry
33 N2 Cong/*Conga* Mayo
63 N7 Conlig Down
12 F8 Conna Cork
32 E2 Connemara National Park Galway
25 K9 Connolly/*Fíoch Rua* Clare
4 F7 Connonagh Cork
62 F3 Connor Antrim
67 P7 Conogher Cross Roads Antrim
60 B2 Convoy/*Conmhaigh* Donegl
61 P7 Cookstown Tyrone
12 H6 Cool Watfd
52 E9 Coola Cross Roads Sligo
37 N9 Coolagary Offaly
51 P5 Coolaney/*Cúil Aine* Sligo
13 K7 Coolanheen Watfd
23 J3 Coolattin Wicklw
21 P2 Coolbaun Kilken
27 K6 Coolbaun Tippry
20 G8 Coolbaun Cross Roads Tippry
65 M9 Coolboy Donegl
12 D3 Coolboy Limrck
23 J3 Coolboy Wicklw
28 D5 Coolderry Offaly
45 L9 Coole Wmeath
12 B8 Coolea Cork
10 F9 Coolea/*Cúil Aodha* Cork
12 E7 Coole Abbey Cork
21 P5 Coolgrange Kilken
23 M3 Coolgreany/*Cúil Ghréine* Wexfd
6 B3 Coolgreen Cork
12 B7 Coolinny Cork
4 E4 Coolkellure Cork
53 J8 Coollegreane Leitrm
17 M3 Coolmeen Clare
59 J9 Coolmore Donegl
42 G8 Coolnafarna Mayo
45 K9 Coolnagun Wmeath
39 M6 Coolock Dublin
28 G6 Coolrain Laois
23 M8 Coolroe Wexfd
27 N2 Coolross Tippry
6 B7 Coolsallagh Cork
44 B10 Coolshaghtena Roscom
43 P10 Coolteige Cross Roscom
8 G8 Coomduff Kerry
3 P3 Coomhola Bridge Cork
4 D4 Coomleagh Cork
18 G3 Coonagh Limrck
54 E5 Cooneen Ferman
43 L3 Coonloogh Sligo
17 J2 Cooraclare/*Cuar an Chláir* Clare
21 Q4 Coorleagh Kilken
3 P7 Coosane Cork
43 P3 Cootehall Roscom
45 Q1 Cootehill/*Muinchille* Cavan
4 H2 Coppeen Cork
11 N4 Copsetown Cross Roads Cork
34 C6 Cor an Dola/*Corrandulla* Galway
16 F2 Corbally Clare
50 H5 Corbally Sligo
30 E2 Corbally Cross Roads Kildre
44 G9 Corboy Longfd
48 E3 Corclogh/*Corrchloch* Mayo
46 G3 Corcreeghagh Louth
49 M8 Corcullin Mayo
10 D3 Cordal Kerry
41 L8 Cordarragh Mayo
38 D8 Corduff Kildre
5 Q1 Cork Cork
6 A5 Cork/*Corcaigh* Cork
68 B8 Corkey Antrim
6 C7 Cork The Island Crematorium Cork
36 D1 Corlea Longfd
26 F5 Corlea Bridge Clare
50 H9 Corlee Mayo
53 N10 Corlough Cavan
36 B6 Cornafulla Roscom
33 L3 Cornamona/*Corr na Móna* Galway
41 Q9 Cornanagh Mayo
37 K8 Corndarragh Offaly
26 F6 Corrakyle Clare
55 P6 Corran Cross Roads Armagh
34 C6 Corrandulla/*Cor an Dola* Galway
40 E5 Corraun/*An Corrán* Mayo
48 E3 Corrchloch/*Corclogh* Mayo
62 F1 Correen Antrim
37 P4 Correllstown Wmeath
36 E8 Corr Hill Offaly
22 C5 Corries Cross Carlow
33 L3 Corr na Móna/*Cornamona* Galway
34 E5 Corrofin Galway
25 L7 Corrofin/*Cora Finne* Clare
53 J9 Corry Leitrm
21 L5 Corstown Cross Roads Kilken
46 D9 Cortown Meath
49 N5 Corvoley Mayo
33 K8 Costelloe/*Casla* Galway
8 H4 Coumduff Kerry
12 F6 Countygate Watfd
15 J3 Courthoyle Wexfd
5 M6 Courtmacsherry/*Cúirt Mhic Shéafraidh* Cork
18 C6 Courtmatrix Limrck
23 M5 Courtown/*Baile na Cúirte* Wexfd
4 D3 Cousane Cork
23 K4 Craan Wexfd
23 K5 Craanford Wexfd
24 H3 Craggagh Clare
26 D8 Cragroe Clare
60 H3 Craig Tyrone
67 M10 Craigavole Lderry
56 C2 Craigavon Armagh
62 C1 Craigs Antrim
62 C1 Craigs Cross Antrim
61 J4 Cranagh Tyrone
23 J8 Crane Wexfd
65 M6 Cranford Donegl
17 M2 Cranny Clare
61 P5 Cranny Lderry
18 F2 Cratloe Clare
34 G9 Craughwell/*Creachmhaoil* Galway
63 M6 Crawfordsburn Down
37 M2 Crazy Corner Wmeath
4 C8 Creagh Cork
55 M8 Creaghanroe Monhan
11 M8 Crean's Cross Roads Cork
18 G5 Crecora Limrck
17 J1 Creegh Clare
35 M1 Creegs Galway
65 K6 Creeslough/*An Craoslach* Donegl
50 D4 Creevagh Mayo
18 C5 Creeves Limrck
25 J3 Cregg Clare
4 G8 Cregg Cork
55 P10 Creggan Armagh
36 D8 Creggan Offaly
61 K7 Creggan Tyrone
40 G9 Cregganbaun Mayo
29 N9 Crettyard Laois
66 H7 Crindle Lderry
28 C4 Crinkill Offaly
58 G6 Croagh Donegl
18 E6 Croagh Limrck
40 B2 Croaghaun Mayo
50 G6 Crockets Town Mayo
37 M7 Croghan Offaly
43 P4 Croghan Roscom

64 E8 **Croithlí**/*Crolly* Donegl
64 E8 **Crolly**/*Croithlí* Donegl
9 L5 **Cromane** Kerry
53 M10 **Cromlin** Leitrm
29 J6 **Cromoge Cross Roads** Laois
16 F8 **Crompaun Bridge** Kerry
37 M1 **Crookedwood** Wmeath
3 L9 **Crookhaven**/*An Cruachán* Cork
5 K1 **Crookstown** Cork
30 E5 **Crookstown** Kildre
18 G6 **Croom**/*Cromadh* Limrck
16 D4 **Cross** Clare
7 K2 **Cross** Watfd
33 P2 **Cross**/*An Chrois* Mayo
15 N3 **Crossabeg** Wexfd
45 Q9 **Crossakeel**/*Crosa Caoil* Meath
5 N2 **Cross Barry** Cork
42 C9 **Crossboyne** Mayo
35 N9 **Crossconnell** Galway
45 K3 **Crossdoney**/*Cros Domhnaigh* Cavan
44 G10 **Crossea** Longfd
45 M5 **Crosserlough** Cavan
57 L3 **Crossgar** Down
67 L7 **Crossgare** Lderry
6 C7 **Crosshaven**/*Bun an Tábhairne* Cork
45 M4 **Cross Keys** Cavan
29 Q3 **Crosskeys** Kildre
45 P9 **Cross Keys** Meath
55 P10 **Crossmaglen** Armagh
5 L4 **Cross Mahon** Cork
50 D7 **Crossmolina**/*Crois Mhaoilíona* Mayo
43 P2 **Crossna** Roscom
25 N2 **Crossooha** Galway
20 H3 **Crosspatrick** Kilken
23 K3 **Crosspatrick** Wicklw
59 Q4 **Cross Roads** Donegl
6 G4 **Crowbally** Cork
62 F7 **Crumlin** Antrim
2 H4 **Crumpane** Cork
25 N7 **Crusheen**/*Croisín* Clare
29 M8 **Crutt** Kilken
28 H8 **Cuffsborough Cross Roads** Laois
10 F9 **Cúil Aodha**/*Coolea* Cork
50 E9 **Cuilkillew** Mayo
56 F1 **Culcavy** Down
66 E3 **Culdaff**/*Cúil Dabhcha* Donegl
43 K2 **Culfadda** Sligo
66 E2 **Culkeeny** Donegl
21 K2 **Cullahill**/*An Chúlchoill* Laois
19 M10 **Cullane** Limrck
46 F1 **Cullaville** Armagh
18 E1 **Culleen** Clare
51 J5 **Culleens** Sligo
10 G5 **Cullen** Cork
19 N7 **Cullen** Tippry
12 B4 **Cullenagh** Cork
15 K7 **Cullenstown** Wexfd
42 C2 **Cullin** Mayo
4 B6 **Cullomane Cross Roads** Cork
62 D1 **Cullybackey** Antrim
55 P9 **Cullyhanna** Armagh
66 D8 **Culmore** Lderry
38 G4 **Culmullin Cross Roads** Meath
61 Q2 **Culnady** Lderry
12 F7 **Currabeha** Cork
15 P3 **Curracloe** Wexfd
5 J2 **Curraclogh** Cork
7 L4 **Curragh** Watfd
39 J2 **Curragha** Meath
4 F5 **Curraghalicky** Cork
35 Q4 **Curraghboy** Roscom
30 D2 **Curragh Camp** Kildre
23 K2 **Curraghlawn** Wicklw
21 Q10 **Curraghmore** Kilken
27 J10 **Curraghmore** Tippry
44 B8 **Curraghroe** Roscom
42 H10 **Curragh West** Galway
12 G8 **Curraglass** Cork
28 D8 **Curragunneen** Tippry
61 Q3 **Curran** Lderry
9 Q3 **Currans** Kerry
19 Q2 **Curreeny** Tippry
10 B4 **Currow** Kerry
42 F2 **Curry** Sligo
68 E7 **Cushendall** Antrim
68 F6 **Cushendun** Antrim
29 N1 **Cushina** Offaly

D

37 M8 **Daingean**/*An Daingean* Offaly
39 P8 **Dalkey**/*Deilginis* Dublin
13 N6 **Dalligan Bridge** Watfd
37 L5 **Dalystown** Wmeath

39 L2 **Damastown** Dublin
67 M7 **Damhead** Lderry
21 N7 **Danesfort** Kilken
6 G3 **Dangan** Cork
20 C9 **Dangandargan** Tippry
22 H9 **Darby's Gap** Wexfd
55 N7 **Darkley** Armagh
54 H10 **Dartry** Monhan
22 G9 **Davidstown** Wexfd
49 M7 **Deel Bridge** Mayo
31 P2 **Delgany**/*Deilgne* Wicklw
40 G10 **Delphi** Mayo
37 Q1 **Delvin**/*Dealbhna* Wmeath
10 H5 **Dernagree** Cork
53 M10 **Derradda** Leitrm
25 L10 **Derragh** Clare
36 D1 **Derraghan Cross Roads** Longfd
24 F7 **Derreen** Clare
8 F10 **Derreen** Kerry
41 M2 **Derreen** Mayo
40 E4 **Derreen**/*An Doirín* Mayo
3 M4 **Derreenacarrin** Cork
4 B7 **Derreenard** Cork
2 G2 **Derreenauliff** Kerry
3 K5 **Derreeny** Cork
36 H8 **Derries** Offaly
38 B8 **Derries** Offaly
36 B7 **Derrineel** Roscom
43 Q1 **Derrinisky** Roscom
38 C7 **Derrinturn** Kildre
66 C9 **Derry** Lderry
56 B1 **Derryadd** Armagh
64 E7 **Derrybeg**/*Doirí Beaga* Donegl
57 L2 **Derryboy** Down
26 E4 **Derrybrien** Galway
66 C9 **Derry City Walls** Lderry
4 E6 **Derryclogh** Cork
28 H4 **Derrycon** Laois
36 G9 **Derrycooly** Offaly
28 F1 **Derrydolney** Offaly
20 G3 **Derryfadda** Tippry
10 F10 **Derryfineen**/*Doire Fhinín* Cork
29 L3 **Derrygile** Laois
37 K7 **Derrygolan** Wmeath
53 M3 **Derrygonnelly** Ferman
36 D1 **Derrygowna** Longfd
13 K2 **Derrygrath** Tippry
37 L8 **Derrygrogan** Offaly
67 P6 **Derrykeighan** Antrim
36 B7 **Derrylahan** Roscom
53 Q8 **Derrylin** Ferman
56 B1 **Derrymacash** Armagh
9 L2 **Derrymore** Kerry
4 E3 **Derrynacaheragh** Cork
32 H6 **Derryrush**/*Doire Iorrais* Galway
32 H3 **Derryvoreada**/*Doire Bhó Riada* Galway
43 J9 **Derrywode** Galway
67 P6 **Dervock** Antrim
6 D2 **Desert** Cork
61 Q4 **Desertmartin** Lderry
53 P4 **Devenish** Ferman
8 E4 **Dingle**/*An Daingean* Kerry
62 H5 **Doagh** Antrim
65 N4 **Doagh Beg**/*Dumhaigh Bhig* Donegl
32 H3 **Doire Bhó Riada**/*Derryvoreada* Galway
10 F10 **Doire Fhínín**/*Derryfineen* Cork
32 H6 **Doire Iorrais**/*Derryrush* Galway
64 E7 **Doirí Beaga**/*Derrybeg* Donegl
27 L10 **Dolla** Tippry
56 D2 **Dollingstown** Down
39 N6 **Dollymount** Dublin
46 E9 **Domhnach Phádraig**/*Donaghpatrick* Meath
39 N4 **Donabate**/*Domhnach Bat* Dublin
47 L9 **Donacarney** Meath
38 E7 **Donadea** Kildre
54 C8 **Donagh** Ferman
63 P7 **Donaghadee** Down
56 D3 **Donaghcloney** Down
28 G8 **Donaghmore** Laois
39 K3 **Donaghmore** Meath
61 N9 **Donaghmore** Tyrone
46 E9 **Donaghpatrick**/*Domhnach Phádraig* Meath
22 E10 **Donard** Wexfd
30 G5 **Donard**/*Dún Ard* Wicklw
20 B8 **Donaskeagh** Tippry
64 D8 **Donegal** Donegl
59 K7 **Donegal**/*Dún na nGall* Donegl
59 K7 **Donegal Castle** Donegl
60 F2 **Donemana** Tyrone

11 P3 **Doneraile**/*Dún ar Aill* Cork
19 Q6 **Donohill** Tippry
38 C3 **Donore** Meath
47 J9 **Donore** Meath
11 M8 **Donoughmore** Cork
40 C3 **Dooagh**/*Dumha Acha* Mayo
49 N6 **Doobehy** Mayo
45 N1 **Doocarrick** Cavan
51 N9 **Doocastle** Mayo
59 J1 **Doocharry**/*An Dúchoraidh* Donegl
40 D4 **Dooega**/*Dumha Éige* Mayo
44 G2 **Doogary** Cavan
60 G9 **Doogary** Tyrone
40 G5 **Dooghbeg**/*Dumhach Bheag* Mayo
48 E9 **Doogort**/*Dumha Goirt* Mayo
55 L9 **Doohamlat** Monhan
54 G9 **Doohat** Monhan
48 F7 **Doohooma**/*Dumha Thuama* Mayo
49 M7 **Dooleeg** Mayo
24 G5 **Doolin**/*Dúlainn* Clare
35 M6 **Doon** Galway
12 G5 **Doon** Tippry
19 N4 **Doon**/*Dún* Limrck
48 C8 **Doona** Mayo
16 F4 **Doonaha** Clare
16 H1 **Doonbeg** Clare
36 E7 **Doon Cross Roads** Offaly
8 G5 **Doonmanagh**/*An Dún Meánach* Kerry
32 F5 **Doonreaghan** Galway
14 C6 **Doornane** Kilken
48 F7 **Dooyork**/*Dumha Dhearc* Mayo
3 K9 **Dough** Cork
34 C4 **Doughiska** Galway
6 B6 **Douglas**/*Dúglas* Cork
60 E5 **Douglas Bridge** Tyrone
20 D4 **Dovea** Tippry
14 B4 **Dowling** Kilken
67 J5 **Downhill** Lderry
65 L5 **Downies**/*Na Dúnaibh* Donegl
12 D6 **Downing** Cork
57 L5 **Downpatrick** Down
53 J8 **Dowra**/*An Damhshraith* Cavan
47 J9 **Dowth** Meath
20 H8 **Drangan**/*Drongán* Tippry
61 N4 **Draperstown** Lderry
61 K2 **Dreen** Kerry
16 C8 **Dreenagh** Kerry
9 M1 **Drehidasillagh** Kerry
4 E6 **Driminidy** Cork
28 H5 **Drimmo** Laois
4 D5 **Drimoleague**/*Drom Dhá Liag* Cork
4 F6 **Drinagh** Cork
32 C4 **Drinagh** Galway
44 C8 **Drinagh** Roscom
15 P5 **Drinagh** Wexfd
50 H4 **Drinaghan** Sligo
44 H6 **Dring** Longfd
11 M10 **Dripsey** Cork
3 N7 **Drishane Bridge** Cork
47 K9 **Drogheda**/*Droichead Átha* Louth
49 J4 **Droichead Bhéal an Átha Buí**/*Bellanaboy Bridge* Mayo
9 K8 **Droichead Drom an Long Foirt**/*Dromalonhurt Bridge* Kerry
9 J9 **Droichead Lios an tSonnaigh**/*Lissatinnig Bridge* Kerry
20 D3 **Drom** Tippry
8 G2 **Drom**/*An Drom* Kerry
11 J5 **Dromagh** Cork
52 F7 **Dromahair**/*Droim Dhá Thiar* Leitrm
9 K8 **Dromalonhurt Bridge**/*Droichead Drom an Long Foirt* Kerry
56 G4 **Dromara** Down
8 G10 **Dromaragh**/*Drom Oireach* Cork
11 Q8 **Dromboy South** Cork
18 D10 **Dromcolliher**/*Drom Collachair* Limrck
16 E10 **Dromcunnig** Kerry
11 Q8 **Dromgarriff** Cork
19 J8 **Dromin** Limrck
47 J6 **Dromin** Louth
11 M1 **Dromina**/*Drom Aidhne* Cork
27 K7 **Dromineer** Tippry
47 K4 **Dromiskin** Louth
11 N6 **Drommahane** Cork

3 L7 **Dromnea** Cork
8 G10 **Drom Oireach**/*Dromaragh* Kerry
4 C5 **Dromore** Cork
56 F7 **Dromore** Down
60 E10 **Dromore** Tyrone
13 K8 **Dromore** Tyrone
51 K4 **Dromore West** Sligo
11 J9 **Dromree Cross Roads** Cork
17 M10 **Dromtrasna** Limrck
54 G10 **Drum** Monhan
36 B6 **Drum** Roscom
66 D9 **Drumahoe** Lderry
55 N10 **Drumakill** Monhan
26 D6 **Drumandoora** Clare
57 J4 **Drumaness** Down
25 K9 **Drumanure** Clare
51 N4 **Drumard** Sligo
57 J5 **Drumaroad** Down
27 J1 **Drumatober** Galway
20 C5 **Drumbane** Tippry
19 M1 **Drumbaun** Tippry
63 J9 **Drumbeg** Down
63 J10 **Drumbo** Down
47 K5 **Drumcar** Louth
26 D8 **Drumcharley** Clare
25 M8 **Drumcliff** Clare
52 C5 **Drumcliff**/*Droim Chliabh* Sligo
46 F6 **Drumcondra**/*Droim Conrach* Meath
45 P10 **Drumcree** Wmeath
22 D5 **Drumfea** Carlow
52 D9 **Drumfin** Sligo
66 B5 **Drumfree** Donegl
34 C6 **Drumgriffin** Galway
59 L6 **Druminnin** Donegl
26 G3 **Drumkeary** Galway
59 Q2 **Drumkeen** Donegl
52 H9 **Drumkeeran**/*Droim Caorthainn* Leitrm
44 F2 **Drumlea** Leitrm
44 F6 **Drumlish**/*Droim Lis* Longfd
36 C7 **Drumlosh** Roscom
52 E9 **Drummacool** Sligo
24 G10 **Drummin** Clare
41 J9 **Drummin** Mayo
43 Q6 **Drummullin** Roscom
44 E3 **Drumna** Leitrm
60 H8 **Drumnakilly** Tyrone
44 D6 **Drumod**/*Drómad* Leitrm
60 C1 **Drumoghill** Donegl
45 P9 **Drumone** Meath
60 D8 **Drumquin** Tyrone
36 F4 **Drumraney** Wmeath
38 G3 **Drumree** Meath
13 J7 **Drumroe** Watfd
44 B1 **Drumshanbo**/*Droim Seanbhó* Leitrm
33 N2 **Drumsheel** Mayo
44 B4 **Drumsna**/*Droim ar Snámh* Leitrm
67 J9 **Drumsurn** Lderry
45 N1 **Drung** Cavan
17 K8 **Duagh**/*Dubháth* Kerry
20 E8 **Dually** Tippry
39 M5 **Dublin** Dublin
39 M7 **Dublin**/*Baile Átha Cliath* Dublin
39 L6 **Dublin Glasnevin Crematorium** Dublin
39 L7 **Dublin Mount Jerome Crematorium** Dublin
39 K8 **Dublin Newlands Cross Crematorium** Dublin
38 B6 **Duffy's Cross Roads** Kildre
36 B6 **Duggarry** Roscom
47 J10 **Duleek**/*Damhliag* Meath
48 F7 **Dumha Dhearc**/*Dooyork* Mayo
40 D4 **Dumha Éige**/*Dooega* Mayo
65 N4 **Dumhaigh Bhig**/*Doagh Beg* Donegl
48 F7 **Dumha Thuama**/*Doohooma* Mayo
62 G6 **Dunadry** Antrim
65 Q3 **Dunaff** Donegl
35 M1 **Dunamon** Roscom
47 L9 **Dunany** Louth
21 P6 **Dunbell** Kilken
39 J5 **Dunboyne** Meath
39 J5 **Dunbyrne** Kildre
14 G7 **Duncannon**/*Dún Canann* Wexfd
8 C4 **Dún Chaoin**/*Dunquin* Kerry
15 L7 **Duncormick** Wexfd
47 K2 **Dundalk**/*Dún Dealgan* Louth
5 N4 **Dunderrow** Cork
38 E1 **Dunderry** Meath

55 J4 **Dundian** Monhan
63 L8 **Dundonald** Down
35 M7 **Dundoogan** Galway
62 G7 **Dundrod** Antrim
57 K6 **Dundrum** Down
39 M8 **Dundrum** Dublin
20 B7 **Dundrum**/*Dún Droma* Tippry
65 J5 **Dunfanaghy**/*Dún Fionnachaidh* Donegl
38 D6 **Dunfierth Cross Roads** Kildre
55 L1 **Dungannon** Tyrone
14 F4 **Dunganstown** Wexfd
21 Q7 **Dungarvan** Kilken
13 N8 **Dungarvan**/*Dún Garbhán* Watfd
61 L1 **Dungiven** Lderry
64 D10 **Dunglow**/*An Clochán Liath* Donegl
6 F4 **Dungourney** Cork
14 C8 **Dunhill** Watfd
26 H3 **Duniry** Galway
28 C8 **Dunkerrin** Offaly
58 G7 **Dunkineely**/*Dún Cionnaola* Donegl
14 D5 **Dunkitt** Kilken
39 N8 **Dún Laoghaire** Dublin
30 F4 **Dunlavin**/*Dún Luáin* Wicklw
47 K6 **Dunleer**/*Dún Léire* Louth
64 G9 **Dunlewy**/*Dún Lúiche* Donegl
67 Q9 **Dunloy** Antrim
67 N4 **Dunluce Castle** Antrim
64 G9 **Dún Lúiche**/*Dunlewy* Donegl
3 L8 **Dunmanus** Cork
4 F4 **Dunmanway**/*Dún Mánmhaí* Cork
12 H9 **Dunmoon** Watfd
34 G1 **Dunmore**/*Dún Mór* Galway
14 F8 **Dunmore East**/*Dún Mór* Watfd
62 H9 **Dunmurry** Antrim
21 M9 **Dunnamaggan** Kilken
61 L6 **Dunnamore** Tyrone
21 M5 **Dunningstown** Kilken
8 C4 **Dunquin**/*Dún Chaoin* Kerry
38 G2 **Dunsany Cross Roads** Meath
38 H3 **Dunshaughlin**/*Dún Seachlainn* Meath
29 K9 **Durrow**/*Darú* Laois
3 N6 **Durrus**/*Dúras* Cork
35 P4 **Dysart** Roscom
37 K4 **Dysart** Wmeath

E

34 C7 **Eadargúil**/*Addergoole* Galway
38 H10 **Eadestown** Kildre
34 B6 **Eanach Dhúin**/*Annaghdown* Galway
20 H6 **Earlshill** Tippry
51 J3 **Easky**/*Iascaigh* Sligo
53 J6 **East Barrs** Leitrm
64 F3 **East Town**/*An Baile Thoir* Donegl
63 L5 **Eden** Antrim
37 Q7 **Edenderry**/*Eadan Doire* Offaly
60 B10 **Ederney** Ferman
44 H9 **Edgeworthstown**/*Meathas Troim* Longfd
66 E8 **Eglinton** Lderry
55 L2 **Eglish** Tyrone
45 P6 **Eighter** Cavan
43 P6 **Elphin**/*Ail Finn* Roscom
19 K8 **Elton** Limrck
26 D1 **Emlagh Cross Roads** Galway
8 F10 **Emlaghmore**/*An timleach Mór* Kerry
19 M8 **Emly**/*Imleach* Tippry
43 Q10 **Emmoo** Roscom
29 M3 **Emo**/*Íoma* Laois
55 J5 **Emyvale**/*Scairb na gCaorach* Monhan
38 D5 **Enfield**/*An Bóthar Buí* Meath
25 M9 **Ennis**/*Inis* Clare
22 H9 **Enniscorthy**/*Inis Córthaidh* Wexfd
5 J4 **Enniskean**/*Inis Céin* Cork
31 N1 **Enniskerry**/*Áth na Sceire* Wicklw
53 P5 **Enniskillen** Ferman

24 H7 **Ennistymon**/*Inis Díomáin* Clare
24 C2 **Eochaill** Galway
24 B2 **Eoghanacht**/*Onaght* Galway
44 C9 **Erra** Roscom
41 K10 **Erriff Bridge** Mayo
28 F9 **Errill** Laois
66 E10 **Ervey Cross Roads** Lderry
54 F6 **Eshnadarragh** Ferman
34 G8 **Esker** Galway
49 M7 **Eskeragh Bridge** Mayo
44 F7 **Esker South** Longfd
9 L10 **Eskine** Kerry
54 F2 **Eskragh** Tyrone
44 D4 **Eslinbridge** Leitrm
2 G4 **Eyeries**/*Na hAorai* Cork
27 M1 **Eyrecourt**/*Dún an Uchta* Galway

F

9 P5 **Faha** Kerry
10 C2 **Fahaduff** Kerry
13 Q6 **Faha Glen** Watfd
9 J1 **Fahamore** Kerry
65 Q7 **Fahan** Donegl
8 C5 **Fahan**/*Fán* Kerry
19 M10 **Fahanasoodry** Limrck
27 L2 **Fahy** Galway
35 L8 **Fahy** Galway
36 F5 **Fairfield** Wmeath
25 N8 **Fair Green** Clare
43 K6 **Fairymount** Roscom
64 G6 **Falcarragh**/*An Fál Carrach* Donegl
8 C5 **Fán**/*Fahan* Kerry
24 H3 **Fanore More** Clare
12 A4 **Farahy** Cork
36 D6 **Fardrum** Wmeath
9 P2 **Farmer's Bridge** Kerry
36 F6 **Farnagh** Wmeath
44 E5 **Farnaght** Leitrm
4 E3 **Farnanes** Cork
5 L1 **Farnanes** Cork
14 E4 **Farnoge** Kilken
5 L1 **Farran** Cork
29 J8 **Farran Cross Roads** Laois
9 Q4 **Farranfore**/*An Fearann Fuar* Kerry
46 B7 **Fartagh Cross Roads** Cavan
44 H1 **Fartrin Cross Roads** Cavan
26 E7 **Feakle**/*An Fhiacail* Clare
24 B2 **Fearann an Choirce** Galway
18 H6 **Fedamore**/*Feadamair* Limrck
16 D4 **Feeard** Clare
25 J3 **Feenagh** Clare
18 E9 **Feenagh** Limrck
43 L1 **Feenaghmore** Sligo
61 K1 **Feeny** Lderry
44 E2 **Fenagh** Leitrm
9 L1 **Fenit**/*An Fhianait* Kerry
22 D4 **Fennagh** Carlow
14 C8 **Fennor** Watfd
37 N1 **Fennor** Wmeath
18 C9 **Feohanagh** Limrck
8 D3 **Feohanagh**/*An Fheothanach* Kerry
3 L1 **Feoramore** Kerry
36 E9 **Ferbane**/*An Féar Bán* Offaly
12 D7 **Fermoy**/*Mainistir Fhear Mai* Cork
23 J7 **Ferns**/*Fearna* Wexfd
23 P2 **Ferrybank** Wicklw
18 F4 **Ferry Bridge** Limrck
20 G10 **Fethard**/*Fiodh Ard* Tippry
14 H8 **Fethard**/*Fiodh Ard* Wexfd
13 Q5 **Fews** Watfd
19 M2 **Fiddane** Tippry
14 B4 **Fiddown**/*Fiodh Dúin* Kilken
9 Q4 **Fieries** Kerry
42 H6 **Figh Bridge** Roscom
13 Q2 **Figlash** Tippry
25 L2 **Finavarra** Clare
45 L7 **Finnea**/*Fiodh an Átha* Wmeath
56 G4 **Finnis** Down
33 L2 **Finny**/*Fionnaithe* Mayo
54 D1 **Fintona** Tyrone
59 K2 **Fintown**/*Baile na Finne* Donegl
16 H8 **Finuge**/*Fionnúig* Kerry
67 P9 **Finvoy** Antrim
33 L2 **Fionnaithe**/*Finny* Mayo
2 E6 **Firkeel** Cork

24 G5 **Fisherstreet** Clare
28 D2 **Fivealley** Offaly
62 H4 **Five Corners** Antrim
52 E6 **Fivemilebourne** Leitrm
5 D2 **Fivemilebridge** Cork
54 D4 **Fivemiletown** Tyrone
26 E6 **Flagmount** Clare
21 Q5 **Flagmount** Kilken
9 J4 **Flemingstown** Kerry
53 N7 **Florence Court** Ferman
8 G8 **Foilmore Bridge** Kerry
3 P8 **Foilnamuck** Cork
19 J9 **Foley's Cross Roads** Limrck
30 C4 **Fontstown** Kildre
46 C10 **Fordstown** Meath
45 N9 **Fore** Wmeath
56 B10 **Forkill** Armagh
25 J3 **Formoyle** Clare
25 J9 **Formoyle** Clare
36 C1 **Formoyle** Longfd
40 F8 **Formoyle** Mayo
11 N8 **Fornaght** Cork
36 D2 **Forthill** Longfd
18 G9 **Fort Middle** Limrck
6 C5 **Fota Wildlife Park** Cork
15 K5 **Foulkesmill** Wexfd
20 F8 **Foulkstown** Tippry
25 M9 **Fountain Cross** Clare
43 P9 **Four Mile House** Roscom
35 P3 **Four Roads** Roscom
44 D2 **Foxfield** Leitrm
42 B3 **Foxford**/*Béal Easa* Mayo
17 P4 **Foynes**/*Faing* Limrck
11 K2 **Freemount**/*Cillin an Chrónáin* Cork
43 L5 **Frenchpark**/*Dún Gar* Roscom
21 L4 **Freshford**/*Achadh Úr* Kilken
30 F5 **Freynestown** Wicklw
18 H5 **Friarstown** Limrck
58 H6 **Frosses**/*Na Frosa* Donegl
35 N1 **Fuerty** Roscom
25 M3 **Funshin More** Galway
33 P9 **Furbo**/*Na Forbacha* Galway
3 N4 **Furkeal** Cork
13 P5 **Furraleigh** Watfd
17 M1 **Furroor** Clare
9 M4 **Fybagh** Kerry

G

17 J6 **Gabbett's Bridge** Kerry
37 L4 **Gainstown** Wmeath
15 L3 **Galbally** Wexfd
19 M9 **Galbally**/*An Gallbhaile* Limrck
20 E6 **Galbertstown** Tippry
16 H7 **Galey Cross Roads** Kerry
62 D2 **Galgorm** Antrim
44 B10 **Gallagh** Roscom
20 H2 **Galmoy** Kilken
28 C2 **Galros Cross Roads** Offaly
38 F3 **Galtrim** Meath
19 P10 **Galtymore Mountain** Tippry
34 D8 **Galway** Galway
34 C8 **Galway**/*Caillimh* Galway
19 N3 **Gannavane** Limrck
54 D10 **Gannon's Cross** Cavan
64 E8 **Gaoth Dobhair**/*Gweedore* Donegl
48 G6 **Gaoth Sáile**/*Gweesalia* Mayo
38 F4 **Garadice** Meath
35 N7 **Garbally Demesne** Galway
13 J2 **Garnavilla** Tippry
37 N6 **Garr** Offaly
42 F10 **Garrafrauns** Galway
50 D5 **Garranard** Mayo
11 P1 **Garrane Cross Roads** Cork
5 J2 **Garranereagh** Cork
42 H9 **Garranlahan** Roscom
16 G3 **Garraun** Clare
27 J2 **Garraun** Galway
9 P3 **Garraun** Kerry
30 F8 **Garrettstown** Carlow
52 H3 **Garrison** Ferman
39 K2 **Garristown**/*Baile Gháire* Dublin
12 F9 **Garrycaheragh** Cork
50 E7 **Garrycloonagh** Mayo
15 J6 **Garrycullen** Wexfd
67 P8 **Garryduff** Antrim
18 G9 **Garryfine** Limrck
22 D5 **Garryhill** Clare
27 J8 **Garrykennedy** Tippry
6 H5 **Garrymore** Cork
27 N9 **Garrynafana** Tippry
6 G6 **Garryvoe** Cork

67 L9 **Garvagh** Lderry
44 D3 **Garvagh** Lderry
54 G2 **Garvaghy** Tyrone
19 L9 **Garyspillane** Limrck
21 K3 **Gattabaun** Kilken
37 M4 **Gaybrook** Wmeath
37 M9 **Geashill**/*Géisill* Offaly
52 F10 **Geevagh**/*An Ghaobhach* Sligo
63 K7 **George Best Airport** Belfst
46 E8 **Georges Cross Roads** Meath
14 A8 **Georgestown** Watfd
3 M6 **Gerahies** Cork
67 N4 **Giant's Causeway** Antrim
46 E9 **Gibstown**/*Baile Ghib* Meath
56 C4 **Gilford** Down
46 G5 **Glack Cross Roads** Louth
3 N8 **Glan** Cork
3 L7 **Glanalin** Cork
9 K7 **Glanbehy Bridge** Kerry
4 C5 **Glan Cross Roads** Cork
4 C5 **Glandart** Cork
4 F7 **Glandore**/*Cuan Dor* Cork
53 L8 **Glangevlin** Cavan
3 M6 **Glanlough** Cork
6 B5 **Glanmire**/*Gleann Maghair* Cork
16 G9 **Glanoe** Kerry
3 K7 **Glanroon** Cork
11 M6 **Glantane** Cork
12 C6 **Glanworth**/*Gleannúir* Cork
68 B10 **Glarryford** Antrim
8 D3 **Glashabeg**/*An Ghlaise Bheag* Kerry
11 R7 **Glashaboy East** Cork
11 Q7 **Glashaboy North** Cork
28 G9 **Glasha Cross Roads** Laois
17 J10 **Glashananoon** Kerry
17 L6 **Glashapullagh** Limrck
46 C3 **Glasleck** Cavan
55 K5 **Glaslough**/*Glasloch* Monhan
36 D4 **Glassan**/*Glasán* Wmeath
32 F1 **Glassillaun** Galway
57 P1 **Glastry** Down
58 B6 **Gleann Cholm Cille**/*Glencolumbkille* Donegl
65 J10 **Gleann Domhain**/*Glendowan* Donegl
49 K4 **Gleann na Muaidhe**/*Glenamoy* Mayo
33 K5 **Gleann Trasna**/*Glentrasna* Galway
66 H6 **Glebe** Lderry
65 L6 **Glen** Lderry
61 P2 **Glen** Lderry
6 G2 **Glenacroghery** Cork
52 F4 **Glenade** Leitrm
27 N8 **Glenahilty** Tippry
49 K4 **Glenamoy**/*Gleann na Muaidhe* Mayo
68 E8 **Glenariff or Waterfoot** Antrim
68 G10 **Glenarm** Antrim
62 F8 **Glenavy** Antrim
9 K6 **Glenbeigh**/*Gleann Beithe* Kerry
52 H6 **Glenboy** Leitrm
23 J9 **Glenbrien** Wexfd
19 L9 **Glenbrohane** Limrck
9 L8 **Glencar** Kerry
52 E5 **Glencar**/*Gleann an Chairthe* Leitrm
58 B6 **Glencolumbkille**/*Gleann Cholm Cille* Donegl
33 Q3 **Glencorrib** Mayo
39 L10 **Glencree** Wicklw
39 M9 **Glencullen** Dublin
31 N3 **Glendarragh** Wicklw
16 C9 **Glenderry** Kerry
6 E3 **Glendine Bridge** Cork
65 J10 **Glendowan**/*Gleann Domhain* Donegl
26 D7 **Glendree** Clare
12 E4 **Glenduff** Cork
68 E6 **Glendun Viaduct** Antrim
31 N6 **Glenealy** Wicklw
50 D4 **Glenedagh** Mayo
66 E4 **Gleneely**/*Gleann Daoile* Donegl
53 K6 **Glenfarne** Leitrm
10 D7 **Glenflesk** Kerry
3 N7 **Glengarriff**/*An Gleann Garbh* Cork
63 J6 **Glengormley** Antrim
12 G8 **Glengoura** Cork
66 G9 **Glenhead** Lderry
61 K5 **Glenhull** Tyrone
40 F9 **Glenkeen Bridge** Mayo
60 B1 **Glenmaquin** Donegl
17 L1 **Glenmore** Clare

14 F4 **Glenmore**/*An Gleann Mhór* Kilken
13 K1 **Glennagat** Tippry
10 G2 **Glennaknockane** Cork
35 J1 **Glennamaddy**/*Gleann na Madadh* Galway
10 G3 **Glennamucklagh East** Cork
13 R4 **Glennaphuca Cross Roads** Watfd
63 K3 **Glenoe** Antrim
20 B6 **Glenough Lower** Tippry
20 B6 **Glenough Upper** Tippry
12 B3 **Glenroe** Limrck
6 F2 **Glentane** Cork
58 H4 **Glenties**/*Na Gleannta* Donegl
66 D4 **Glentogher** Donegl
33 K5 **Glentrasna**/*Gleann Trasna* Galway
67 Q10 **Glenvale** Antrim
65 P6 **Glenvar** Donegl
65 J8 **Glenveagh Castle** Donegl
64 H9 **Glenveagh National Park** Donegl
12 B9 **Glenville**/*Gleann an Phréacháin* Cork
17 L5 **Glin**/*An Gleann* Limrck
32 F6 **Glinsce**/*Glinsk* Galway
43 L10 **Glinsk** Galway
32 F6 **Glinsk**/*Glinsce* Galway
6 C5 **Glounthaune** Cork
63 L3 **Glynn** Antrim
22 C9 **Glynn** Carlow
15 M3 **Glynn** Wexfd
10 E5 **Gneeveguilla** Kerry
40 E4 **Gob an Choire**/*Achill Sound* Mayo
20 C9 **Golden**/*An Gabhailin* Tippry
39 N9 **Golden Ball** Dublin
3 L9 **Goleen**/*An Góilin* Cork
20 C7 **Goold's Cross** Tippry
22 B6 **Goresbridge**/*An Droichead Nua* Kilken
23 M5 **Gorey**/*Guaire* Wexfd
13 J3 **Gormanstown** Tippry
47 M10 **Gormanstown**/*Baile Mhic Gormáin* Meath
26 C4 **Gort**/*An Gort* Galway
61 L7 **Gortaclady** Tyrone
3 J1 **Gortagowan** Kerry
64 G6 **Gortahork**/*Gort an Choirce* Donegl
20 C3 **Gortalough** Tippry
64 G6 **Gort an Choirce**/*Gortahork* Donegl
27 N2 **Gortarevan** Offaly
7 J4 **Gortaroo** Cork
53 M6 **Gortatole** Ferman
61 M7 **Gorteagh** Tyrone
35 J6 **Gorteen** Galway
29 N9 **Gorteen** Kilken
18 E9 **Gorteen** Limrck
43 K2 **Gorteen** Sligo
13 M9 **Gorteen**/*An Goirtin* Watfd
28 H1 **Gorteen Bridge** Offaly
14 E6 **Gorteens** Kilken
27 J5 **Gorteeny** Galway
2 G4 **Gortgarriff** Cork
52 F7 **Gortgarrigan** Leitrm
10 C3 **Gortglass** Kerry
66 F10 **Gortilea Cross Roads** Lderry
60 G5 **Gortin** Tyrone
44 E5 **Gortletteragh** Leitrm
4 D2 **Gortloughra Bridge** Cork
50 D3 **Gortmore** Mayo
33 J6 **Gortmore**/*An Gort Mór* Galway
35 L1 **Gortnadeeve** Galway
21 K5 **Gortnagap Cross Roads** Kilken
24 B3 **Gort na gCapall** Galway
17 N3 **Gortnahaha** Clare
66 H10 **Gortnahey** Lderry
20 H5 **Gortnahoo** Tippry
4 F2 **Gortnahoughtee** Cork
49 N6 **Gortnahurra** Mayo
9 Q1 **Gortnaleaha** Kerry
26 C7 **Gortnamearacaun** Clare
43 M7 **Gortnasillagh** Roscom
9 L7 **Gortrelig** Kerry
25 N3 **Gortskeagh** Galway
3 L6 **Gouladoo** Cork
22 G6 **Gour Bridge** Cork
32 E1 **Gowlaun** Galway
22 D8 **Gowlin** Carlow
21 Q6 **Gowran**/*Gabhrán* Kilken
62 D2 **Gracehill** Antrim
13 P5 **Graigearush** Watfd

19 J10 **Graigue Cross Roads** Limrck
22 C8 **Graiguenamanagh**/*Gráig na Manach* Kilken
31 J4 **Granabeg** Wicklw
45 J7 **Granard**/*Gránard* Longfd
30 B2 **Graney** Kildre
37 Q6 **Grange** Kildre
14 B5 **Grange** Kilken
21 M6 **Grange** Kilken
47 M2 **Grange** Louth
13 K2 **Grange** Tippry
7 L3 **Grange** Watfd
15 M7 **Grange** Wexfd
52 C4 **Grange**/*An Ghráinseach* Sligo
30 B2 **Grange Beg** Kildre
28 G8 **Grange Beg** Laois
47 K6 **Grangebellew** Louth
18 C7 **Grange Bridge** Limrck
30 E6 **Grange Con** Wicklw
38 H2 **Grange Cross Roads** Meath
22 E2 **Grangeford** Carlow
46 H7 **Grangegeeth** Meath
52 D10 **Graniamore** Sligo
26 C2 **Grannagh** Galway
55 L1 **Granville** Tyrone
31 L7 **Greenan** Wicklw
54 H8 **Greenans Cross Roads** Monhan
39 L1 **Greenanstown** Meath
61 J6 **Greencastle** Tyrone
66 G4 **Greencastle**/*An Caisleán Nua* Donegl
28 G8 **Green Cross Roads** Laois
63 K5 **Greenisland** Antrim
47 N1 **Greenore**/*An Grianfort* Louth
11 P8 **Grenagh** Cork
63 P9 **Greyabbey** Down
17 L1 **Greygrove** Clare
66 F8 **Greysteel** Lderry
55 L2 **Greystone** Tyrone
31 P2 **Greystones**/*Na Clocha Liatha* Wicklw
19 L10 **Griston** Limrck
36 F7 **Grogan** Offaly
63 N6 **Groomsport** Down
53 K7 **Gubaveeny** Cavan
14 B6 **Guilcagh Cross Roads** Watfd
61 Q3 **Gulladuff** Lderry
10 E5 **Gullaun** Kerry
52 F5 **Gurteen** Leitrm
14 H5 **Gusserane** Wexfd
64 E8 **Gweedore**/*Gaoth Dobhair* Donegl
48 G6 **Gweesalia**/*Gaoth Sáile* Mayo
6 E7 **Gyleen** Cork

H

46 H1 **Hackballs Cross** Louth
30 H8 **Hacketstown**/*Baile Haicéid* Carlow
5 P2 **Halfway** Cork
14 F7 **Halfway House** Watfd
46 E10 **Halltown Cross Roads** Meath
55 P5 **Hamiltonsbawn** Armagh
62 H8 **Hannahstown** Antrim
14 C3 **Harristown** Kilken
34 B4 **Headford**/*Áth Cinn* Galway
10 D7 **Headfort** Kerry
15 M6 **Heavenstown Cross Roads** Wexfd
16 D8 **Heirhill** Kerry
63 M6 **Helen's Bay** Down
19 K6 **Herbertstown**/*Baile Hiobaird* Limrck
36 D9 **Highstreet** Offaly
6 D2 **Hightown** Cork
62 H10 **Hillhall** Down
38 B4 **Hill of Down** Meath
56 F2 **Hillsborough** Down
43 Q5 **Hill Street** Roscom
56 F8 **Hilltown** Down
15 K5 **Hilltown** Wexfd
15 N6 **Hilltown** Wexfd
18 C4 **Hogan's Bridge** Limrck
19 Q4 **Hollyford** Wicklw
23 L4 **Hollyfort** Wexfd
26 D3 **Hollymount** Galway
42 B10 **Hollymount** Mayo
30 G3 **Hollywood**/*Cillin Chaoimhin* Wicklw
19 J7 **Holycross** Limrck
20 D6 **Holycross**/*Mainistir na Croiche* Tippry

53 L6 **Holywell** Ferman
63 L7 **Holywood** Down
14 G9 **Hook Lighthouse** Watfd
46 D7 **Horath Cross Roads** Meath
15 P6 **Horetown** Wexfd
20 F6 **Horse & Jockey**/*An Marcach* Tippry
36 H6 **Horseleap**/*Baile Átha an Urchair* Wmeath
19 L7 **Hospital**/*An tOspidéal* Limrck
39 P6 **Howth**/*Binn Éadair* Dublin
21 N10 **Hugginstown** Kilken
18 E2 **Hurlers Cross** Clare

I

9 K5 **Illaunstookagh** Kerry
25 K8 **Inagh**/*Eidhneach* Clare
6 E7 **Inch** Cork
6 H3 **Inch** Cork
65 Q8 **Inch** Donegl
19 Q3 **Inch** Tippry
23 M3 **Inch** Wexfd
9 K4 **Inch**/*Inse* Kerry
17 M9 **Inchabaun** Limrck
38 C4 **Inchamore Bridge** Meath
21 L3 **Inchbeg** Kilken
29 N5 **Inch Cross Roads** Laois
10 D10 **Inchee Bridge** Kerry
4 F3 **Inchicahan Cross Roads** Cork
4 F1 **Inchigeelagh**/*Inse Geimhleach* Cork
12 B6 **Inchinapallas** Cork
12 G3 **Inchnamuck** Tippry
33 L9 **Indreabhán**/*Inveran* Galway
5 M3 **Inishannon**/*Inis Eonáin* Cork
50 G5 **Inishcrone**/*Inis Crabhann* Sligo
62 A2 **Inishrush** Lderry
46 G2 **Iniskeen**/*Inis Caoin* Monhan
21 Q9 **Inistioge**/*Inis Tíog* Kilken
58 H7 **Inver**/*Inbhear* Donegl
33 L9 **Inveran**/*Indreabhán* Galway
42 F4 **Ireland West Airport Knock** Mayo
30 C2 **Irish National Stud** Kildre
42 E10 **Irishtown** Mayo
53 P2 **Irvinestown** Ferman
58 H5 **Ivy Bridge** Donegl

J

31 P8 **Jack White's Cross Roads** Wicklw
29 N3 **Jamestown** Laois
44 B4 **Jamestown** Leitrm
21 M3 **Jenkinstown** Kilken
47 L2 **Jenkinstown** Louth
56 C7 **Jerrettspass** Armagh
14 G5 **John F Kennedy Ancestral Home** Wexfd
42 D4 **Johnsfort** Mayo
44 D6 **Johnstonsbridge** Longfd
6 B6 **Johnstown** Cork
38 G9 **Johnstown** Kildre
46 F10 **Johnstown** Meath
15 L6 **Johnstown** Wexfd
23 M2 **Johnstown** Wicklw
31 P9 **Johnstown** Wicklw
20 H3 **Johnstown**/*Baile Sheáin* Kilken
38 D6 **Johnstown Bridge** Kildre
15 N5 **Johnstown Castle** Wexfd
21 P4 **Johnswell** Kilken
56 C10 **Jonesborough** Armagh
47 L9 **Julianstown** Meath

K

11 K4 **Kanturk**/*Ceann Toirc* Cork
9 P7 **Kate Kearney's Cottage** Kerry
56 F5 **Katesbridge** Down
43 Q1 **Keadew**/*Céideadh* Roscom
55 M7 **Keady** Armagh
9 L10 **Kealariddig** Kerry

2 H5 **Kealincha Bridge** Cork
4 B3 **Kealkill** Cork
4 E2 **Kealvaugh**/*Caolmhagh* Cork
33 P7 **Keeagh**/*An Chaothach* Galway
40 C3 **Keel**/*An Caol* Mayo
8 G9 **Keelnagore** Kerry
35 K1 **Keeloges** Galway
49 M8 **Keenagh** Mayo
36 E1 **Keenagh**/*Caonach* Longfd
13 K8 **Keereen** Watfd
22 D2 **Kellistown Cross Roads** Carlow
62 E3 **Kells** Antrim
8 H7 **Kells** Kerry
21 M8 **Kells**/*Ceanannas* Kilken
46 C8 **Kells**/*Ceanannas* Meath
21 Q2 **Kelly's Bridge** Kilken
30 G7 **Kelshabeg** Wicklw
9 Q10 **Kenmare**/*Neidín* Kerry
28 C3 **Kennedy's Cross Roads** Offaly
46 H10 **Kentstown** Meath
15 N5 **Kerloge** Wexfd
9 Q4 **Kerry** Kerry
17 P6 **Kerryikyle** Limrck
9 N2 **Kerry the Kingdom** Kerry
59 Q10 **Kesh** Ferman
44 C2 **Keshcarrigan**/*Ceis Charraigín* Leitrm
7 M3 **Kiely's Cross Roads** Watfd
36 H4 **Kilane** Wmeath
23 M3 **Kilanerin** Wexfd
16 C5 **Kilbaha**/*Cill Bheathach* Clare
22 D2 **Kilballyhue** Carlow
26 F10 **Kilbane** Clare
4 G1 **Kilbarry** Cork
14 D7 **Kilbarry** Watfd
26 C4 **Kilbeacanty** Galway
14 B8 **Kilbeg** Watfd
37 J6 **Kilbeggan**/*Cill Bheagáin* Wmeath
35 M1 **Kilbegnet** Roscom
12 E3 **Kilbeheny** Limrck
34 E2 **Kilbenan Cross Roads** Galway
29 Q5 **Kilberry** Kildre
46 F9 **Kilberry** Meath
13 P3 **Kilbrack** Watfd
18 E5 **Kilbreedy** Limrck
18 H9 **Kilbreedy** Limrck
20 C8 **Kilbreedy** Tippry
33 J6 **Kilbrickan**/*Cill Bhriocáin* Galway
20 E3 **Kilbrickane** Tippry
29 J7 **Kilbricken** Laois
42 D4 **Kilbride** Mayo
31 J1 **Kilbride** Wicklw
31 P7 **Kilbride** Wicklw
38 D1 **Kilbride**/*Cill Bhríde* Meath
39 K4 **Kilbride Cross Roads** Meath
12 C8 **Kilbrien** Cork
13 M6 **Kilbrien** Watfd
11 L3 **Kilbrin** Cork
5 M5 **Kilbrittain**/*Cill Briotáin* Cork
34 D9 **Kilcaimin** Galway
29 M1 **Kilcappagh** Offaly
58 D7 **Kilcar**/*Cill Charthaigh* Donegl
14 E7 **Kilcaragh Cross Roads** Watfd
31 J8 **Kilcarney** Wicklw
31 J8 **Kilcarney Cross Roads** Wicklw
17 J3 **Kilcarroll** Clare
13 P1 **Kilcash** Tippry
35 Q7 **Kilcashel** Roscom
29 K1 **Kilcavan** Laois
26 E2 **Kilchreest**/*Cill Chríost* Galway
26 E7 **Kilclaran** Clare
57 N4 **Kilclief** Down
16 D5 **Kilcloher** Clare
37 L7 **Kilclonfert** Offaly
38 F6 **Kilcock**/*Cill Choca* Kildre
4 B8 **Kilcoe** Cork
45 K6 **Kilcogy** Cavan
14 E7 **Kilcohan** Watfd
34 E10 **Kilcolgan**/*Cill Cholgáin* Galway
5 K4 **Kilcolman** Cork
17 P6 **Kilcolman** Limrck
7 M3 **Kilcolman**/*Cill Cholmáin* Watfd
27 P6 **Kilcomin** Offaly
12 H2 **Kilcommon** Tippry
19 Q2 **Kilcommon** Tippry
34 C9 **Kilconierin** Galway
34 D2 **Kilconly** Galway

35 L7 **Kilconnell**/*Cill Chonaill* Galway
11 Q3 **Kilconnor** Cork
56 G7 **Kilcoo** Down
53 J4 **Kilcoo Cross Roads** Ferman
31 P3 **Kilcoole**/*Cill Chomhghuill* Wicklw
12 E9 **Kilcor** Cork
19 R9 **Kilcorkan** Clare
28 E2 **Kilcormac**/*Cill Chormaic* Offaly
11 J6 **Kilcorney** Cork
23 J9 **Kilcotty** Wexfd
6 H6 **Kilcredan** Cork
43 K10 **Kilcroan Cross Roads** Galway
3 L7 **Kilcrohane** Cork
12 G9 **Kilcronat** Cork
30 E3 **Kilcullen**/*Cill Chuillinn* Kildre
8 H2 **Kilcummin** Kerry
10 B5 **Kilcummin** Kerry
47 J2 **Kilcurly** Louth
47 J1 **Kilcurry** Louth
10 C2 **Kilcusnaun** Kerry
38 C2 **Kildalkey** Meath
29 Q3 **Kildangan** Kildre
30 C2 **Kildare**/*Cill Dara* Kildre
22 F5 **Kildavin**/*Cill Damháin* Carlow
14 B7 **Kildermody** Watfd
18 F4 **Kildimo New** Limrck
18 F4 **Kildimo Old** Limrck
12 B4 **Kildorrery**/*Cill Dairbhre* Cork
61 N7 **Kildress** Tyrone
66 B10 **Kildrum** Donegl
8 D4 **Kildurrihy**/*Cill Ura* Kerry
20 B9 **Kilfeakle** Tippry
16 F3 **Kilfearagh** Clare
25 J6 **Kilfenora**/*Cill Fhionnúrach* Clare
19 K10 **Kilfinnane**/*Cill Fhionáin* Limrck
18 F6 **Kilfinny** Limrck
16 F10 **Kilflyn** Kerry
10 C10 **Kilgarvan**/*Cill Gharbháin* Kerry
35 M5 **Kilglass** Galway
35 Q2 **Kilglass** Roscom
50 H4 **Kilglass** Sligo
9 N6 **Kilgobnet** Kerry
13 M7 **Kilgobnet** Watfd
30 E4 **Kilgowan** Kildre
18 E5 **Kilgrogan** Limrck
30 C7 **Kilkea** Kildre
21 N10 **Kilkeasy** Kilken
16 F2 **Kilkee**/*Cill Chaoi* Clare
47 Q1 **Kilkeel** Down
42 E5 **Kilkelly**/*Cill Cheallaigh* Mayo
21 N5 **Kilkenny**/*Cill Chainnigh* Kilken
21 N5 **Kilkenny Castle** Kilken
36 E4 **Kilkenny West** Wmeath
5 N5 **Kilkerran** Cork
35 J2 **Kilkerrin** Galway
32 G7 **Kilkieran**/*Cill Chiaráin* Galway
21 N4 **Kilkieran Cross Roads** Kilken
4 B8 **Kilkilleen** Cork
17 K10 **Kilkinlea Lower** Limrck
26 C10 **Kilkishen**/*Cill Chisín* Clare
45 P2 **Kill** Cavan
32 C3 **Kill** Galway
14 B8 **Kill** Watfd
38 G9 **Kill**/*An Chill* Kildre
36 F5 **Killachonna** Wmeath
12 C4 **Killaclug** Cork
18 F9 **Killacolla** Limrck
53 P3 **Killadeas** Ferman
35 N5 **Killaderry** Galway
40 F9 **Killadoon** Mayo
17 P3 **Killadysert**/*Cill an Dísirt* Clare
26 C5 **Killafeen** Galway
15 M7 **Killag** Wexfd
17 N8 **Killaghteen** Limrck
13 J7 **Killahaly** Watfd
21 K5 **Killahy Cross Roads** Kilken
50 F5 **Killala**/*Cill Ala* Mayo
45 Q9 **Killallon** Meath
26 H10 **Killaloe**/*Cill Dalua* Clare
60 H1 **Killaloo** Lderry
21 K9 **Killalure** Clare
26 D6 **Killanena** Clare
22 F8 **Killann**/*Cill Anna* Wexfd
16 H1 **Killard** Clare
52 G7 **Killarga** Leitrm
10 B6 **Killarney**/*Cill Airne* Kerry
10 B8 **Killarney National Park** Kerry
36 H4 **Killaroo** Wmeath

45 J2 **Killashandra**/*Cill na Seanrátha* Cavan
44 D9 **Killashee** Longfd
42 D3 **Killasser** Mayo
33 L1 **Killateeaun**/*Coill an tSiáin* Mayo
28 D3 **Killaun** Offaly
41 N8 **Killavally** Mayo
12 F8 **Killavarilly** Cork
11 R9 **Killavarrig** Cork
51 P9 **Killavil** Sligo
34 H2 **Killavoher** Galway
11 Q5 **Killavullen**/*Cill an Mhuilinn* Cork
52 H5 **Killea** Leitrm
20 D2 **Killea** Tippry
14 F8 **Killea** Watfd
62 F6 **Killead** Antrim
6 H4 **Killeagh**/*Cill Ia* Cork
24 C3 **Killeany**/*Cill Éinne* Galway
22 D6 **Killedmond** Carlow
12 C4 **Killee Bridge** Cork
17 P9 **Killeedy** Limrck
11 Q5 **Killeen** Galway
40 F8 **Killeen** Mayo
27 P4 **Killeen** Tippry
61 Q9 **Killeen** Tyrone
25 N1 **Killeenaran** Galway
20 C9 **Killeenasteena** Tippry
25 P2 **Killeenavarra** Galway
34 F10 **Killeeneenmore** Galway
4 C6 **Killeenleagh** Cork
8 H10 **Killeenleagh**/*Cillín Liath* Kerry
11 R9 **Killeens Cross** Cork
54 G8 **Killeevan** Monhan
35 P5 **Killeglan** Roscom
37 K10 **Killeigh**/*Cill Aichidh* Offaly
60 B6 **Killen** Tyrone
23 M6 **Killenagh** Wexfd
29 N3 **Killenard** Laois
27 P3 **Killenaule** Tippry
20 G7 **Killenaule**/*Cill Náile* Carlow
43 M4 **Killerdoo** Roscom
30 E9 **Killerrig Cross Roads** Carlow
37 M7 **Killeshil** Offaly
30 B9 **Killeshin** Laois
60 B6 **Killeter** Tyrone
34 H10 **Killilan Bridge** Galway
17 J4 **Killimer** Clare
27 K2 **Killimor**/*Cill Íomair* Galway
25 L6 **Killinaboy**/*Cill Inine Baoith* Clare
11 L10 **Killinardrish** Cork
14 C4 **Killinaspick** Kilken
57 M1 **Killinchy** Down
23 M9 **Killincooly** Wexfd
9 J2 **Killiney** Kerry
39 P8 **Killiney**/*Cill Iníon Léinin* Dublin
15 P6 **Killinick** Wexfd
45 Q5 **Killinkere** Cavan
25 N3 **Killinny** Galway
38 B9 **Killinthomas** Kildre
31 P4 **Killiskey** Wicklw
10 H10 **Killnamartery**/*Cill na Martra* Cork
44 G8 **Killoe** Longfd
50 E3 **Killogeary** Mayo
36 E6 **Killogeenaghan** Wmeath
8 E10 **Killoluaig**/*Cill Ó Luaigh* Kerry
25 P3 **Killomoran** Galway
37 N8 **Killoneen** Offaly
35 M9 **Killoran** Galway
9 M5 **Killorglin**/*Cill Orglan* Kerry
35 J5 **Killoscobe** Galway
57 M6 **Killough** Down
33 P1 **Killour** Mayo
56 E10 **Killowen** Down
39 L4 **Killsallaghan** Dublin
37 P3 **Killucan**/*Cill Liúcainne* Wmeath
43 Q4 **Killukin** Roscom
37 J10 **Killurin** Offaly
15 M3 **Killurin** Wexfd
2 C1 **Killurly**/*Cill Urlai* Kerry
20 G10 **Killusty** Tippry
62 D3 **Killybegs** Antrim
58 F7 **Killybegs**/*Na Cealla Beaga* Donegl
60 G8 **Killyclogher** Tyrone
44 H2 **Killygar** Leitrm
60 B4 **Killygordon**/*Cúil na gCuirridín* Donegl
67 L9 **Killykergan** Lderry
55 L5 **Killylea** Armagh
57 M3 **Killyleagh** Down
55 K6 **Killyneill** Monhan

28 D3 **Killyon** Offaly
6 F6 **Kilmacahill** Cork
31 N2 **Kilmacanoge** Wicklw
11 N3 **Kilmaclenine Cross Roads** Cork
14 D5 **Kilmacow**/*Cill Mhic Bhúith* Kilken
65 L8 **Kilmacrenan**/*Cill Mhic Réanain* Donegl
13 Q5 **Kilmacthomas**/*Coill Mhic Thomáisín* Watfd
43 N1 **Kilmactranny** Sligo
21 M10 **Kilmaganny**/*Cill Mogeanna* Kilken
34 B2 **Kilmaine** Mayo
46 D6 **Kilmainham Wood** Meath
25 L10 **Kilmaley**/*Cill Mháile* Clare
39 N10 **Kilmalin** Wicklw
19 J9 **Kilmallock**/*Cill Mocheallóg* Limrck
21 K6 **Kilmanagh** Kilken
17 K10 **Kilmaniheen** Kerry
35 Q3 **Kilmass** Roscom
30 C5 **Kilmead** Kildre
14 C6 **Kilmeadan** Watfd
38 D9 **Kilmeage** Kildre
18 D9 **Kilmeedy**/*Cill Míde* Limrck
38 F2 **Kilmessan**/*Cill Mheasáin* Meath
2 D6 **Kilmichael** Cork
4 G1 **Kilmichael** Cork
17 L2 **Kilmihil**/*Cill Mhicil* Clare
11 Q8 **Kilmona** Cork
3 Q10 **Kilmoon** Cork
55 P3 **Kilmore** Armagh
19 J1 **Kilmore** Clare
57 K3 **Kilmore** Down
16 E7 **Kilmore** Kerry
42 B3 **Kilmore** Mayo
44 B5 **Kilmore** Roscom
15 M7 **Kilmore** Wexfd
38 F4 **Kilmore Cross Roads** Meath
15 M8 **Kilmore Quay** Wexfd
44 D9 **Kilmore Upper** Longfd
17 K8 **Kilmorna** Kerry
30 B7 **Kilmorony** Laois
42 G5 **Kilmovee** Mayo
23 M8 **Kilmuckridge**/*Cill Mhucraise* Wexfd
14 B9 **Kilmurrin** Watfd
24 F10 **Kilmurry** Clare
5 J1 **Kilmurry** Cork
18 E9 **Kilmurry** Limrck
30 F7 **Kilmurry** Wicklw
18 F1 **Kilmurry**/*Cill Mhuire* Clare
17 L3 **Kilmurry McMahon** Clare
24 B2 **Kilmurvy**/*Cill Mhuirbhigh* Galway
22 G6 **Kilmyshall** Wexfd
13 J8 **Kilnacarriga** Watfd
18 G1 **Kilnacreagh** Clare
44 C3 **Kilnagross** Leitrm
35 M8 **Kilnahown** Galway
45 L5 **Kilnaleck**/*Cill na Leice* Cavan
23 L8 **Kilnamanagh** Wexfd
25 L8 **Kilnamona**/*Cill na Móna* Clare
5 M3 **Kilpatrick** Cork
18 H5 **Kilpeacon Cross Roads** Limrck
31 P3 **Kilpedder** Wicklw
8 E3 **Kilquane**/*Cill Chuáin* Kerry
22 H2 **Kilquiggin** Wicklw
67 Q7 **Kilraghts** Antrim
15 Q6 **Kilrane** Wexfd
67 N10 **Kilrea** Lderry
58 G4 **Kilrean** Donegl
35 K9 **Kilreekill** Galway
34 C8 **Kilroghter**/*Coill Uachtar* Galway
24 C3 **Kilronan**/*Cill Rónáin* Galway
43 Q10 **Kilroosky** Roscom
19 N8 **Kilross** Tippry
16 H3 **Kilrush**/*Cill Rois* Clare
43 K10 **Kilsallagh** Galway
40 H7 **Kilsallagh** Mayo
47 K5 **Kilsaran** Louth
38 C6 **Kilshanchoe** Kildre
9 J1 **Kilshannig** Kerry
24 H6 **Kilshanny** Clare
13 N2 **Kilsheelan** Tippry
5 L5 **Kilshinahan** Cork
46 B9 **Kilskeer** Meath
53 Q3 **Kilskeery** Tyrone
42 C6 **Kiltamagh**/*Cailíte Mach* Mayo
41 M8 **Kiltarsaghaun** Mayo
26 C3 **Kiltartan** Galway

22 F7 **Kiltealy**/*Cill Téile* Wexfd
38 H9 **Kilteel** Kildre
19 L6 **Kilteely**/*Cill Tíle* Limrck
43 Q10 **Kilteevan Cross Roads** Roscom
30 G8 **Kiltegan** Wicklw
23 J6 **Kilthomas Cross Roads** Wexfd
39 N9 **Kiltiernan** Dublin
25 P1 **Kiltiernan** Galway
37 K7 **Kiltober** Wmeath
36 B4 **Kiltoom** Roscom
45 L10 **Kiltoom** Wmeath
35 N9 **Kiltormer** Galway
34 H8 **Kiltullagh**/*Cill Tulach* Galway
53 J4 **Kiltyclogher**/*Coillte Clochair* Leitrm
21 J9 **Kilvemnon** Tippry
42 E10 **Kilvine** Mayo
12 H8 **Kilwatermoy** Watfd
63 K2 **Kilwaughter** Antrim
38 H7 **Kilwoghan** Kildre
12 D6 **Kilworth**/*Cill Uird* Cork
12 D5 **Kilworth Camp** Cork
36 H6 **Kimalady** Offaly
17 L5 **Kinard** Limrck
53 P7 **Kinawley** Ferman
64 C9 **Kincaslough**/*Cionn Caslach* Donegl
50 D5 **Kincon** Mayo
59 L1 **Kingarrow**/*An Cionn Garbh* Donegl
18 H3 **King John's Castle** Limrck
46 D4 **Kingscourt**/*Dún an Rí* Cavan
45 Q9 **King's Cross Roads** Meath
61 Q7 **Kingsmill** Tyrone
52 F2 **Kinlough**/*Cionn Locha* Leitrm
40 E9 **Kinnadoohy** Mayo
37 P4 **Kinnegad**/*Cionn Átha Gad* Wmeath
28 E3 **Kinnitty**/*Cion Eitigh* Offaly
5 P4 **Kinsale**/*Cionn tSáile* Cork
7 K4 **Kinsalebeg** Watfd
39 N5 **Kinsaley** Dublin
33 K7 **Kinvarra**/*Cinn Mhara* Galway
25 N2 **Kinvarra**/*Cinn Mharra* Galway
4 G5 **Kippagh Bridge** Cork
63 Q10 **Kircubbin** Down
67 P7 **Kirkhills** Antrim
57 P2 **Kirkistown** Down
10 G4 **Kishkeam** Cork
41 K7 **Knappagh** Mayo
8 E9 **Knight's Town** Kerry
17 K4 **Knock** Clare
28 F7 **Knock** Tippry
42 D7 **Knock**/*An Cnoc* Mayo
25 L8 **Knockacaurhin** Clare
10 B5 **Knockacullig** Kerry
50 E7 **Knockadangan Bridge** Mayo
18 C7 **Knockaderry** Limrck
19 K7 **Knockainy**/*Cnoc Áine* Limrck
13 P3 **Knockalafalla** Watfd
43 M8 **Knockalaghta** Roscom
17 L2 **Knockalough** Clare
31 J8 **Knockananna** Wicklw
42 F8 **Knockanarra** Mayo
30 H6 **Knockanarrigan** Wicklw
4 H2 **Knockane** Cork
12 B3 **Knockanevin** Cork
50 E7 **Knockanillaun** Mayo
13 J9 **Knockanore** Watfd
17 K7 **Knockanure** Kerry
28 G7 **Knockaroe** Laois
54 G6 **Knockatallan** Monhan
12 E6 **Knockatrasnane** Cork
24 H8 **Knockatullaghaun** Clare
35 M10 **Knockaun** Galway
12 H6 **Knockaunarast** Watfd
17 J9 **Knockaunbrack** Kerry
9 L5 **Knockaunnaglashy** Kerry
9 K6 **Knockaunroe** Kerry
8 E4 **Knockavrogeen**/*Cnoc an Bhróigin* Kerry
17 M8 **Knockawahig** Limrck
13 M5 **Knockboy** Watfd
26 E9 **Knockbrack** Cork
60 B1 **Knockbrack** Donegl
16 F10 **Knockbrack** Kerry
46 B3 **Knockbride** Cork
46 H3 **Knockbridge** Louth
20 F9 **Knockbrit** Tippry
5 L5 **Knockbrown** Cork
5 N1 **Knockburden** Cork

16 G9 **Knockburrane Cross Roads** Kerry
61 Q3 **Knockcloghrim** Lderry
35 Q2 **Knockcroghery**/*Cnoc an Chrochaire* Roscom
18 H8 **Knockdarnan** Limrck
37 L2 **Knockdrin** Wmeath
11 N6 **Knockdrislagh** Cork
10 G4 **Knockeenadallane** Cork
10 D1 **Knockeencreen** Kerry
10 B2 **Knockeen Cross Roads** Kerry
24 G5 **Knockfin Cross Roads** Clare
13 K2 **Knocklofty** Tippry
19 L8 **Knocklong** Limrck
25 P7 **Knockmael West** Clare
21 K2 **Knockmannon Cross Roads** Kilken
50 F9 **Knockmore** Mayo
12 F8 **Knockmourne** Cork
41 L4 **Knockmoyle Bridge** Mayo
17 N5 **Knocknabooly** Limrck
10 E4 **Knocknaboul Cross** Kerry
68 E6 **Knocknacarry** Antrim
30 D8 **Knocknacree Cross Roads** Kildre
5 M4 **Knocknacurra** Cork
17 K10 **Knocknagashel**/*Cnoc na gCaiseal* Kerry
26 G8 **Knocknagower** Clare
10 F5 **Knocknagree** Cork
9 N1 **Knocknahaha** Kerry
24 G10 **Knocknahila** Clare
5 M1 **Knocknahilan** Cork
48 G3 **Knocknalina**/*Cnocán na Líne* Mayo
48 G3 **Knocknalower**/*Cnoc na Lobhar* Mayo
6 G5 **Knocknaskagh** Cork
24 H7 **Knockpatrick** Clare
6 C4 **Knockraha** Cork
13 M7 **Knockroe** Watfd
9 J9 **Knockroe**/*Cnocrua* Kerry
5 J5 **Knocks** Cork
29 J4 **Knocks** Laois
5 J5 **Knockskagh** Cork
11 J2 **Knockskavane** Cork
21 N9 **Knocktopher**/*Cnoc an Tóchair* Kilken
15 L6 **Knocktown Cross Roads** Wexfd
43 P2 **Knockvicar** Roscom
5 M4 **Knoppoge Bridge** Cork
46 H9 **Knowth** Meath
11 Q6 **Knuttery** Cork
29 N6 **Kyle** Laois
26 G3 **Kylebrack** Galway
19 N4 **Kylegarve** Limrck
35 Q9 **Kylemore** Galway
32 H7 **Kylesalia**/*Coill Sáile* Galway

L

26 C2 **Laban** Galway
17 M4 **Labasheeda**/*Leaba Shíoda* Clare
60 C9 **Lack** Ferman
10 E10 **Lackabaun**/*An Leaca Bhán* Cork
29 Q2 **Lackagh** Kildre
19 M3 **Lackamore** Tippry
27 J9 **Lackamore** Tippry
21 Q4 **Lackan** Carlow
43 Q8 **Lackan** Roscom
31 J2 **Lackan** Wicklw
45 K10 **Lackan** Wmeath
35 P3 **Lackan Cross** Roscom
5 J2 **Lackareagh** Cork
10 D1 **Lackbrooder** Kerry
14 H3 **Lacken** Wexfd
12 B8 **Lackendarragh North** Cork
28 F6 **Lackey** Laois
6 G5 **Ladysbridge**/*Droichead na Scuab* Cork
15 Q7 **Lady's Island** Wexfd
67 Q4 **Lagavara** Antrim
20 C10 **Lagganstown** Tippry
55 M1 **Laghey Corner** Tyrone
59 K8 **Laghy**/*An Lathaigh* Donegl
11 M6 **Laharan Cross Roads** Cork
50 D9 **Lahardaun**/*Leathardán* Mayo
24 G7 **Lahinch**/*An Leacht* Clare
17 L4 **Lakyle** Clare
21 L10 **Lamoge** Kilken

44 C10 **Lanesborough**/*Béal Átha Liag* Roscom
26 D5 **Lannaght** Clare
38 E3 **Laracor** Meath
38 F6 **Laragh** Kildre
46 D1 **Laragh** Monhan
31 L5 **Laragh**/*Láithreach* Wicklw
11 L10 **Larchill Cross Roads** Cork
49 K6 **Largan** Mayo
43 Q6 **Largan** Roscom
51 J7 **Largan** Sligo
58 E7 **Largy** Donegl
52 E3 **Largydonnell** Leitrm
63 L2 **Larne** Antrim
54 H8 **Latnamard** Monhan
25 N10 **Latoon Bridge** Clare
19 N7 **Lattin** Tippry
46 B1 **Latton** Monhan
3 K3 **Lauragh**/*Láithreach* Kerry
56 B4 **Laurelvale** Armagh
35 P9 **Laurencetown**/*An Baile Mór* Galway
51 N7 **Lavagh** Sligo
56 C4 **Lawrencetown** Down
47 M9 **Laytown**/*An Inse* Meath
64 B9 **Leabgarrow**/*An Leadhb Gharbh* Donegl
6 D4 **Leamlara** Cork
4 F7 **Leap**/*An Léim* Cork
36 B3 **Lecarrow** Roscom
66 F4 **Leckemy** Donegl
32 H1 **Leenane**/*An Líonán* Galway
36 G1 **Legan or Lenamore** Longfd
44 G5 **Leggah** Longfd
63 J7 **Legoniel** Belfst
22 B3 **Leighlinbridge**/*Leithghlinn an Droichid* Carlow
38 B5 **Leinster Bridge** Kildre
32 H8 **Leitir Calaidh**/*Lettercallow* Galway
32 G9 **Leitir Mealláin**/*Lettermullan* Galway
58 H2 **Leitir Mhic an Bhaird**/*Lettermacaward* Donegl
32 H8 **Leitir Móir**/*Lettermore* Galway
17 K1 **Leitrim** Clare
56 H6 **Leitrim** Down
44 B3 **Leitrim**/*Liatroim* Leitrm
17 K6 **Leitrim East** Kerry
4 D5 **Leitry Bridge** Cork
39 J6 **Leixlip** Kildre
36 F8 **Lemanaghan** Offaly
13 P6 **Lemybrien**/*Léim Uí Bhriain* Watfd
14 F8 **Leperstown** Watfd
16 E10 **Lerrig** Kerry
59 J6 **Letterbarra** Donegl
53 N5 **Letterbreen** Ferman
32 H8 **Lettercallow**/*Leitir Calaidh* Galway
32 E2 **Letterfrack**/*Leitir Fraic* Galway
24 H9 **Letterkelly** Clare
65 M10 **Letterkenny**/*Leitir Ceanainn* Donegl
67 L7 **Letterloan** Lderry
58 H2 **Lettermacaward**/*Leitir Mhic an Bhaird* Donegl
41 K4 **Lettermaghera** Mayo
32 H8 **Lettermore**/*Leitir Móir* Galway
32 G9 **Lettermullan**/*Leitir Mealláin* Galway
34 G3 **Levally** Galway
41 Q10 **Levally** Mayo
14 C6 **Licketstown** Kilken
60 D3 **Lifford**/*Leifear* Donegl
60 F4 **Ligfordrum or Douglas** Tyrone
66 H8 **Limavady** Lderry
18 H3 **Limerick**/*Luimneach* Limrck
18 H3 **Limerick Hunt Museum** Limrck
19 P7 **Limerick Junction** Tippry
65 Q5 **Linsfort** Donegl
3 P10 **Lios Ó Móine**/*Lissamona* Cork
8 G4 **Lios Póil**/*Lispole* Kerry
63 M10 **Lisbane** Down
54 B5 **Lisbellaw** Ferman
45 N1 **Lisboduff** Cavan
62 H10 **Lisburn** Antrim
24 G7 **Liscannor**/*Lios Ceannúir* Clare
41 K8 **Liscarney** Mayo
11 M2 **Liscarroll**/*Lios Cearúill* Cork
38 B1 **Lisclogher Cross Roads** Wmeath
60 G2 **Liscloon** Tyrone

8 G4 **Lisdargan**/*Lios Deargáin* Kerry
24 H5 **Lisdoonvarna**/*Lios Dúin Bhearna* Clare
21 L2 **Lisdowney** Kilken
45 Q7 **Lisduff** Cavan
11 Q9 **Lisduff** Cork
28 E2 **Lisduff** Offaly
44 E9 **Lisduff Cross Roads** Longfd
27 M8 **Lisgarode** Tippry
6 E3 **Lisgoold** Cork
45 P5 **Lisgrea Cross Roads** Cavan
17 P1 **Lisheen** Clare
35 N10 **Lisheenaguile** Galway
43 L2 **Liskeagh** Sligo
45 K9 **Lismacaffry** Wmeath
11 K3 **Lismire** Cork
12 H7 **Lismore**/*Lios Mór* Watfd
35 P4 **Lismoyle** Roscom
55 N6 **Lisnadill** Armagh
19 K3 **Lisnagry** Limrck
14 C7 **Lisnakill Cross** Watfd
54 H10 **Lisnalong** Monhan
61 P3 **Lisnamuck** Lderry
53 N2 **Lisnarick** Ferman
54 C7 **Lisnaskea** Ferman
5 P6 **Lispatrick** Cork
8 G4 **Lispole**/*Lios Póil* Kerry
25 K10 **Lisroe** Clare
13 M1 **Lisronagh** Tippry
45 J8 **Lisryan** Longfd
10 H10 **Lissacresig** Cork
43 L8 **Lissalway** Roscom
3 P10 **Lissamona**/*Lios Ó Móine* Cork
35 P10 **Lissanacody** Galway
43 K7 **Lissananny** Roscom
5 L4 **Lissaphooca Cross Roads** Cork
9 J9 **Lissatinnig Bridge**/*Droichead Lios an tSonnaigh* Kerry
4 H7 **Lissavard** Cork
16 G7 **Lisselton Cross Roads** Kerry
17 N1 **Lissycasey** Clare
9 N1 **Listellick** Kerry
14 E3 **Listerlin** Kilken
57 K3 **Listooder** Down
16 H8 **Listowel**/*Lios Tuathail* Kerry
19 N9 **Lisvarrinane** Tippry
6 C5 **Little Island** Cork
20 F6 **Littleton**/*An Baile Beag* Tippry
16 F9 **Lixnaw**/*Leic Snámha* Kerry
62 G6 **Loanends** Antrim
46 F7 **Lobinstown** Meath
64 E9 **Loch an Iúir**/*Loughanure* Donegl
45 J5 **Loch Gowna**/*Loch Gamhna* Cavan
17 M5 **Loghill** Limrck
12 H6 **Logleagh** Watfd
7 N2 **Loiscearán**/*Loskeran* Watfd
8 G4 **Lios Deargáin**/*Lisdargan* Kerry
2 H1 **Lomanagh** Kerry
11 M5 **Lombardstown** Cork
66 C9 **Londonderry** Lderry
66 C9 **Londonderry Tower Museum** Lderry
28 E4 **Longford** Offaly
44 E8 **Longford**/*An Longfort* Longfd
19 J6 **Longford Bridge** Limrck
20 G4 **Longfordpass Bridge** Tippry
38 C4 **Longwood** Meath
27 M4 **Lorrha**/*Lothra* Tippry
22 C5 **Lorum** Carlow
7 N2 **Loskeran**/*Loiscearán* Watfd
35 L7 **Loughaclerybeg** Galway
12 H2 **Loughacutteen** Tippry
37 J4 **Loughanavally** Wmeath
64 E9 **Loughanure**/*Loch an Iúir* Donegl
33 M9 **Loughaunbeg**/*An Lochán Beag* Galway
56 D5 **Loughbrickland** Down
45 K5 **Loughduff** Cavan
9 K5 **Lougher** Kerry
55 P3 **Loughgall** Armagh
43 J6 **Loughglinn**/*Loch Glinne* Roscom
68 B7 **Loughguile** Antrim
57 N4 **Loughinisland** Down
61 Q7 **Loughmacory** Tyrone
20 E3 **Loughmore** Tippry
46 D1 **Loughmorne** Monhan
26 F1 **Loughrea**/*Baile Locha Riach* Galway
39 P2 **Loughshinny** Dublin

40 G7 **Louisburgh**/*Cluain Cearbán* Mayo
46 H3 **Louth**/*Lú* Louth
62 E9 **Lower Ballinderry** Antrim
3 M8 **Lowertown** Cork
56 E5 **Lowtown** Down
39 J6 **Lucan** Dublin
51 L4 **Lugdoon** Sligo
29 N7 **Luggacurren** Laois
31 J6 **Lugnaquilla Mountain** Wicklw
14 D3 **Lukeswell** Kilken
38 C8 **Lullymore** Kildre
42 F4 **Lurga** Mayo
56 C2 **Lurgan** Armagh
36 F6 **Lurgan** Offaly
43 M5 **Lurgan** Roscom
65 P6 **Lurganboy** Donegl
52 G5 **Lurganboy** Leitrm
39 N3 **Lusk**/*Lusca* Dublin
44 D10 **Lyneen Bridge** Longfd
16 H10 **Lyracrumpane** Kerry
11 P7 **Lyradane** Cork
11 L6 **Lyre** Cork
12 G9 **Lyre** Cork
10 D2 **Lyre** Kerry
12 F6 **Lyrenaglogh** Watfd

M

33 K4 **Maam Cross**/*An Teach Dóite* Galway
58 G3 **Maas** Donegl
41 M7 **Mace** Mayo
65 N3 **Machair Dromann**/*Magheradrumman* Donegl
65 L5 **Machair Loiscthe**/*Rosepenna* Donegl
53 P7 **Mackan** Ferman
67 L7 **Macosquin** Lderry
12 E6 **Macroney** Cork
11 J10 **Macroom**/*Maigh Chromtha* Cork
45 Q2 **Madabawn** Cavan
21 N6 **Maddockstown** Kilken
30 C8 **Maganey** Kildre
62 F10 **Maghaberry** Antrim
57 J7 **Maghera** Down
61 Q2 **Maghera** Lderry
25 P8 **Maghera Cross Roads** Clare
65 N3 **Magheradrumman**/*Machair Dromann* Donegl
61 Q4 **Magherafelt** Lderry
56 D2 **Magheralin** Down
66 B10 **Magheramason** Tyrone
63 L3 **Magheramorne** Antrim
54 E8 **Magheraveely** Ferman
62 A10 **Maghery** Armagh
58 F1 **Maghery**/*An Machaire* Donegl
54 B6 **Maguiresbridge** Ferman
18 C8 **Mahoonagh** Limrck
33 Q7 **Maigh Cuilinn**/*Moycullen* Galway
48 F4 **Maigh Raithin**/*Moyrahan* Mayo
32 F6 **Maighros**/*Moyrus* Galway
9 Q3 **Maine Bridge** Kerry
38 F7 **Mainham** Kildre
8 H10 **Máistir Gaoithe**/*Mastergeehy* Kerry
39 N4 **Malahide**/*Mullach Íde* Dublin
58 A6 **Málainn Bhig**/*Malin Beg* Donegl
58 B6 **Málainn Mhóir**/*Malin More* Donegl
66 D2 **Malin**/*Málainn* Donegl
58 A6 **Malin Beg**/*Málainn Bhig* Donegl
58 B6 **Malin More**/*Málainn Mhóir* Donegl
11 P5 **Mallow**/*Mala* Cork
62 H6 **Mallusk** Antrim
33 K1 **Mám Trasna**/*Maumtrasna* Mayo
4 G4 **Manch Bridge** Cork
36 D7 **Mannion's Cross Roads** Galway
65 N10 **Manorcunningham**/*Mainear Ui Chuinneagain* Donegl
52 G6 **Manorhamilton**/*Cluainin* Leitrm
20 F4 **Manselstown** Tippry
47 J4 **Mansfieldstown** Louth
43 N6 **Mantua** Roscom
41 Q6 **Manulla** Mayo
53 M7 **Marble Arch Caves** Ferman
20 G7 **Mardyke** Tippry

55 Q6 **Markethill** Armagh
13 L2 **Marlfield** Tippry
22 H7 **Marshalstown** Wexfd
68 C10 **Martinstown** Antrim
19 K9 **Martinstown** Limrck
46 C10 **Martinstown Cross Roads** Meath
46 D9 **Marty** Meath
8 H10 **Mastergeehy**/*Máistir Gaoithe* Kerry
20 C10 **Masterstown** Tippry
11 P9 **Matehy** Cork
4 E7 **Maulatrahane** Cork
4 C3 **Maulavanig** Cork
3 M8 **Maulawaddra** Cork
33 K3 **Maum**/*An Mám* Galway
33 K1 **Maumtrasna**/*Mám Trasna* Mayo
25 K8 **Mauricesmills** Clare
15 N6 **Mayglass** Wexfd
38 G6 **Maynooth**/*Maigh Nuad* Kildre
42 B8 **Mayo** Mayo
56 E8 **Mayobridge** Down
62 G10 **Mazetown** Antrim
68 C10 **McGregor's Corner** Antrim
67 N10 **McLaughlins Corner** Antrim
18 H6 **Meanus** Limrck
27 M2 **Meelick** Galway
10 H2 **Meelin** Cork
64 F6 **Meenaclady**/*Mín an Chladaigh* Donegl
58 C5 **Meenacross**/*Mín na Croise* Donegl
58 G1 **Meenacross**/*Mín na Croise* Donegl
58 D6 **Meenaneary**/*Mín an Aoire* Donegl
64 D9 **Meenbannad**/*Mín Beannaid* Donegl
10 D1 **Meenbannivane** Kerry
64 F6 **Meenlaragh**/*Mín Lárach* Donegl
10 F1 **Meennaraheeny** Cork
31 M8 **Meeting of the Waters** Wicklw
56 C9 **Meigh** Armagh
34 B8 **Menlough**/*Mionlach* Galway
35 J5 **Menlough**/*Mionlach* Galway
55 L6 **Middletown** Armagh
42 D5 **Midfield** Mayo
6 E5 **Midleton**/*Mainistir an Corann* Cork
22 H8 **Milehouse** Wexfd
30 F3 **Milemill** Kildre
19 Q3 **Milestone** Tippry
55 N5 **Milford** Armagh
18 E10 **Milford**/*Áth an Mhuilinn* Cork
63 K2 **Millbrook** Antrim
4 E7 **Milleen Bridge** Cork
65 M7 **Millford**/*Baile na nCallóglach* Donegl
63 P7 **Millisle** Down
12 E5 **Millstreet** Cork
13 L6 **Millstreet** Watfd
10 H6 **Millstreet**/*Sráid an Mhuilinn* Cork
62 E5 **Mill Town** Antrim
55 Q4 **Milltown** Armagh
45 J1 **Milltown** Cavan
58 H7 **Milltown** Donegl
65 M5 **Milltown** Donegl
39 J7 **Milltown** Dublin
34 E1 **Milltown** Galway
35 K3 **Milltown** Galway
38 D10 **Milltown** Kildre
14 C3 **Milltown** Kilken
67 K6 **Milltown** Lderry
67 M8 **Milltown** Lderry
37 J3 **Milltown** Wmeath
8 E4 **Milltown**/*Baile an Mhuilinn* Kerry
9 N4 **Milltown**/*Baile an Mhuilinn* Kerry
18 G10 **Milltown Cross Roads** Cork
24 G9 **Milltown Malbay**/*Sráid na Cathrach* Clare
37 N5 **Milltownpass**/*Bealach Bhaile an Mhuileann* Wmeath
58 D6 **Mín an Aoire**/*Meenaneary* Donegl
64 F6 **Mín an Chladaigh**/*Meenaclady* Donegl
6 B8 **Minane Bridge** Cork
64 D9 **Mín Beannaid**/*Meenbannad* Donegl
57 L6 **Minerstown** Down
64 F6 **Mín Lárach**/*Meenlaragh* Donegl

58 C5 **Mín na Croise**/*Meenacross* Donegl
58 G1 **Mín na Croise**/*Meenacross* Donegl
34 B8 **Mionlach**/*Menlough* Galway
12 D4 **Mitchelstown**/*Baile Mhistéala* Cork
12 F3 **Mitchelstown Caves** Tippry
16 H3 **Moanmore** Clare
19 M8 **Moanmore** Tippry
36 F6 **Moate**/*An Móta* Wmeath
44 G8 **Moat Farrell** Longfd
13 L7 **Modelligo** Watfd
11 M9 **Model Village** Cork
11 P10 **Model Village** Cork
27 N7 **Modreeny** Tippry
6 G4 **Mogeely** Cork
21 N4 **Mohil** Kilken
44 D4 **Mohill**/*Maothail* Leitrm
8 F10 **Moing Uí Dhúda**/*Muingydowda* Kerry
7 M2 **Móin na mBróthar**/*Monamraher* Watfd
56 D1 **Moira** Down
9 P9 **Moll's Gap** Kerry
23 J8 **Monagear** Wexfd
55 J7 **Monaghan**/*Muineachán* Monhan
55 J7 **Monaghan County Museum** Monhan
12 F8 **Monagoun** Cork
13 J6 **Monalour** Watfd
14 E7 **Monamintra Cross Roads** Watfd
23 L7 **Monamolin** Wexfd
7 M2 **Monamraher**/*Móin na mBróthar* Watfd
19 N6 **Monard** Tippry
23 K4 **Monaseed** Wexfd
18 G6 **Monaster** Limrck
43 K4 **Monasteraden** Sligo
47 J7 **Monasterboice** Louth
29 P2 **Monasterevin**/*Mainistir Eimhin* Kildre
53 N4 **Monea** Ferman
11 P6 **Monee Cross Roads** Cork
16 C5 **Moneen** Clare
34 D4 **Moneen** Galway
29 N9 **Moneenroe** Kilken
29 J1 **Monettia Bog** Laois
4 H1 **Moneycusker** Cork
67 M9 **Moneydig** Lderry
27 P8 **Moneygall**/*Muine Gall* Offaly
53 L7 **Moneygashel** Cavan
62 C4 **Moneyglass** Antrim
61 Q6 **Moneymore** Lderry
64 G8 **Money More**/*Muine Mór* Donegl
61 N3 **Moneyneany** Lderry
63 L9 **Moneyreagh** Down
56 F6 **Moneyslane** Down
37 M2 **Monilea** Wmeath
34 G6 **Monivea**/*Muine Mheá* Galway
63 J5 **Monkstown** Antrim
6 C6 **Monkstown** Cork
19 K1 **Montpelier** Limrck
14 C5 **Mooncoin**/*Móin Choinn* Kilken
30 D6 **Moone**/*Maoin* Kildre
7 K4 **Moord** Watfd
27 L1 **Moorfield Cross Roads** Galway
62 F3 **Moorfields** Antrim
61 R1 **Moran's Cross Roads** Lderry
18 F7 **Morenane** Limrck
10 C9 **Morley's Bridge** Kerry
47 L8 **Mornington** Meath
19 Q6 **Morpeth Bridge** Tippry
19 K10 **Mortlestown** Limrck
5 L2 **Moskeagh** Cork
47 M10 **Mosney Camp** Meath
63 J6 **Mossley** Antrim
67 Q5 **Moss-Side** Antrim
13 Q3 **Mothel** Watfd
47 M2 **Mountain Bay** Louth
43 Q1 **Mountallen** Roscom
35 K4 **Mountbellew Bridge**/*An Creagán* Galway
28 F1 **Mountbolus** Offaly
6 C2 **Mountcatherine** Cork
59 J7 **Mountcharles**/*Moin Séarlas* Donegl
10 F1 **Mountcollins** Limrck
60 H7 **Mountfield** Tyrone
23 L7 **Mounthoward Cross Roads** Wexfd
60 F7 **Mountjoy** Tyrone
13 J6 **Mountmelleray** Watfd
29 L3 **Mountmellick**/*Móinteach Mílic* Laois

29 M4 **Mountmellick**/*Móinteach Mílic* Laois
55 Q7 **Mountnorris** Armagh
45 M6 **Mount Nugent** Cavan
29 J6 **Mountrath**/*Maighean Rátha* Laois
16 H1 **Mountrivers Bridge** Clare
26 H7 **Mountshannon**/*Baile Uí Bheoláin* Clare
63 P9 **Mount Stewart** Down
35 N3 **Mount Talbot** Roscom
52 C3 **Mount Temple** Sligo
36 F6 **Mount Temple** Wmeath
6 G3 **Mount Uniacke** Cork
56 G10 **Mourne Park** Down
16 F3 **Moveen** Clare
66 G5 **Moville**/*Bun an Phobail* Donegl
25 N3 **Moy** Galway
55 M2 **Moy** Tyrone
32 D2 **Moyard** Galway
16 H3 **Moyasta** Clare
20 E6 **Moycarky** Tippry
33 Q7 **Moycullen**/*Maigh Cuilinn* Galway
44 E10 **Moydow** Longfd
55 M1 **Moygashel** Tyrone
20 F8 **Moyglass** Tippry
22 D2 **Moyle** Carlow
22 G3 **Moylisha** Wicklw
35 J4 **Moylough** Galway
51 M9 **Moylough** Sligo
26 C9 **Moymore** Clare
46 C7 **Moynalty**/*Maigh nEalta* Meath
38 F4 **Moynalvy** Meath
44 G4 **Moyne** Longfd
43 J6 **Moyne** Roscom
20 F4 **Moyne** Tippry
31 J8 **Moyne** Wicklw
4 D5 **Moyny Bridge** Cork
48 F4 **Moyrahan**/*Maigh Raithin* Mayo
17 N6 **Moyreen** Limrck
32 F6 **Moyrus**/*Maighros* Galway
66 H9 **Moys** Lderry
38 C5 **Moyvally** Kildre
36 G3 **Moyvore** Wmeath
36 G5 **Moyvoughly** Wmeath
10 B7 **Mucklon** Kildre
10 B7 **Muckross** Kerry
10 B7 **Muckross House** Kerry
66 D8 **Muff**/*Magh* Donegl
64 G8 **Muine Mór**/*Money More* Donegl
10 C1 **Muinganear** Kerry
9 L6 **Muingaphuca** Kerry
9 Q1 **Muingnaminnane** Kerry
17 J10 **Muingwee** Kerry
8 F10 **Muingydowda**/*Moing Uí Dhúda* Kerry
39 K5 **Mulhuddart** Dublin
50 E5 **Mullafarry** Mayo
24 F10 **Mullagh** Clare
35 L10 **Mullagh** Galway
40 H8 **Mullagh** Mayo
38 G4 **Mullagh** Meath
46 B6 **Mullagh**/*An Mullach* Cavan
55 Q10 **Mullaghbane** Armagh
52 D2 **Mullaghmore** Sligo
43 K3 **Mullaghroe** Sligo
67 L8 **Mullan** Lderry
67 P9 **Mullan Head** Antrim
51 K8 **Mullany's Cross** Sligo
47 K7 **Mullary Cross Roads** Louth
43 L6 **Mullen** Roscom
11 R6 **Mullenaboree** Cork
21 K10 **Mullennaglogh** Tippry
21 Q10 **Mullennakill** Kilken
22 H2 **Mullinacuff** Wicklw
21 J8 **Mullinahone**/*Muileann na hUamhan* Tippry
14 D4 **Mullinavat**/*Muileann an Bhata* Kilken
37 L1 **Mullingar**/*An Muileann gCearr* Wmeath
41 Q9 **Mullingar Bridge** Mayo
40 G4 **Mulrany**/*An Mhala Raithní* Mayo
37 L1 **Multyfarnham**/*Muilte Farannáin* Wmeath
18 G4 **Mungret**/*Mungairit* Limrck
17 K7 **Murher** Kerry
6 G2 **Murley's Cross Roads** Cork
15 N5 **Murntown** Wexfd

8 D3 **Murreagh**/*An Mhulríoch* Kerry
41 J7 **Murrisk** Mayo
19 L3 **Murroe** Limrck
24 H3 **Murrough** Clare
40 D3 **Mweelin**/*An Mhaoilinn* Mayo
10 B2 **Mweennalaa** Kerry
4 F8 **Myross** Cork
6 C8 **Myrtleville** Cork
22 E4 **Myshall**/*Míseal* Carlow

N

38 F10 **Naas**/*An Nás* Kildre
11 L6 **Nad** Cork
65 L5 **Na Dúnaibh**/*Downies* Donegl
33 P9 **Na Forbacha**/*Furbo* Galway
37 P10 **Nahana** Offaly
58 F3 **Naran** Donegl
30 D4 **Narraghmore**/*An Fhorrach Mhór* Kildre
40 E4 **Na Sraithini**/*Sraheens Bridge* Mayo
39 L1 **Naul**/*An Aill* Dublin
46 F10 **Navan**/*An Uaimh* Meath
33 P2 **Neale**/*An Éill* Mayo
28 E6 **Nealstown** Laois
2 G3 **Nedanone** Kerry
27 L9 **Nenagh**/*An tAonach* Tippry
15 J4 **Newbawn** Wexfd
20 G6 **New Birmingham** Tippry
54 G9 **Newbliss**/*Cúil Darach* Monhan
35 L3 **Newbridge** Galway
18 C5 **Newbridge** Limrck
30 E2 **Newbridge**/*An Droichead Nua* Kildre
66 C10 **New Buildings** Lderry
57 J7 **Newcastle** Down
34 H7 **Newcastle** Galway
13 K4 **Newcastle** Tippry
39 J8 **Newcastle**/*An Caisleán Nua* Dublin
31 P4 **Newcastle**/*An Caisleán Nua* Wicklw
17 P8 **Newcastle West**/*An Caisléan Nua* Limrck
5 K3 **Newcestown** Cork
13 L1 **Newchapel** Tippry
37 K5 **Newell's Bridge** Wmeath
47 J9 **Newgrange Megalithic Passage Tomb** Meath
45 N4 **New Inn** Cavan
35 K8 **New Inn** Galway
29 M4 **New Inn** Laois
20 D10 **Newinn**/*Loch Ceann* Tippry
21 N9 **Newmarket** Kilken
11 J3 **Newmarket**/*Áth Trasna* Cork
10 D3 **Newmarket Cross Roads** Cork
18 D1 **Newmarket-on-Fergus**/*Cora Chaitlín* Clare
4 H7 **Newmills** Cork
59 P1 **Newmills** Donegl
61 P9 **Newmills** Tyrone
19 L2 **Newport**/*An Port Nua* Tippry
41 K5 **Newport**/*Baile Uí Fhiacháin* Mayo
14 G3 **New Ross**/*Ros Mhic Thriúin* Wexfd
56 C8 **Newry** Down
35 L9 **Newtown** Galway
38 E6 **Newtown** Kildre
21 J5 **Newtown** Kilken
29 N9 **Newtown** Laois
19 K8 **Newtown** Limrck
41 P7 **Newtown** Mayo
46 G6 **Newtown** Meath
27 N2 **Newtown** Offaly
35 P7 **Newtown** Roscom
43 M9 **Newtown** Roscom
19 P9 **Newtown** Tippry
27 K8 **Newtown** Tippry
28 E8 **Newtown** Tippry
7 L3 **Newtown** Watfd
13 M8 **Newtown** Watfd
13 R5 **Newtown** Watfd
15 J7 **Newtown** Wexfd
15 M7 **Newtown** Wexfd
63 J6 **Newtownabbey** Antrim
13 J2 **Newtownadam** Tippry
63 M8 **Newtownards** Down

54 D8 **Newtownbutler** Ferman
36 C2 **Newtown Cashel** Longfd
50 F8 **Newtown Cloghans** Mayo
68 C9 **Newtown-Crommelin** Antrim
65 Q9 **Newtown Cunningham**/*An Baile Nua Chuinneagain* Donegl
44 E8 **Newtown Forbes**/*An Lios Breac* Longfd
44 G1 **Newtown Gore** Leitrm
55 P8 **Newtownhamilton** Armagh
37 K6 **Newtownlow** Wmeath
25 M2 **Newtownlynch** Galway
31 P3 **Newtown Mount Kennedy**/*Baile an Chinnéidigh* Wicklw
17 K7 **Newtownsandes**/*Maigh Mheáin* Kerry
18 F10 **Newtownshandrum**/*Baile Nua Sheandroma* Cork
60 F5 **Newtownstewart** Tyrone
11 N4 **New Twopothouse Village**/*Tigh Nua an Dá Phota* Cork
14 E5 **Nicholastown** Kilken
21 K10 **Ninemilehouse**/*Tigh na Naoi Mile* Tippry
46 E6 **Nobber**/*An Obair* Meath
6 B9 **Nohaval** Cork
28 E7 **Nore Bridge** Tippry
46 C3 **Northlands** Cavan
5 K6 **North Ring** Cork
25 K5 **Noughaval** Clare
25 N9 **Noughaval** Clare
30 C3 **Nurney** Kildre
22 C3 **Nurney**/*An Urnai* Carlow
39 J4 **Nuttstown Cross Roads** Meath

O

16 G8 **Oaghley** Kerry
18 G1 **Oatfield** Clare
24 G7 **O'Brien's Bridge** Clare
19 K1 **O'Briensbridge**/*Droichead Uí Bhriain* Clare
26 D9 **O'Callaghansmills** Clare
35 P9 **Oghill** Galway
26 G8 **Ogonnelloe** Clare
23 J10 **Oilgate**/*Maolán na nGabhar* Wexfd
12 B9 **Old Bride Bridge** Cork
19 M5 **Old Bridge** Limrck
67 N4 **Old Bushmills Distillery** Antrim
45 P7 **Oldcastle**/*An Seanchaisleán* Meath
38 G3 **Old Cross Keys** Meath
13 K3 **Oldgrange** Tippry
5 P6 **Old Head** Cork
30 E3 **Old Kilcullen** Kildre
29 Q8 **Oldleagh** Laois
22 B3 **Oldleighlin** Carlow
43 K5 **Old Lung Bridge** Roscom
47 J8 **Old Mellifont Abbey** Meath
6 E5 **Old Midleton Distillery** Cork
13 N7 **Old Pike Bridge** Watfd
14 H3 **Old Ross** Wexfd
39 L3 **Oldtown** Dublin
29 K8 **Old Town** Laois
35 Q8 **Old Town** Roscom
36 C6 **Oldtown** Roscom
22 E8 **Old Town** Wexfd
11 P4 **Old Twopothouse Cross Roads** Cork
60 G8 **Omagh** Tyrone
56 D10 **Omeath**/*Ó Méith* Louth
24 B2 **Onaght**/*Eoghanacht* Galway
19 N6 **Oola**/*Úlla* Limrck
34 D9 **Oranmore**/*Orán Mór* Galway
46 E8 **Oristown**/*Baile Órthaí* Meath
61 N7 **Orritor** Tyrone
36 G9 **Oughter** Offaly
33 N5 **Oughterard**/*Uachtar Ard* Galway

23 K8 **Oulart**/*An tAbhallort* Wexfd
13 J1 **Outeragh** Tippry
46 C2 **Ouvry Cross Roads** Monhan
11 N10 **Ovens** Cork
51 J4 **Owenbeg** Sligo
25 P2 **Owenbristy** Galway
41 J9 **Owenmore Bridge** Mayo
51 J5 **Owenykeevan or Tawnamaddoo** Sligo
33 Q4 **Ower** Galway
14 A3 **Owning** Kilken

P

41 M10 **Páirc an Teampaill**/*Churchfield* Mayo
22 E10 **Palace** Wexfd
30 D9 **Palatine** Carlow
19 M6 **Palatine Street** Limrck
35 L6 **Pallas** Galway
29 K5 **Pallas** Laois
37 L7 **Pallasboy** Wmeath
20 C4 **Pallas Cross** Tippry
19 M6 **Pallas Green** Limrck
19 M5 **Pallas Green New** Limrck
18 E4 **Pallaskenry**/*Pailis Chaonrai* Limrck
23 L3 **Pallis** Wexfd
39 K7 **Palmerstown** Dublin
61 J2 **Park** Lderry
41 Q4 **Park** Mayo
15 L7 **Park** Wexfd
12 B6 **Parkacunna** Cork
5 K3 **Parkbane** Cork
22 G4 **Park Bridge** Wicklw
52 E7 **Parkes Castle** Leitrm
62 G5 **Parkgate** Antrim
25 N2 **Parkmore** Galway
3 J2 **Parknasilla** Kerry
18 H2 **Parteen** Clare
41 P9 **Partry**/*Partrai* Mayo
35 N2 **Passage** Roscom
14 G6 **Passage East**/*An Pasáiste* Watfd
6 C6 **Passage West**/*An Pasáiste* Cork
18 G5 **Patrickswell**/*Tobar Phádraig* Limrck
22 B5 **Paulstown**/*Baile Phóil* Kilken
35 L9 **Peak** Galway
62 E4 **Peters Bridge** Antrim
26 D3 **Peterswell**/*Tobar Pheadair* Galway
59 P9 **Pettigo**/*Paiteagó* Donegl
6 A4 **Piercetown** Cork
15 N5 **Piercetown** Wexfd
3 Q4 **Pierson's Bridge** Cork
27 N3 **Pike** Tippry
38 F3 **Pike Corner** Meath
28 H7 **Pike of Rush Hall** Laois
14 B4 **Piltown**/*Baile an Phoill* Kilken
65 N10 **Pluck** Donegl
60 G4 **Plumbridge** Tyrone
25 N2 **Pollagh** Galway
36 F8 **Pollagh** Offaly
35 L9 **Pollatlugga** Galway
48 H3 **Pollatomish**/*Poll a' tSómais* Mayo
48 H3 **Poll a' tSómais**/*Pollatomish* Mayo
35 P8 **Pollboy** Galway
43 J10 **Pollshask** Galway
61 L8 **Pomeroy** Tyrone
41 Q3 **Pontoon** Mayo
41 Q3 **Pontoon Bridge** Mayo
19 P6 **Pope's Bridge** Tippry
47 L6 **Port** Louth
48 H2 **Port a' Chlóidh**/*Portacloy* Mayo
48 H2 **Portacloy**/*Port a' Chlóidh* Mayo
56 B3 **Portadown** Armagh
57 N3 **Portaferry** Down
66 E2 **Portaleen** Donegl
29 M2 **Portarlington**/*Cuil an tSùdaire* Laois
57 Q2 **Portavogie** Down
67 N4 **Portballintrae** Antrim
49 J2 **Port Durlainne**/*Porturlin* Mayo
62 B2 **Portglenone** Antrim
27 L3 **Portland** Tippry
29 L5 **Portlaoise**/*Port Laoise* Laois
14 B5 **Portlaw**/*Port Lách* Watfd
8 D10 **Portmagee**/*An Caladh* Kerry

39 N5 **Portmarnock**/*Port Mearnóg* Dublin
63 M2 **Portmuck** Antrim
65 J5 **Portnablaghy**/*Port na Blaiche* Donegl
40 D7 **Portnakilly** Mayo
37 L1 **Portnashangan** Wmeath
58 F3 **Portnoo**/*Port Nua* Donegl
39 P3 **Portraine**/*Port Reachrainn* Dublin
27 J8 **Portroe**/*An Port Rua* Tippry
67 M5 **Portrush** Antrim
65 N5 **Portsalon**/*Port an tSalainn* Donegl
67 L5 **Portstewart** Lderry
27 L4 **Portumna**/*Port Omna* Galway
49 J2 **Porturlin**/*Port Durlainne* Mayo
5 J1 **Poulanargid** Cork
10 D8 **Poulgorm Bridge** Kerry
13 K1 **Poulnamucky** Tippry
12 B8 **Powers Bridge** Cork
31 N1 **Powerscourt Gardens** Wicklw
31 M2 **Powerscourt Waterfall** Wicklw
27 J4 **Power's Cross** Galway
56 C6 **Poyntz Pass** Armagh
12 B8 **Prap** Cork
14 G5 **Priesthaggard** Wexfd
60 E7 **Priest's Bridge** Tyrone
13 L5 **Priesttown** Tippry
38 E8 **Prosperous**/*An Chorrchoill* Kildre
27 K7 **Puckaun** Tippry

Q

5 K2 **Quarry Cross Roads** Cork
62 E1 **Quarrytown** Antrim
25 L2 **Quay** Clare
6 C6 **Queenstown Story** Cork
16 G4 **Querrin** Clare
66 E6 **Quigley's Point**/*Rinn Uí Choigligh* Donegl
24 F10 **Quilty**/*Coillte* Clare
25 P10 **Quin**/*Cuinche* Clare
28 D8 **Quinlisk's Cross Roads** Tippry

R

21 N4 **Radestown** Kilken
57 L2 **Raffrey** Down
51 N2 **Raghly** Sligo
45 P8 **Rahaghy** Meath
36 H8 **Rahan**/*Raithean* Offaly
37 Q3 **Raharney**/*Ráth Fhearna* Wmeath
30 G9 **Raheen** Carlow
5 M2 **Raheen** Cork
10 D6 **Raheen** Kerry
12 H2 **Raheen** Tippry
15 J3 **Raheen** Wexfd
36 G5 **Raheen** Wmeath
23 M8 **Raheenlusk** Wexfd
3 N7 **Raheenroe** Cork
57 M4 **Raholp** Down
50 D8 **Rake Street** Mayo
14 G6 **Ramsgrange** Wexfd
26 H2 **Ranamackan** Galway
62 D4 **Randalstown** Antrim
28 C2 **Rapemills** Offaly
60 C2 **Raphoe**/*Ráth Bhoth* Donegl
10 G3 **Rascalstreet** Cork
67 P10 **Rasharkin** Antrim
59 P1 **Rashedoge** Donegl
43 N4 **Ratallen Cross Roads** Roscom
28 D3 **Rath** Offaly
38 B10 **Rathangan**/*Ráith Iomgháin* Kildre
9 Q2 **Rathanny** Kerry
44 H10 **Rathaspick** Wmeath
20 F9 **Rathbrit** Tippry
27 N3 **Rathcabban** Tippry
38 D1 **Rathcarran**/*Ráth Chairn* Meath
38 D1 **Ráth Chairn**/*Rathcarran* Meath
38 F7 **Rathcoffey** Kildre
43 N9 **Rathconor** Roscom
37 J3 **Rathconrath** Wmeath
11 J6 **Rathcool** Cork
39 J8 **Rathcoole**/*Ráth Cúil* Dublin
38 D4 **Rathcore** Meath

12 D8 **Rathcormack**/*Ráth Chormaic* Cork
43 M7 **Rathcroghan Cross Roads** Roscom
25 K10 **Rathcrony** Clare
39 K3 **Rath Cross Roads** Meath
30 H7 **Rathdangan**/*Ráth Daingin* Wicklw
28 G9 **Rathdowney**/*Ráth Domhnaigh* Laois
31 M7 **Rathdrum**/*Ráth Droma* Wicklw
36 H1 **Rathduff** Longfd
17 P9 **Ratheenagh** Limrck
38 D9 **Rathernan** Kildre
47 J6 **Rathescar Cross Roads** Louth
39 J1 **Rathfeigh** Meath
6 C3 **Rathfilode** Cork
56 E7 **Rathfriland** Down
22 F9 **Rathfylane** Wexfd
29 L9 **Rathgarry** Laois
13 P3 **Rathgormuck** Watfd
34 B1 **Rathgranagher** Mayo
19 N8 **Rathkea** Tippry
18 D6 **Rathkeale**/*Ráth Caola* Limrck
46 F8 **Rathkenny** Meath
43 N8 **Rathkeva** Roscom
13 L2 **Rathkevin** Tippry
43 M6 **Rathkineely** Roscom
50 E3 **Rathlackan**/*Ráth Leacáin* Mayo
50 H3 **Rathlee** Sligo
30 F9 **Rathlyon** Carlow
13 Q5 **Rathmaiden** Watfd
65 N8 **Rathmelton**/*Ráth Mealtain* Donegl
46 D10 **Rathmore** Meath
10 F6 **Rathmore**/*An Ráth Mhór* Kerry
38 H10 **Rathmore**/*An Ráth Mhór* Kildre
14 F9 **Rathmoylan** Watfd
38 D4 **Rathmoylon** Meath
65 P7 **Rathmullan**/*Ráth Maolain* Donegl
31 P5 **Rathnew**/*Ráth Naoi* Wicklw
22 E9 **Rathnure** Wexfd
50 E5 **Rathoma** Mayo
6 F3 **Rathorgan** Cork
45 J10 **Rathowen**/*Ráth Eoghainn* Wmeath
50 F6 **Rathroeen** Mayo
3 P7 **Rathruane** Cork
16 E9 **Rathscannel** Kerry
22 E2 **Rathtoe** Carlow
30 F8 **Rathvilly**/*Ráth Bhile* Carlow
37 P3 **Rathwire** Wmeath
39 J3 **Ratoath**/*Ráth Tó* Meath
3 M8 **Ratooragh** Cork
47 K1 **Ravensdale** Louth
56 G1 **Ravernet** Down
65 P7 **Ray** Donegl
4 C7 **Rea Cross Roads** Cork
46 C4 **Reaghstown** Louth
7 M3 **Reanaclogheen**/*Ré na gChoichin* Watfd
25 J10 **Reanagishagh** Clare
10 B1 **Reanagowan Cross Roads** Kerry
10 G10 **Reananerree**/*Ré na nDoiri* Cork
4 G6 **Reanascreena** Cork
19 N3 **Rearcross** Tippry
36 C10 **Reask** Galway
4 F6 **Reavouler Bridge** Cork
32 H4 **Recess**/*Sraith Salach* Galway
61 L10 **Reclain** Tyrone
66 F6 **Redcastle** Donegl
31 N8 **Redcross**/*An Chrois Dhearg* Wicklw
23 J10 **Redgate** Wexfd
54 D10 **Redhills**/*An Cnoc Rua* Cavan
27 M3 **Redwood** Tippry
3 N2 **Releagh Bridge** Kerry
7 M3 **Ré na gChoichin**/*Reanaclogheen* Watfd
10 G10 **Ré na nDoiri**/*Reananerree* Cork
32 D1 **Renvyle** Galway
3 J6 **Rerrin** Cork
67 N5 **Revallagh North** Antrim
7 N7 **Rhode**/*Ród* Offaly
55 P4 **Richhill** Armagh
6 E3 **Riesk** Cork
6 C7 **Ringaskiddy**/*Rinn an Scidigh* Cork
67 L8 **Ringsend** Lderry
29 J5 **Ringstown** Laois
13 N9 **Ringville**/*An Rinn* Watfd
64 D8 **Rinnafarset**/*Rinn na Feirste* Donegl
24 G8 **Rinneen** Clare

4 E8 **Rinneen** Cork
64 D8 **Rinn na Feirste**/*Rinnafarset* Donegl
34 D9 **Rinville** Galway
23 M5 **Riverchapel** Wexfd
5 Q3 **Riverstick** Cork
6 B5 **Riverstown** Cork
27 P4 **Riverstown** Tippry
52 D9 **Riverstown**/*Baile Idir Dhá Abhainn* Sligo
9 Q3 **Riverville Cross Roads** Kerry
24 G5 **Roadford** Clare
38 D8 **Robertstown**/*Baile Riobaird* Kildre
38 E1 **Robinstown** Meath
15 L6 **Robinstown** Wexfd
14 C4 **Rochestown** Kilken
14 F5 **Rochestown** Kilken
13 J2 **Rochestown** Tippry
37 M5 **Rochfortbridge**/*Droichead Chaisleán Loiste* Wmeath
10 G1 **Rockchapel** Cork
54 H10 **Rockcorry**/*Buiochar* Monhan
31 N7 **Rocketstown** Wicklw
18 G9 **Rockhill** Limrck
12 B5 **Rockmills** Cork
20 D8 **Rock of Cashel** Tippry
43 Q5 **Rodeen** Roscom
34 E10 **Roevehagh** Galway
27 N1 **Rooaun** Galway
42 H2 **Roosky** Mayo
44 C6 **Roosky**/*Rúscaigh* Roscom
35 Q7 **Rooty Cross Roads** Roscom
33 K8 **Ros an Mhíl**/*Rossaveel* Galway
14 G3 **Rosbercon** Wexfd
22 E2 **Roscat** Carlow
35 P1 **Roscommon**/*Ros Comáin* Roscom
28 D7 **Roscrea**/*Ros Cré* Tippry
48 H3 **Ros Dumhach**/*Ross Port* Mayo
20 E9 **Rosegreen** Tippry
36 G5 **Rosemount** Wmeath
29 J3 **Rosenallis** Laois
65 L5 **Rosepenna**/*Machair Loiscthe* Donegl
33 J7 **Ros Muc**/*Rosmuck* Galway
33 J7 **Rosmuck**/*Ros Muc* Galway
20 C5 **Rosmult** Tippry
65 M5 **Rosnakill** Donegl
45 M7 **Ross** Meath
19 Q9 **Rossadrehid** Tippry
10 B4 **Rossanean** Kerry
33 K8 **Rossaveel**/*Ros an Mhíl* Galway
58 E3 **Rossbeg** Donegl
9 J6 **Ross Behy** Kerry
3 P8 **Rossbrin** Cork
33 P6 **Rosscahill** Galway
4 G7 **Ross Carbery**/*Ros Ó gCairbre* Cork
51 P3 **Rosses Point**/*An Ros* Sligo
52 H4 **Rossinver**/*Ros Inbhir* Leitrm
15 Q6 **Rosslare**/*Ros Láir* Wexfd
15 Q6 **Rosslare Harbour**/*Calafort Ros Láir* Wexfd
54 F7 **Rosslea** Ferman
3 J5 **Rossmackowen** Cork
4 G1 **Rossmore** Cork
4 H5 **Rossmore** Cork
22 B2 **Rossmore** Laois
20 B6 **Rossmore** Tippry
29 N4 **Rossmore Cross Roads** Laois
3 M3 **Rossnagrena** Cork
59 J9 **Rossnowlagh** Donegl
48 H3 **Ross Port**/*Ros Dumhach* Mayo
41 P4 **Ross West** Mayo
6 E6 **Rostellan** Cork
56 E10 **Rostrevor** Down
40 H4 **Rosturk** Mayo
42 B10 **Roundfort** Mayo
32 E6 **Roundstone**/*Cloch na Rón* Galway
31 N4 **Roundwood**/*An Tóchar* Wicklw
61 J5 **Rousky** Tyrone
25 M7 **Ruan** Clare
57 P1 **Rubane** Down
39 P3 **Rush**/*An Ros* Dublin
11 K9 **Rusheen** Cork
32 D1 **Rusheenduff** Galway
13 L3 **Russellstown** Watfd
34 G6 **Ryehill** Galway
11 L8 **Rylane** Cork

S

39 J8 **Saggart** Dublin
66 C9 **St Columb's Cathedral** Lderry
57 K2 **Saintfield** Down
60 D1 **St Johnston**/*Baile Suingean* Donegl
39 L5 **St Margaret's** Dublin
22 C9 **St Mullin's** Carlow
6 E6 **Saleen** Cork
8 G10 **Sallahig** Kerry
38 F9 **Sallins**/*Na Solláin* Kildre
6 B4 **Sallybrook** Cork
20 B2 **Sallypark** Tippry
34 B9 **Salthill**/*Bóthar na Trá* Galway
14 H7 **Saltmills** Wexfd
61 N8 **Sandholes** Tyrone
39 M8 **Sandyford** Dublin
39 M5 **Santry** Dublin
21 L4 **Sart Cross Roads** Kilken
57 M4 **Saul** Down
10 E2 **Scalp Bridge** Kerry
35 P2 **Scardaun** Roscom
42 C10 **Scardaune** Mayo
23 N3 **Scarnagh Cross Roads** Wexfd
26 F8 **Scarriff**/*An Scairbh* Clare
38 C3 **Scarriff Bridge** Roscom
10 C4 **Scartaglin**/*Scairteach an Ghlinne* Kerry
13 M6 **Scart Bridge** Watfd
56 C5 **Scarva** Down
3 N8 **Schull**/*An Scoil* Cork
55 K8 **Scotch Corner** Monhan
55 Q2 **Scotch Street** Armagh
54 E10 **Scotshouse** Monhan
54 H6 **Scotstown**/*Baile an Scotaigh* Monhan
10 D5 **Scrahanfadda** Kerry
44 B8 **Scramoge** Roscom
12 B6 **Scrarour** Cork
23 K10 **Screen** Wexfd
36 H9 **Screggan** Offaly
66 H10 **Scriggan** Lderry
46 C9 **Scurlockstown** Meath
57 K5 **Seaforde** Down
56 D4 **Seapatrick** Down
13 N2 **Seskin** Tippry
60 G10 **Seskinore** Tyrone
4 E3 **Shanacrane** Cork
6 G6 **Shanagarry** Cork
25 P5 **Shanaglish** Galway
17 P5 **Shanagolden**/*Seanghualainn* Limrck
29 J7 **Shanahoe** Laois
24 H9 **Shanavogh East** Clare
35 J7 **Shanballard** Galway
6 C7 **Shanbally** Cork
35 K1 **Shanbally** Galway
13 P7 **Shanbally** Watfd
19 N3 **Shanballyedmond** Tippry
42 F10 **Shanballymore** Galway
12 A5 **Shanballymore**/*An Seanbhaile Mór* Cork
38 C3 **Shanco Bridge** Meath
26 H2 **Shangarry** Galway
39 P9 **Shankill** Dublin
4 G3 **Shanlaragh** Cork
46 G5 **Shanlis Cross Roads** Louth
17 N4 **Shannakea** Clare
18 D2 **Shannon** Clare
18 E2 **Shannon**/*Sionainn* Clare
36 B8 **Shannonbridge**/*Droichead na Sionainne* Offaly
36 C10 **Shannon Harbour**/*Caladh na Sionainne* Offaly
29 P7 **Shanragh** Laois
12 G4 **Shanrahan Cross Roads** Tippry
18 C9 **Shanrath** Limrck
46 C1 **Shantonagh** Monhan
28 C3 **Sharavogue** Offaly
46 C2 **Shercock**/*Searcóg* Cavan
13 Q2 **Sheskin** Watfd
20 B5 **Shevry** Tippry
22 H3 **Shillelagh**/*Siol Éalaigh* Wicklw
28 C6 **Shinrone**/*Sui an Róin* Offaly
57 M3 **Shrigley** Down
16 H6 **Shrone** Kerry
19 N7 **Shronell** Tippry
16 H6 **Shronowen** Kerry
34 B3 **Shrule**/*Sruthair* Mayo
4 E4 **Sillahertane** Cork
55 Q10 **Silver Bridge** Armagh
27 K10 **Silvermines**/*Béal Átha Gabhann* Tippry
55 K6 **Silver Stream** Monhan
60 D4 **Sion Mills** Tyrone

18 F1 **Sixmilebridge/** *Droichead Abhainn Ó gCearnaigh* Clare
61 J9 **Sixmilecross** Tyrone
63 N7 **Six Road Ends** Down
4 B4 **Skahanagh** Cork
6 C2 **Skahanagh North** Cork
6 C3 **Skahanagh South** Cork
4 C7 **Skeagh** Cork
36 H3 **Skeagh Beg** Wmeath
26 C3 **Skehanagh** Galway
34 H5 **Skehanagh** Galway
12 E4 **Skeheen** Cork
11 Q4 **Skenakilla Cross Roads** Cork
39 P1 **Skerries/** *Na Sceirí* Dublin
4 D8 **Skibbereen/** *An Sciobairín* Cork
38 H1 **Skreen** Meath
51 M4 **Skreen** Sligo
14 G9 **Slade** Watfd
46 H9 **Slane/** *Baile Shláine* Meath
57 J8 **Slieve Donard** Down
35 L2 **Slievemurray** Galway
4 H2 **Slieveowen** Cork
14 E5 **Slieverue** Kilken
5 Q2 **Sligga Bridge** Cork
52 C6 **Sligo/** *Sligeach* Sligo
52 C6 **Sligo Abbey** Sligo
46 H6 **Smarmore** Louth
8 C3 **Smerwick/** *Ard na Caithne* Kerry
54 G7 **Smithborough** Monhan
21 P2 **Smithstown** Kilken
2 H1 **Sneem/** *An tSnaidhm* Kerry
52 D9 **Sooey** Sligo
9 M1 **Spa** Kerry
25 N8 **Spancehill** Clare
24 F9 **Spanish Point/** *Rinn na Spáinneach* Clare
61 K4 **Sperrin** Tyrone
33 N9 **Spiddal/** *An Spidéal* Galway
29 M8 **Spink Bridge** Laois
36 H6 **Spittaltown** Wmeath
66 C9 **Spring Town** Lderry
31 M3 **Sraghmore** Wicklw
41 N9 **Srah/** *An tSraith* Mayo
48 F5 **Srah/** *An tSraith* Mayo
28 F5 **Srahanboy** Laois
49 K2 **Srahataggle/** *Sraith a' tSeagail* Mayo
42 B5 **Sraheens** Mayo
40 E4 **Sraheens Bridge/** *Na Sraithíní* Mayo
48 H6 **Srahmore** Mayo
48 H8 **Srahnamanragh Bridge** Mayo
49 K2 **Sraith a' tSeagail/** *Srahataggle* Mayo
32 H4 **Sraith Salach/** *Recess* Galway
13 J6 **Sruh** Watfd
47 J5 **Stabannan** Louth
46 G9 **Stackallan** Meath
62 C5 **Staffordstown** Antrim
47 M10 **Stamullin** Meath
38 E7 **Staplestown** Kildre
39 M9 **Stepaside** Dublin
61 Q8 **Stewartstown** Tyrone
39 M8 **Stillorgan** Dublin
54 F8 **Stone Bridge** Monhan
19 J5 **Stonepark** Limrck
62 G8 **Stonyford** Antrim
21 N8 **Stonyford/** *Áth Stúin* Kilken
63 L8 **Stormont** Down
60 D3 **Strabane** Tyrone
8 H2 **Stradbally** Kerry
29 N5 **Stradbally/** *An tSráidbhaile* Laois
13 Q7 **Stradbally/** *An tSráidbhaile* Watfd
42 B4 **Strade** Mayo
45 N3 **Stradone/** *Sraith an Domhain* Cavan
38 G8 **Straffan/** *Teach Srafáin* Kildre
22 H6 **Strahart** Wexfd
63 J4 **Straid** Antrim
17 N9 **Strand** Limrck
51 P3 **Strandhill/** *An Leathros* Sligo
57 N4 **Strangford** Down
67 Q6 **Stranocum** Antrim
59 P3 **Stranorlar/** *Srath an Urláir* Donegl
30 F6 **Stratford/** *Áth na Sráide* Wicklw
36 H5 **Streamstown** Wmeath
45 J9 **Street** Wmeath
20 F2 **Strogue Cross Roads** Tippry
43 Q7 **Strokestown/** *Béal na mBuillí* Roscom

43 Q7 **Strokestown Park** Roscom
66 H4 **Stroove** Donegl
11 M8 **Stuake** Cork
5 Q5 **Summer Cove** Cork
38 E4 **Summerhill/** *Cnoc an Linsigh* Meath
30 D3 **Suncroft** Kildre
29 N8 **Swan** Laois
53 N8 **Swanlinbar/** *An Muileann Iarainn* Cavan
54 H9 **Swan's Cross Roads** Monhan
61 Q1 **Swatragh** Lderry
42 D4 **Swinford/** *Béal Átha na Muice* Mayo
39 M4 **Swords/** *Sord* Dublin

T

35 P6 **Taghmaconnell** Roscom
15 L5 **Taghmon/** *Teach Munna* Wexfd
36 G1 **Taghshinny** Longfd
15 Q6 **Tagoat** Wexfd
3 J1 **Tahilla** Kerry
39 K8 **Tallaght** Dublin
44 H4 **Tallanstown** Louth
12 G8 **Tallow/** *Tulach an Iarainn* Watfd
12 H8 **Tallowbridge** Watfd
53 Q5 **Tamlaght** Ferman
61 R1 **Tamlaght O'Crilly** Lderry
55 N1 **Tamnamore** Tyrone
56 B4 **Tandragee** Armagh
36 E3 **Tang** Wmeath
18 H9 **Tankardstown** Limrck
38 G2 **Tara** Meath
36 H7 **Tara** Offaly
17 K5 **Tarbert/** *Tairbeart* Kerry
13 K4 **Tar Bridge** Tippry
17 K3 **Tarmon** Clare
11 L1 **Tarrant's Cross Roads** Cork
55 N6 **Tassagh** Armagh
10 G3 **Taur** Cork
65 M5 **Tawny** Donegl
42 F4 **Tawnyinah** Mayo
52 G8 **Tawnylea** Leitrm
27 P2 **Taylor's Cross** Offaly
3 P5 **Tedagh** Cork
54 H6 **Tedavnet** Monhan
58 C7 **Teelin/** *Teileann* Donegl
54 B9 **Teemore** Ferman
8 G2 **Teer/** *An Tír* Kerry
8 E10 **Teeranearagh/** *An Trian Íarach* Kerry
8 C4 **Teeravane/** *Tíorabháin* Kerry
4 H1 **Teerelton** Cork
25 M10 **Teermaclane** Clare
33 K3 **Teernakill Bridge/** *Tír na Cille* Galway
8 H8 **Teeromoyle** Kerry
46 C5 **Teevurcher** Meath
58 C7 **Teileann/** *Teelin* Donegl
51 L4 **Templeboy** Sligo
19 Q1 **Templederry** Tippry
13 N1 **Templeetney** Tippry
20 E2 **Templemore/** *An Teampall Mór* Tippry
3 L1 **Templenoe** Kerry
37 L6 **Templeoran** Wmeath
14 B3 **Templeorum** Kilken
62 G5 **Templepatrick** Antrim
22 F7 **Templeshanbo** Wexfd
20 F2 **Templetouhy/** *Teampall Tuaithe* Tippry
14 H8 **Templetown** Wexfd
6 B4 **Templeusque** Cork
54 C4 **Tempo** Ferman
15 N7 **Tenacre Cross Roads** Wexfd
65 L8 **Termon/** *An Tearmann* Donegl
44 D8 **Termonbarry** Roscom
47 L7 **Termonfeckin/** *Tearmann Feichín* Louth
27 L4 **Terryglass/** *Tír Dhá Ghlas* Tippry
37 N2 **Tevrin** Wmeath
62 B7 **The Battery** Tyrone
47 M2 **The Bush** Louth
21 Q3 **The Butts** Carlow
66 D10 **The Cross** Lderry
30 D2 **The Curragh** Kildre
62 E7 **The Diamond** Antrim
62 A7 **The Diamond** Tyrone
37 N3 **The Downs** Wmeath
68 B7 **The Drones** Antrim
39 M2 **The Five Roads** Dublin
24 H9 **The Hand Cross Roads** Clare
23 K7 **The Harrow** Wexfd
15 K3 **The Leap** Wexfd

61 R6 **The Loup** Lderry
36 E3 **The Pigeons** Wmeath
27 N5 **The Pike** Tippry
6 H2 **The Pike** Watfd
13 P7 **The Pike** Watfd
61 N8 **The Rock** Tyrone
22 C10 **The Rower** Kilken
62 G1 **The Sheddings** Antrim
61 M4 **The Six Towns** Lderry
57 J4 **The Spa** Down
14 B4 **The Sweep** Kilken
57 J1 **The Temple** Down
19 K10 **Thomastown** Limrck
46 D7 **Thomastown** Meath
20 B9 **Thomastown** Tippry
21 P8 **Thomastown/** *Baile Mhic Andáin* Kilken
21 M4 **Threecastles** Kilken
54 H7 **Three Mile House** Monhan
31 L8 **Threewells** Wicklw
20 E5 **Thurles/** *Durlas* Tippry
43 K5 **Tibohine** Roscom
16 B8 **Tiduff** Kerry
13 M2 **Tikincor** Watfd
38 D7 **Timahoe** Kildre
29 M6 **Timahoe/** *Tigh Mochua* Laois
5 L6 **Timoleague/** *Tigh Molaige* Cork
30 E6 **Timolin** Kildre
23 J2 **Tinahely/** *Tigh na hÉille* Wicklw
36 F7 **Tinamuck** Offaly
23 J8 **Tinnacross Cross Roads** Cork
15 M3 **Tinnakilla** Wexfd
22 C2 **Tinryland** Carlow
47 J7 **Tinure Cross Roads** Louth
8 C4 **Tíorabháin/** *Teeravane* Kerry
19 P7 **Tipperary/** *Tiobraid Árann* Tippry
61 P2 **Tirkane** Lderry
33 K3 **Tír na Cille/** *Teernakill Bridge* Galway
5 L6 **Tirnanean** Cork
55 J6 **Tirnaneill** Monhan
25 P4 **Tirneevin** Galway
53 J8 **Tober** Cavan
36 G6 **Tober** Offaly
30 F5 **Toberbeg** Wicklw
51 M8 **Tobercurry/** *Tobar an Choire* Sligo
26 D2 **Toberelatan** Galway
61 P3 **Tobermore** Lderry
11 J2 **Tobernaclougha Cross Roads** Cork
34 B2 **Tobernadarry** Mayo
52 C9 **Toberscanavan** Sligo
19 P5 **Toem** Tippry
4 F3 **Togher** Cork
47 L6 **Togher** Louth
38 D4 **Togher** Meath
37 N7 **Togher** Offaly
31 J4 **Togher** Wicklw
16 D9 **Togherbane** Kerry
34 B8 **Tóin na Brocaí/** *Tonabrocky* Galway
40 F3 **Tóin re Gaoth/** *Tonregee* Mayo
15 N7 **Tonhaggard** Wexfd
34 B8 **Tonabrocky/** *Tóin na Brocaí* Galway
41 M8 **Tonlegee** Mayo
40 F3 **Tonregee/** *Tóin re Gaoth* Mayo
45 Q3 **Tonyduff** Cavan
4 G3 **Toom** Cork
25 J4 **Toomaghera** Clare
35 K3 **Toomard** Galway
32 F5 **Toombeola** Galway
62 B4 **Toome** Antrim
4 H1 **Tooms** Cork
27 N9 **Toomyvara/** *Tuaim Uí Mheára* Tippry
19 N2 **Toor** Tippry
13 L5 **Tooraneena** Watfd
17 M6 **Tooraree** Limrck
11 R6 **Tooreen** Cork
19 N2 **Tooreenbrien Bridge** Tippry
10 E4 **Tooreencahill** Kerry
10 H2 **Tooreendermot** Cork
12 A8 **Toorgarriff** Cork
41 N10 **Toormakeady/** *Tuar Mhic Éadaigh* Mayo
3 M8 **Toormore** Cork
17 N10 **Toornafulla** Limrck
37 K6 **Torque** Wmeath
14 D7 **Towergare** Watfd
6 D7 **Trabolgan** Cork
6 B8 **Tracton** Cork
3 L5 **Trafrask** Cork
9 N2 **Tralee/** *Trá Lí* Kerry
14 D8 **Tramore/** *Trá Mhór* Watfd

34 H3 **Trasternagh** Galway
2 G5 **Travara Bridge** Cork
4 B5 **Trawlebane** Cork
33 M1 **Trean/** *Tréan* Mayo
33 M1 **Tréan/** *Trean* Mayo
65 L9 **Treantagh** Donegl
45 M1 **Treehoo Cross Roads** Cavan
9 J2 **Trench Bridge** Kerry
43 J8 **Trien** Roscom
54 B2 **Trillick** Tyrone
38 E2 **Trim/** *Baile Átha Troim* Meath
38 E2 **Trim Castle** Meath
35 L7 **Trust** Galway
34 E3 **Tuam/** *Tuaim* Galway
26 F8 **Tuamgraney/** *Tuaim Gréine* Clare
41 N10 **Tuar Mhic Éadaigh/** *Toormakeady* Mayo
25 P6 **Tubber** Galway
21 J4 **Tubbrid** Kilken
12 H3 **Tubbrid** Tippry
26 C8 **Tulla/** *An Tulach* Clare
48 G7 **Tullachán Dubh/** *Tullaghanduff* Mayo
4 E2 **Tullagh** Cork
25 J10 **Tullaghaboy** Clare
52 E2 **Tullaghan** Leitrm
48 G7 **Tullaghanduff/** *Tullachán Dubh* Mayo
21 Q10 **Tullagher** Kilken
21 L10 **Tullaghought** Kilken
21 P7 **Tullaherin** Kilken
4 K10 **Tullakeel** Kerry
37 J8 **Tullamore/** *Tulach Mhór* Offaly
9 J2 **Tullaree** Kerry
21 K5 **Tullaroan** Kilken
25 L9 **Tullassa** Clare
16 D4 **Tullig** Clare
9 L5 **Tullig** Kerry
16 G9 **Tullig** Kerry
22 F2 **Tullow/** *An Tulach* Carlow
33 L9 **Tully/** *An Tulaigh* Galway
47 J8 **Tullyallen** Louth
15 L6 **Tullycanna** Wexfd
52 F8 **Tullycoly** Leitrm
32 E1 **Tully Cross** Galway
61 P8 **Tullyhogue** Tyrone
11 K1 **Tullylease** Cork
45 P1 **Tullyvin** Cavan
42 F9 **Tulrohaun** Mayo
43 N7 **Tulsk/** *Tuilsce* Roscom
3 K2 **Tuosist** Kerry
37 N2 **Turin** Wmeath
25 L3 **Turlough** Clare
41 Q5 **Turlough** Mayo
34 E6 **Turloughmore** Galway
4 E1 **Turnaspidogy** Cork
11 Q3 **Turnpike Cross** Cork
44 C10 **Turreen** Longfd
15 P6 **Twelveacre Cross Roads** Wexfd
20 D6 **Twoford Bridges** Tippry
20 F5 **Twomileborris** Tippry
29 K2 **Twomile Bridge** Laois
27 J2 **Tynagh** Galway
55 L5 **Tynan** Armagh
61 P10 **Tyrone Crystal** Tyrone
37 L6 **Tyrrellspass/** *Bealach an Tirialaigh* Wmeath

U

60 F7 **Ulster American Folk Park** Tyrone
4 F8 **Unionhall/** *Bréantrá* Cork
62 F9 **Upper Ballinderry** Antrim
20 B4 **Upperchurch** Tippry
61 Q2 **Upperlands** Lderry
5 M3 **Upton** Cork
2 G5 **Urhin** Cork
42 G6 **Urlaur** Mayo
20 H4 **Urlingford/** *Áth na nUrlainn* Kilken

V

30 H3 **Valleymount** Wicklw
8 D4 **Ventry/** *Ceann Trá* Kerry
29 P4 **Vicarstown** Laois
60 E4 **Victoria Bridge** Tyrone
13 K8 **Villierstown/** *An Baile Nua* Watfd
45 Q6 **Virginia/** *Achadh an Iúir* Cavan

W

37 N9 **Walsh Island** Offaly
6 E3 **Walshtown** Cork
38 H1 **Walterstown** Meath
39 L4 **Ward** Dublin
56 D2 **Waringstown** Down
5 P2 **Warner's Cross Roads** Cork
56 D10 **Warrenpoint** Down
30 G1 **Watch House Cross Roads** Kildre
22 G4 **Watch House Village** Wexfd
5 P1 **Waterfall** Cork
14 E8 **Waterford** Watfd
14 E6 **Waterford/** *Port Láirge* Watfd
14 D6 **Waterford Crystal** Watfd
6 C3 **Watergrasshill/** *Cnocán na Biolraí* Cork
2 E1 **Waterville/** *An Coireán* Kerry
59 N3 **Welchtown** Donegl
15 K6 **Wellingtonbridge/** *Droichead Eoin* Wexfd
5 J6 **West Cork Model Railway Village** Cork
41 L7 **Westport/** *Cathair na Mart* Mayo
41 K7 **Westport Quay** Mayo
14 D9 **Westtown** Watfd
64 F3 **West Town/** *An Baile Thiar* Donegl
15 N4 **Wexford/** *Loch Garman* Wexfd
30 D1 **Wheelam Cross Roads** Kildre
63 K6 **Whiteabbey** Antrim
11 Q8 **Whitechurch** Cork
13 L7 **Whitechurch** Watfd
14 G5 **Whitechurch** Wexfd
55 Q7 **Whitecross** Armagh
26 H7 **Whitegate/** *An Geata Bán* Clare
6 D7 **Whitegate/** *An Geata Bán* Cork
9 M4 **White Gate Cross Roads** Kerry
44 D8 **Whitehall** Roscom
45 M10 **Whitehall** Wmeath
63 M4 **Whitehead** Antrim
6 A4 **White's Cross** Cork
62 D3 **Whitesides Corner** Antrim
47 N2 **Whites Town** Louth
31 Q6 **Wicklow/** *Cill Mhantáin* Wicklw
31 K4 **Wicklow Mountains National Park** Wicklw
46 F8 **Wilkinstown/** *Baile Uilcín* Meath
25 K7 **Willbrook** Clare
43 J10 **Williamstown** Galway
21 L10 **Windgap/** *Bearna na Gaoithe* Kilken
38 C7 **Windmill Cross Roads** Kildre
29 N8 **Wolfhill** Laois
63 K5 **Woodburn** Antrim
31 M9 **Woodenbridge** Wicklw
26 D10 **Woodfield Bridge** Clare
26 H4 **Woodford/** *An Chráig* Galway
35 K7 **Woodlawn/** *Móta* Galway
14 F7 **Woodstown** Watfd

Y

46 G9 **Yellow Furze** Meath
27 J8 **Youghal** Tippry
7 K4 **Youghal/** *Eochaill* Cork